Fred Seidman

## *About the Author*

ANTHONY DIAS BLUE is the author of several
books, including *American Wine: A Comprehensive Guide* and *Buyer's Guide to American
Wines.* A leading food and wine expert, Mr.
Blue regularly appears on television and radio.
In 2001, he was awarded a James Beard Award
for his radio show, *Lifestyle Minute.* Mr. Blue
lives in Pacific Palisades, California, with his
wife, Kathryn.

# THE COMPLETE BOOK OF MIXED DRINKS

ANTHONY DIAS BLUE

# THE
# COMPLETE
# BOOK OF
# MIXED
# DRINKS

*More Than 1,000 Alcoholic and*
*Nonalcoholic Cocktails*

REVISED EDITION

Quill
*An Imprint of* HarperCollins*Publishers*

First Quill edition published 2002.

Designed by Dorothy S. Baker
Line drawings of glasses by Jennifer Harper
Line drawings by Frank Ronan

Library of Congress Cataloging-in-Publication Data
Dias Blue, Anthony.
    The complete book of mixed drinks : more than 1,000 alcoholic
and nonalcoholic cocktails / Anthony Dias Blue.—Rev. ed.
    p. cm.
    Includes index.
    ISBN 0-06-009914-3
    1. Cocktails. 2. Nonalcoholic cocktails. I. Title.
TX951 .D48 2002
641.8'74—dc21
                                                        2002026493

04 05 06 ❖/RRD 10 9 8 7 6 5 4

*In loving memory of my parents, Gertrud and Sidney Blue,*
*who taught me about the nuances of taste and*
*the pure pleasure of a well-mixed drink.*

# Contents

# Acknowledgments

Doing the revision and update of this book has been no less enlightening, entertaining, and delicious than it was on the first go-round. So much has changed in the intervening decade since the first book was written that it has been almost like starting from scratch.

Gallons of thanks go to Tanya Ward Goodman, who has painstakingly researched the whole project as well as unearthed the latest and hottest new concoctions. Tanya was ably assisted by David Gadd, an expert on many subjects. I also want to thank again the talented and devoted young women—Sally Horchow, Elizabeth Weinreb, Lindsay Moran, and Lisa Giannini—who worked on the first edition. They have all left an indelible mark on the manuscript.

Thanks go to Susan Friedland, who was perceptive enough to suggest the project, even before cocktails started being trendy again. Thanks to *Bon Appétit* and *American Way*, both of which give me a platform for my writings on spirits and cocktails, and to the San Francisco World Spirits Competition, where I get to taste all the new brands.

Thanks also to my staff, especially Gayle Marsh, Cecilia Ceja, and Mia Fassero, who covered for me when I was busy shaking and stirring; and to my wife, Kathy, and my children, Caitlin, Toby, Jessica, and Amanda, whose patience is legendary.

# Introduction

It is a golden age for cocktails in America. Everywhere you look there is a bar with one or more creative mixologists behind it—stirring, straining, blending, and shaking. Even your neighborhood sushi bar now offers a "full bar," as the kimonoed hostess politely points out. At home, the modern American is not only laying in a fabulous wine cellar, but fully stocking the bar. Every host and hostess needs to be up to speed on the latest cocktail creations. Not since the early to mid-20th century has our nation been so enthralled with mixed drinks.

Those who were of drinking age in the '70s remember what it was like before this latest mixology boom took hold. Cocktails, closely associated with the previous generation (the one that had among its members the likes of Willy Loman, Van Johnson, June Cleaver, and your father or grandfather), were considered passé, self-indulgent, and unhealthy. Bottled water was in; booze was out. Running was in; the three-martini lunch was out.

The standard order at the bar in those troubled times was "Perrier with lime," or for those living their lives in the fast lane, a glass of Chardonnay. "Light" was the watchword of the lean-and-mean set. Bars had become a great place to display droopy plants. Like bomb shelters, they no longer served any real purpose.

But just as the pendulum reached this extreme, the cocktail, long given up for dead, was struggling to its feet on college campuses. A new generation, unintimidated by the resurgent Perrier-and-lime puritanism of the '70s and '80s, was discovering the joys of a well-mixed cocktail.

When this book was first written, it was just the beginning of the return to the mixed drink. The Long Island Iced Tea (a creation of the dance clubs of the Hamptons) had just vaulted to prominence. Shooters and all manner of bizarre concoctions were waiting to enliven your weekend.

Now, more than a decade later, cocktails are no longer a symbol of rebellion or counterculture behavior. They are an integral part of our 21st-century lifestyle—an accepted and expected aspect of our social transactions. As a result, some of the wilder and crazier drinks have disappeared. The trend is, at the same time, both traditional and modern. The return of the martini—the most classic of all drinks—is the best demonstration of this. Here we have the ultimate cocktail—invented nearly a century ago—spawning an explosion of creative spin-offs. First there was the substitution of vodka for gin; then came the invention of such now classic creations as the Cosmopolitan and the Apple Martini. To give proper respect to the martini phenomenon, I have added an entire chapter on martinis to this new edition.

The rebirth of the cocktail has provided inspiration to the spirits industry to introduce a stream of exciting new products. There are spectacular superpremium versions of standard spirits—single-malt scotch, small-batch bourbon, ultrapremium vodka, exceptional new gin, complex new rum, extraordinary aged tequila—as well as dazzling new products that create exciting mixed drink possibilities. Flavored vodkas, flavored gins, new schnapps, spiced rums, and dramatic new liqueurs have pushed the envelope for mixed drinks. More potential ingredients mean more new ideas and a greater possibility of new inventions.

The cocktail—and all the social interaction it brings with it—is back. Over the last half of the 20th century it has come full circle—from "in" to "out" to "in." It has jumped generations and moved from two-fisted drinkers to the young, hip, and happening set. It is the best time ever for mixed drinks, and it is the best time ever for a comprehensive book on the subject.

*The Complete Book of Mixed Drinks* can be a road map to greater enjoyment and understanding of this phenomenon. For the proactive, it can be a guide to making some of the best new combinations at home, and for those who prefer to have their drinks mixed for them, it can help to demystify the drink menus in today's trendy bars. And don't overlook the introductions to each chapter. They will inform and amuse you, and turn you into a font of knowledge.

*Santé!* Salute! Cheers!
Anthony Diaz Blue,
*March 2002*

# THE
# COMPLETE
# BOOK OF
# MIXED
# DRINKS

# STOCKING THE BAR

As with cooking, mixing drinks requires a full complement of good equipment. It's difficult making a beurre blanc sauce on a hot plate, and making a pineapple daiquiri is virtually impossible without a blender. The best ingredients and the right equipment are necessary to get the most use out of this book.

Throughout this book, I have tried to use generic ingredient names, not brand names. There are several reasons for this. First of all, this book, unlike numerous other drink books, is not beholden to any wine or liquor producer. Second, there are many good choices available within each category. I must point out, however, that cut-rate bargain brands are usually no bargain. Quality ingredients are essential to drawing the most out of the recipes in this book.

## About the Bar

### BASIC EQUIPMENT

The following devices are part of the complete bar. Except for the blender, these are all simple and inexpensive tools.

BLENDER A powerful, heavy-duty blender is needed to grind the ice needed for frozen drinks. The basic kitchen blender may not be strong enough to do the job.

BOTTLE OPENER A standard lever type of bottle opener is essential, the simpler the better.

CAN OPENER A "church key," or standard kitchen opener, is ideal for opening juice cans.

CHAMPAGNE STOPPER    A good champagne stopper will preserve the carbonation in champagne and sparkling wine for at least 24 hours. The best type has a spring mechanism and two metal pieces that hook under the lip of a typical champagne bottle.

CORKSCREW    The classic wine opener is the waiter's corkscrew, a basic lever. There are many versions of this simple tool, and they vary widely in quality. My favorite corkscrew is the Screwpull, a remarkably well designed device full of space-age technology. If you have to open large numbers of bottles, the best corkscrew is the Leverpull by Screwpull. Many California wine folk use the Ah-So, the opener with the two prongs. This device can push the cork into the wine if you're not careful, but it doesn't puncture the cork, which is quite helpful to people who want to recork wine bottles for future use. My least favorite opener is the wing type, mainly because the corkscrew is usually too tightly wound. All the best corkscrews have an open spiral with a channel down the middle.

GLASS PITCHER    A glass pitcher is always handy, and is a very attractive way to serve drinks for more than two guests. It is also useful for pouring water and juices.

ICE BUCKET    The ice bucket is the most practical and attractive way to keep ice at your bar. Use tongs to dispense the ice.

JIGGER    A jigger provides ounce measurements and is absolutely essential. The best jigger is the double-headed, stainless steel variety that delineates 1 and 1½-ounce measurements.

MEASURING CUP    A small Pyrex glass 1-cup measure is perfect for recipes that call for amounts greater than 2 ounces.

MEASURING SPOONS    A standard kitchen set will work perfectly.

MIXING GLASS    The best of these have a pouring spout, but any tall, 16-ounce glass will work.

MIXING SPOON    Preferable is a long stainless steel spoon with a thin twisted handle that can be used for mixing, stirring, and sometimes, muddling.

MUDDLER    This term refers to squeezing the juice from herbs or fruit and blending it with dry ingredients. A mortar and pestle is usually used for muddling, but you can also use the mixing spoon.

PARING KNIFE  A paring knife is needed for cutting fruit wedges and twists. It will also help to make your garnishes pretty fancy.

SHAKER  There are two popular types of shakers: the Boston and the standard. The Boston shaker has two pieces, a glass receptacle and a stainless steel container of comparable but slightly larger size. When shook, the glass is capped by the metal top and the liquid is transferred back and forth from one receptacle to the other. The standard shaker has three pieces: a stainless steel strainer, a lid, and a receptacle. The top often has a small capped spout. Shakers are used to combine ingredients that need more homogenizing than stirring can provide. Carbonated beverages are never put in a shaker—they lose their bubbles.

STRAINER  The Hawthorn strainer is usually used. It has a spring that holds it in the top of a standard mixing glass or shaker.

Also invaluable are such assorted accessories as cocktail napkins, straws, coasters, and toothpicks.

# Direction Definitions

BLEND  Blending requires a powerful electric blender in order to puree the ice and other ingredients to a smooth consistency. Do not blend for more than 5 minutes.

CRUSHED ICE  Also called "cracked" ice, these are ice cubes that have been pulverized with a mallet or other heavy object.

MIX  Mixing thoroughly combines ingredients and is usually done in a mixing glass. The purpose is to chill the alcohols quickly without diluting them. Mix with a glass stirring rod or bar spoon and several ice cubes.

MUDDLE  Muddling requires the use of a mortar and pestle to grind fresh herbs or fruit with sugar.

SHAKE  First combine the ingredients and crushed ice in a shaker. Then shake the canister vigorously to quickly chill the mixture without diluting it.

STRAIN A Hawthorn strainer will fit over either a mixing glass or shaker. The purpose is to separate ice and other solids from the mixture before serving.

# Drink Terminology

APERITIF A drink traditionally served before a meal to whet the appetite. It is usually a flavored bitters or vermouth.

CHASER A mixer, beer, or nonalcoholic drink that is swallowed soon after a straight shot of whiskey, bourbon, tequila, or other spirit.

COBBLER A tall drink usually served in a tall collins glass filled with crushed ice and garnished with fresh fruit and mint sprigs.

COLLINS A tall drink of ice, sugar, citrus juice, and a spirit, topped off with club soda or ice water. The famous Tom Collins is made with gin.

COOLER The basic formula includes a wine or spirit, a carbonated beverage, and a citrus rind for garnish. The citrus garnish is usually one continuous spiral that hooks over the rim of the glass.

CRUSTA A drink served in a wineglass or a short glass, with the optional sugar-coated rim. The inside of the glass is lined with a strip of citrus rind.

DAISY The daisy is an oversized cocktail, usually with more alcohol than a normal cocktail. It is often sweetened with a fruit syrup and served over crushed ice. The margarita is an example of a daisy.

EGGNOG A traditional Christmas holiday punch that is served cold in tall glasses or in punch cups. It is a creamy concoction with grated nutmeg on top.

FIX A small cobbler, sour-type drink made with sugar, lemon juice, alcohol, and crushed ice. It can also be made with pineapple syrup.

FIZZ A drink traditionally served in the late morning. It is always topped off with club soda or sparkling wine.

FLOAT To "float" a liqueur or other spirit, pour it gently into the glass over the back of a spoon and do not mix.

FLIP  Originally, flips were served hot by plunging a red-hot flip iron into the drink. Now they are served as a cold, creamy drink made with eggs, sugar, alcohol, and citrus juice.

GROG  The grog originated as a mixture of rum and water issued to sailors of the Royal Navy. Now it is any rum-based drink made with fruit and sugar.

JULEP  A julep consists of bourbon, sugar, and mint leaves. It originated in Kentucky, and is usually made with Kentucky bourbon.

MIST  Any drink in which the spirit is poured into a glass over crushed ice.

NEAT  A spirit served straight, without mixers or ice.

ON THE ROCKS  Poured over ice cubes.

PUFF  An afternoon drink of equal parts spirit and milk, topped off with club soda and served over ice.

PUNCH  A drink mixture prepared in large quantities. It can include any combination of spirits, sweeteners, juices, wine, flavorings, and fruit garnishes.

SHOOTER  A straight shot of any spirit.

SLING  A tall drink made with lemon juice, sugar, and spirits and topped off with club soda.

SMASH  A short julep, served in an old-fashioned glass.

SOUR  Usually served in a sour or old-fashioned glass, a sour is made with lime or lemon juice, sugar, and spirits.

SWIZZLE  The swizzle originated in the Caribbean, where long twigs were twirled in a pitcher or glass until the container was frosty. Today a glass rod is usually used.

TODDY  The toddy was originally a hot drink. It was a mixture of sweetener, spirit, spices, and hot water. Now it may be served cold, and is distinguished from a sling by using plain water instead of club soda.

TONIC  A tall drink with ice, spirit, and tonic water.

# Measurements

## STANDARD MEASUREMENTS

| 1 quart | = | 32 ounces | = | 2 pints | = | 4 cups |
|---|---|---|---|---|---|---|
| 1 pint | = | 16 ounces | = | 2 cups | | |
| 1 cup | = | 8 ounces | = | ½ pint | | |
| 1 jigger | = | 1½ ounces | | | | |
| 1 wineglass | = | 6 ounces | | | | |
| 1 teaspoon | = | ⅛ ounce | | | | |
| 1 dash | = | ⅙ teaspoon | | | | |
| 1 tablespoon | = | 3 teaspoons | | | | |
| 1 tablespoon | = | ½ ounce | | | | |
| 4 tablespoons | = | ¼ cup | = | 2 ounces | | |
| 8 tablespoons | = | ½ cup | = | 4 ounces | | |
| 16 cups | = | 4 quarts | = | 1 fluid gallon | | |

## SPIRIT BOTTLE MEASURES

| METRIC (BOTTLE SIZE) | FLUID (OUNCES) | BOTTLES (PER CASE) |
|---|---|---|
| 50 ml. | 1.7 | 120 |
| 200 ml. | 6.8 | 48 |
| 500 ml. | 16.9 | 24 |
| 750 ml. | 25.4 | 12 |
| 1 liter | 33.8 | 12 |
| 1.5 liters | 50.8 | 6 |

# Calorie Chart
*calories/ounce*

## ALCOHOLIC BEVERAGES

| | | | |
|---|---|---|---|
| Ale | 18 | Brandy | 72 |
| Beer (imported) | 16 | Canadian whiskey | 86 |
| Beer (U.S.) | 14 | Gin | 75 |
| Bourbon | 86 | Irish whiskey | 84 |

| | | |
|---|---|---|
| Liqueurs | 75 to 175 | |
| Port | 40 | |
| Rum | 97 | |
| Rye whiskey | 92 | |
| Scotch whisky | 78 | |
| Sherry | 37 | |
| Tequila | 95 | |
| Vermouth (dry) | 28 | |
| Vermouth (sweet) | | 42 |
| Vodka | 87 | |
| Wine (dry) | 25 | |
| Wine (sweet) | 50 | |

**MIXERS**

| | |
|---|---|
| Club soda | 0 |
| Cola | 17 |
| Cream (heavy) | 106 |
| Diet soda | 0 |
| Ginger ale | 9 |
| Tonic water | 9 |
| Lemon juice | 8 |
| Lime juice | 8 |
| Orange juice | 14 |
| Pineapple juice | 17 |

# Bar-Supply Checklist

| SPIRITS | MIXERS | GARNISHES |
|---|---|---|
| Amaretto | Club soda | Black olives |
| Baileys Irish Cream | Cola | Cherries |
| Beer | Cream of coconut | Cocktail onions |
| Blended whiskey | Ginger ale | Fresh limes |
| Bourbon | Grenadine syrup | Grated nutmeg |
| Coffee liqueur | Lemon juice | Green olives |
| Dry red wine | Orange juice | Lemon spirals |
| Dry sparkling wine | Pineapple juice | Lemon twists |
| Dry vermouth | Rose's lime juice | Orange wedges |
| Dry white wine | 7 UP | Salt |
| Gin | Simple sugar syrup | Sugar |
| Grand Marnier | (see recipe p.33) | |
| Irish whiskey | Sweet 'n' sour | |
| Rum | Tabasco sauce | |
| Scotch whisky | Tonic water | |
| Sweet vermouth | Worcestershire sauce | |
| Tequila | | |
| Triple sec | | |

IRISH COFFEE

HURRICANE

HIGHBALL

COLLINS

POUSSE-CAFÉ

OLD-FASHIONED

SHOT

PARFAIT

PILSNER

# Glassware

ALL-PURPOSE BALLOON GLASS  A popular 10- to 14-ounce stemmed glass with a large bowl. It is often used when a recipe calls for a large wineglass.

COCKTAIL GLASS  A stemmed glass with sloping sides and a wide mouth that will hold from 3 to 6 ounces.

COLLINS GLASS  Similar to the highball glass, but able to hold from 10 to 14 ounces.

CORDIAL GLASS  A small-stemmed glass, often with extremely sloped sides used for serving highly potent cordials and liqueurs.

DELMONICO GLASS  Another name for the sour glass.

DOUBLE OLD-FASHIONED GLASS  A larger old-fashioned glass. The double will hold from 14 to 16 ounces.

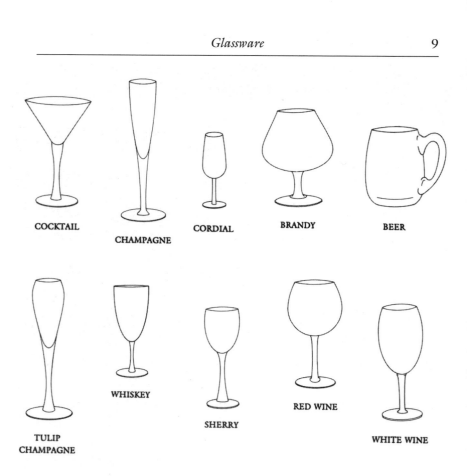

COCKTAIL

CHAMPAGNE

CORDIAL

BRANDY

BEER

TULIP CHAMPAGNE

WHISKEY

SHERRY

RED WINE

WHITE WINE

FLUTE   A tall, graceful stemmed glass used for champagne and sparkling wine.

HIGHBALL GLASS   An 8- to 10-ounce glass with straight sides. Highballs, fizzes, eggnogs, and swizzles are often served in it.

HURRICANE GLASS   A tall glass shaped like a hurricane lamp with a pinched-in center. Usually used for tropical drinks.

IRISH COFFEE GLASS   A short-stemmed glass that widens at the top and often has a handle.

OLD-FASHIONED GLASS   A short, straight-sided glass that will hold from 8 to 10 ounces.

PARFAIT GLASS   A tall glass with a pinched center. Similar to a hurricane glass but smaller. Often used for drinks containing fruit or ice cream, it holds 7½ ounces.

PILSNER GLASS   A tall, slope-sided beer glass that can hold from 10 to 12 ounces.

PONY GLASS   A pony glass is a stemmed glass that will hold up to 2 ounces. Liqueurs and brandies are often served in it.

POUSSE-CAFÉ GLASS   A slim glass with a narrow mouth and, often, a square-footed stem used specifically for the layered liqueur drink pousse café, but also used for a variety of other liqueur-based cocktails.

SHERRY GLASS   A petite wine glass suitable for small amounts of fortified wine such as sherry or port.

SHOT GLASS   A shot glass can come in all shapes and sizes, but it never holds more than 2 ounces.

SNIFTER   A short-stemmed glass with a large bowl used to serve brandy, cognac, and liqueurs. The larger the bowl the better, as it is easier to sniff the spirit's aroma.

SOUR GLASS   A stemmed, short, flute-style glass that is used to serve all types of sours. It holds from 5 to 6 ounces.

TULIP CHAMPAGNE GLASS   A tall-stemmed glass that widens at the top to make a tulip shape. It is used to serve champagne and sparkling wine.

# Mixology Tips

- Try to chill all ingredients before using.

- Don't overfill shakers and mixers. Mix drinks in half portions to avoid this.*

- Never use the same ice more than once.

- Always shake vigorously.

- If you live in an area where the water is too hard or is unpleasant-tasting, make ice with bottled water.

- Be organized. Assemble all ingredients before beginning to mix a drink.

- Don't make cocktails in advance; serve them as soon as they are prepared.

- Use quality ingredients as well as fresh fruit and herbs.

*Unless otherwise stated, the recipes appearing here yield 8-ounce servings.

# VODKA

The incredible success of vodka in the American market has its roots, surprisingly enough, in the Russian Revolution. Before 1917 this clear, fiery spirit was essentially a regional drink, confined to Russia and Poland. It was known as *zhizennia voda* ("water of life") when it first appeared in medieval times, but the Russians eventually shortened the name to "vodka," a diminutive of the word for water. The new name meant, literally, "dear little water."

Water is the most important ingredient in vodka and perhaps the only way to lend this incredibly pure spirit a bit of character. The Russians claim that "living water" from their rivers and lakes is what makes their vodkas stand apart from those produced elsewhere. The quest for pure water has taken the Finns to underground streams, inspired the Americans to invent more elaborate water softeners and filtration systems, and even led the Canadians to melt chunks of icebergs, the theory being that the older the water, the purer it will be.

For a hundred years before the Russian Revolution, the Smirnoff family had been Russia's leading distillers. They became extremely wealthy and developed a close relationship with the czar and the rest of the royal household, but the violent upheaval of 1917 changed all that. Only one of Peter Smirnoff's three sons—Vladimir—managed to escape the onslaught. After fleeing through Turkey and Poland, he eventually settled in Paris.

Vladimir Smirnoff had been stripped of his fortune, but he still had the ability to make great vodka. With the help of other Russian émigrés, he started a small distillery.

Vodka certainly didn't take the world by storm, but it sold steadily in modest quantities in various markets. Soon after Prohibition ended in the United States in 1933, a Smirnoff distillery was established in Connecticut. But until the end of World War II, sales languished at about 6,000 cases per year.

After the war, vodka began to take hold among Hollywood trend-setters. Before too long people began to realize how adaptable vodka was as a base for mixed drinks. When the move toward "light" products began in earnest, vodka was in the forefront of the movement.

America had been a whiskey-drinking nation from the beginning, but, in the late 1940s "brown goods" began to fade drastically. White spirits were moving aggressively into the picture, with vodka the prime mover.

The turning point came at the beginning of the 1950s with the booming popularity of such concoctions as the Moscow Mule, the Screwdriver, the Vodka Martini, and, most beloved of all, the Bloody Mary.

Today, vodka sits perched atop the spirits world, with no challenger in sight. U.S. sales in the 1980s have reached beyond the 40-million-case mark, and show no sign of abating. Seven brands, headed by Smirnoff, account for nearly 50 percent of American vodka sales, but there are an additional 300 brands jostling for position in this lucrative market.

An important submarket that has developed over the past ten years or so is the "premium" vodka business. Marked by glorious packaging efforts and rather high prices, these vodkas show no sign of losing popularity. Perhaps we can attribute this surge of interest in luxury brands to the indulgent '90s which have left us all with a taste for rich desserts, four-dollar cups of coffee, well-aged beef, and, presumably, premium spirits.

Many of these premium vodka imports are distinctively flavored and are less likely to be used in mixed drinks. They are popular with people who drink them straight or on the rocks and treat them with the same respect one might lavish on fine brandy or single-malt Scotch whisky. Incidentally, these excellent products are even smoother and more appealing when they are served directly from the freezer.

Here are a few intriguing vodkas, listed by country of origin:

## RUSSIA

Vodka has been produced for over a thousand years in Russia, where it is most certainly the unofficial national drink. Once believed to contain its own "spirit," vodka was often passed around at religious ceremonies in gallon-sized "cups." Early Russian vodkas were made from rye, then later from potatoes. Though current production relies once again primarily on rye, there are exceptions. Stolichnaya, Russia's premier vodka, is made from wheat and the soft and pure glacial waters of Lake Ladoga, an icy body of water north of Leningrad, close to the Finnish border. Before bottling, the vodka is filtered through both quartz and activated charcoal. The result of this process is a vodka that has a rich but elegant "nose," a slightly thick texture, and clean, soft, gentle flavors.

"Stoli" comes in both 80 and 100 proof. Flavored versions include Limonnaya, Ohranj, Persik (peach), Razberi, Strasberi, and Vanil. Stolichnaya Gold is a recently introduced luxury bottling. The flavored versions are lovely on the rocks and add a burst of flavor to the panoply of new candy-colored martini drinks.

Stolichnaya Okhotnichya ("hunter's vodka") is a 90-proof spirit flavored with spices and herbs. This vodka has been infused with ginger, tormentil, ash-wood roots, cloves, pepper, juniper, coffee beans, anise, white port, sugar, and orange peel, among other things. This liqueur-like drink is spicy and herbal, with a strong licorice flavor undertone. It is particularly attractive on the rocks as an after-dinner drink.

Stolichnaya Pertsovka, dark amber in color, has been infused with red, white, and black peppers. A 70-proof spirit, it is aged for some months in wood. The result is a spicy, rich, hot vodka that is excellent on the rocks or as an ingredient in a fiery Bloody Mary.

Introduced into the U.S. market in 1989, Tarkhuna is a Russian spirit that has been flavored with tarkhuna grass, a fragrant herb that grows wild in the Soviet Georgian countryside. It is light green in color, gentle and herbal, with a flavor that is quite reminiscent of tarragon.

Ikon vodka, first produced outside of Moscow in 1862 by Vassil Vassilivitch Alexandrov, is quadruple-distilled and filtered through Russian birch.

Classic Jewel of Russia vodka comes in a gorgeous, colorless glass bottle marked with a red wax seal. Distilled from hard-winter wheat and rye, this smooth vodka is ideal in mixed drinks.

The Ultra Jewel of Russia vodka merits its hand-painted, limited-edition bottle by going through yet another filtration process. The smooth texture of Ultra is delectable in a vodka martini or on the rocks. Two flavored vodkas from Jewel of Russia, the Berry Infusion and Bilberry Infusion, provide the rich flavor of handpicked wild cranberries and Russian bilberries. Both infusions make tasty aperitifs and can be used to add a nice spark of flavor to a Cosmopolitan or other mixed drink.

## POLAND

The Polish are insistent that their country, and not Mother Russia, was the birthplace of vodka. There is evidence to corroborate the claims of both nations. In any case, there is a long history of vodka production in Poland.

Wodka Wyborowa, a vodka made from rye, has been an important part of the Polish lifestyle since 1489. A soft and elegant spirit with a lush, smooth texture, this fine vodka comes in both 80 and 100 proof. It is delicious on the rocks or in a snifter.

Although most vodkas today are made from grain, there are still some that follow the ancient practice of using potatoes as a base. Luksusowa is an attractive and very smooth spirit that is triple-distilled from potatoes. It presents no problems for most people who are allergic to grain.

Another famous Polish vodka, Zubrowka, was outlawed in the U.S. in 1978. The blade of bison grass contained in this vodka was found to contain coumarin, an anticoagulant drug that had not been approved, in this form, by the FDA. It returned to U.S. markets in 1999 under the name Zubrowka Bison Grass vodka, and each bottle is still graced by a real blade of bison grass. Legend has it that the grass is an aphrodisiac, which may account for the surge in Poland's bison population.

Recent entries in the "luxury vodka" category include the elegantly bottled Belvedere, distilled from rye, and Chopin, crafted from organically grown Polish Stobrawa potatoes. Both vodkas are produced in the region of Masovia.

## FINLAND

Finland's vodka tradition dates back to the 16th century, when Finnish soldiers, returning from wars in other parts of Europe, brought home with them the technology of distillation.

At the end of the last century, several small distilleries were constructed. One of these, in Rajamaki, is where Finlandia is manufactured today.

Made from high-quality Finnish grain, Finlandia is produced in 80- and 100-proof versions and is crisp, fresh, and very clean. It has a smooth texture and comes in a handsome modern bottle designed by Finnish sculptor Tapio Wirkala. Finlandia, always an excellent mixer as well as being quite attractive on its own, has introduced lime- and cranberry-flavored vodkas.

## SWEDEN

Sweden has produced vodka for centuries, but Absolut is a product that was created in the mid-1970s with the American consumer in mind. This nicely packaged, clean-flavored vodka had been the fastest-growing imported vodka on the market for a number of years; then a first-rate advertising campaign featuring artwork by over 350 luminaries, including Andy Warhol, Keith Haring, and Edward Ruscha, helped it become the best-selling of *all* vodka imports. Absolut is lovely in mixed drinks and also quite delicious on the rocks.

Absolut is made in 80 and 100 proof. A completely clear, flavored version, Absolut Peppar, which is infused with jalapeño pepper and paprika, is available, as are Absolut Citron, a lively lemon-flavored product; Absolut Kurant, which owes its tart-sweet flavor to the black currant, a distant cousin of the grape; and Absolut Mandarin, a sweet vodka flavored with mandarin orange and other citrus fruits.

## DENMARK

The award-winning Fris takes its name from the Danish word for frost. Made from grain and distilled six times before being put through a three-step filtration process, Fris is a remarkably clean vodka. Fris Lime is a refreshing addition to cocktails. Denaka is an 80-proof smooth vodka from Denmark that has a creamy, soft texture, a flavor featuring tones of vanilla and caramel, and a soft, lush finish. Danzka is a traditionally made vodka packaged in a unique aluminum canteen. It is also available in three flavored versions: citron, grapefruit, and currant.

## HOLLAND

Ketel One is distilled in a "copper pot still" to produce a smooth flavor. Handmade in small batches by the Nolet family from a 300-year-old recipe, the vodka was imported to the U.S. in 1992 and has grown steadily in popularity. The recently introduced Ketel One Citroen imparts a lemon-orange zing to your favorite cocktails.

Vincent arrived in the U.S. in 1999. Named for the artist Vincent van Gogh, this vodka boasts slim and elegant bottles that feature his paintings, including the famed *Starry Night*. In response to the "Apple Martini" craze, Vincent Wild Appel was released in the summer of 2001.

## ENGLAND

James Burrough, the maker of Beefeater London Dry Gin since 1820, also distills a lovely vodka that is just as painstakingly produced as the company's gin. Made from choice English corn and barley and filtered through charcoal made from Sussex oak trees, Burrough's English Vodka is a spicy and distinctively rich product that is excellent when served on the rocks or "neat."

Tanqueray Sterling has been double-distilled and filtered over granite. Packaged in a frosted bottle with the same shape as the famous Tanqueray gin bottle, the vodka is soft and lush, velvety, complex, and quite elegant.

A bit of a novelty is Blavod, a black vodka which derives its inky coloring from the herb catechu. While the Blavod tastes no different from other vodkas, it certainly makes a design statement.

## FRANCE

Another powerful entry in the ultrapremium vodka sweepstakes is Grey Goose, a distillate made using mineral water from the Gente Springs of Cognac. Purified with champagne limestone, the vodka is packaged in an elegant frosted bottle scattered with flying geese. Grey Goose Vodka L'Orange is delicious over ice or mixed into a French Cosmopolitan.

## ITALY

Mezzaluna is made from semolina grain, the same grain used to make pasta. This gives the vodka a unique and slightly nutty flavor. It's triple-distilled and quadruple-filtered, which makes Mezzaluna as clean and clear as most other vodkas, but the distinctive flavor of semolina sets it apart.

## CANADA

Pearl Vodka, introduced in 1999, is made from Canadian winter wheat and Rocky Mountain water. Distilled five times in micro-batches, the vodka is packaged in a distinctive clear bottle with a pearl-topped cork stopper. It has won numerous awards, including "Best of Category" at the 2000 World Spirits Competition.

## JAPAN

The Suntory Company was started in 1899 by Shinjiro Torii, and its first product was Akadama sweet wine. Today this giant corporation produces wine, beer, whiskey, soft drinks, soup, and pharmaceuticals, among other things.

Suntory makes a crisp and very clean vodka that is packaged in a beautiful, squared-off bottle decorated with Japanese calligraphy and a handsome drawing of trees. The 80-proof version is elegant and smooth, with a dry, refreshing finish, the 100-proof variety is fiery and intense, but still retains a fresh, clean quality. These vodkas are excellent in mixed drinks and charming on the rocks.

## UNITED STATES

Skyy Vodka, a San Francisco–based spirit, is delicious and beautifully presented in a cobalt blue bottle. Skyy Citrus makes an excellent addition to Cosmopolitans and is also quite tasty served very cold and straight up.

Rain, distilled in Kentucky from organic grain and limestone water, hit the shelves in a raindrop-shaped bottle with a blue glass stopper.

Blue Ice is a superpremium vodka made from Idaho potatoes. It is distilled and bottled in Rigby, Idaho, by Silver Creek Distillery, the only manufacturer of potato vodka in North America. The vodka is delicious alone or mixed into a cocktail.

Charbay vodkas, distilled by Domaine Charbay winery in Ukiah, California, are delicious flavored vodkas made from the freshest fruits. The Charbay Meyer Lemon adds extra sweetness to a traditional Lemon Drop, while the Charbay Ruby Red Grapefruit simply sings in a Sea Breeze. Enjoy these vodkas, along with the Charbay Key Lime and Charbay Blood Orange, on their own, with a splash of tonic, or mixed into one of the drinks below.

# Classics

## Black Russian

1½ ounces vodka
¾ ounce coffee liqueur
1 scoop crushed ice

Combine all ingredients in a shaker or blender. Mix well and pour into a chilled old-fashioned glass.

## Bloody Mary

2 ounces vodka
4 to 6 ounces tomato juice
1 teaspoon lemon juice
¼ teaspoon Worcestershire sauce
Several dashes of Tabasco
Pinch of white pepper
Several pinches of celery salt, or
     to taste
½ teaspoon chopped dill (fresh or
     dried)

In a shaker or blender, mix all ingredients with ice. Strain the mixture into a chilled collins glass. Add additional ice cubes if necessary.

## Bombay Mary

1½ ounces vodka
4 ounces tomato juice
½ teaspoon curry powder, or to
    taste
Pinch of ground coriander
Pinch of celery seed or celery salt
Dash of soy sauce, or to taste
Dash of Worcestershire sauce
Dash of Tabasco
Dash of lemon juice
1 scoop crushed ice

Stir together all ingredients in a
14-ounce double old-fashioned
glass.

## Cajun Martini

1½ to 3 ounces vodka
1 thin garlic slice
Several slices of pickled jalepeño
    pepper
Several pickled cocktail onions
Dash of dry vermouth

Let the vodka steep for about an
hour, with garlic, pepper, and
onions, in a sealed container in the
refrigerator or freezer. Combine
the steeped vodka and vermouth in
a mixing glass with ice. Strain into
a chilled cocktail glass. Garnish
with the pepper slice or onions,
blotted to remove vinegar taste.

## Harvey Wallbanger

1½ ounces vodka
4 ounces orange juice
½ ounce Galliano

Pour the vodka and orange juice
into a chilled collins glass with several ice cubes. Stir well. Top off the
glass with a Galliano float.

## Kamikaze

1½ ounces vodka
Splash of lime juice
Splash of triple sec
Lime wedge

Mix the vodka, lime juice, and
triple sec in a shaker with crushed
ice. Strain the mixture into a martini glass and garnish with the lime
wedge.

## Moscow Mule

2 to 3 ounces vodka
1 teaspoon lime juice
Ginger beer
Lime slice or wedge

Pour the vodka and lime juice into
a chilled highball glass with several
ice cubes. Stir. Top off with the
ginger beer and garnish with the
lime.

## Salty Dog I

Pinch of salt
Pinch of granulated sugar
Lime wedge
2 ounces vodka
Grapefruit juice

On a sheet of wax paper, mix together the salt and sugar. With the lime wedge, moisten the rim of an old-fashioned glass. Press the rim of the glass onto the wax paper until it is evenly coated. Fill the glass with several ice cubes, the vodka, and the grapefruit juice. Stir well and serve.

## Screwdriver

2 ounces vodka
5 ounces orange juice

Combine vodka and orange juice, along with one scoop of ice, in a collins glass. Mix well.

## Sea Breeze I

2 ounces vodka
3 ounces grapefruit juice
3 ounces cranberry juice
1 scoop crushed ice

Mix all ingredients in a shaker. Pour the mixture into a chilled highball glass.

## Vodka Gimlet I

2 ounces vodka
½ ounce Rose's lime juice

Combine all ingredients in a mixing glass with several ice cubes. Stir and strain into a chilled cocktail glass.

## Vodka Gimlet II

1½ ounces vodka
1 ounce fresh lime juice
½ ounce sugar syrup

Mix all ingredients in a shaker with ice. Strain the mixture into a chilled cocktail glass.

## Vodka Screwdriver

1½ ounces vodka
4 ounces orange juice
Orange slice

Pour the vodka and the orange juice into a chilled double old-fashioned glass filled with ice cubes. Stir and garnish with the orange slice.

## Vodka Sour

1½ to 2 ounces vodka
¾ ounce lemon juice
1 teaspoon sugar syrup
Lemon slice
1 maraschino cherry

Mix the first three ingredients in a shaker with ice. Strain the mixture into a chilled whiskey sour glass. Garnish with the lemon slice and the cherry.

## White Russian

1½ ounces vodka
1 ounce white crème de cacao
¾ ounce heavy cream
1 scoop crushed ice

In a shaker, mix all ingredients. Strain into a chilled cocktail glass.

# Creative Concoctions

## Belmont Stakes

1½ ounces vodka
½ ounce gold rum
½ ounce strawberry liqueur
½ ounce lime juice
½ teaspoon grenadine
1 scoop crushed ice
Orange slice

Mix all ingredients, except the orange slice, in a shaker. Strain the mixture into a chilled cocktail glass and garnish with the orange slice.

## Bloodhound

1½ ounces vodka
½ ounce dry sherry
4 ounces tomato juice
Dash of lemon juice
Pinch of salt
Pinch of white pepper
Lime slice

In a collins glass with ice, combine all ingredients, except the lime slice. Mix well and garnish with the lime slice.

## Bloody Marie

1½ to 2 ounces vodka
4 ounces tomato juice
¼ ounce lemon juice
½ teaspoon Pernod
Several dashes of Worcestershire
    sauce
Several dashes of Tabasco
Salt
Freshly ground white pepper

Mix all ingredients, except the salt and pepper, with ice in a mixing glass. Strain the mixture into a chilled double old-fashioned glass. Add salt and pepper to taste.

## Bull Shot

1½ to 2 ounces vodka
4 ounces beef consommé or beef
    bouillon
1 teaspoon lemon juice
Several dashes of Worcestershire
    sauce
Several dashes of Tabasco
½ teaspoon horseradish
Pinch of celery salt or celery seed

In a mixing glass, combine all ingredients with several ice cubes. Mix well and pour into a chilled double old-fashioned glass.

## Cape Codder

1½ ounces vodka
Dash of lime juice
4 ounces cranberry juice
1 teaspoon sugar syrup, or to
    taste
1 scoop crushed ice

In a shaker, combine all ingredients. Mix well and strain into a chilled double old-fashioned glass.

## Caitlin Cocktail

1½ ounces vodka
1½ ounces white port
1 teaspoon Campari
Dash of grenadine

Stir all ingredients in a mixing glass with ice. Pour the mixture into a chilled cocktail glass.

## Chiquita

1½ ounces vodka
½ ounce banana liqueur
¼ cup sliced bananas
½ ounce lime juice
1 teaspoon orgeat or sugar syrup
1 scoop crushed ice

In a shaker, mix all ingredients until smooth. Pour the mixture into a chilled deep-saucer champagne glass.

## Clam Digger

2 ounces vodka
4 ounces V8
2 ounces clam juice
2 teaspoons lemon juice
Several dashes of Tabasco
Dash of Worcestershire sauce
Pinch of freshly ground white
  pepper
1 scoop crushed ice

Mix all ingredients in a mixing glass. Pour the mixture into a chilled highball glass.

## Cock 'n' Bull Shot

1½ ounces vodka
2 ounces chicken consommé
2 ounces beef bouillon, beef
  consommé, or beef broth
½ ounce lemon juice
Dash of Tabasco
Dash of Worcestershire sauce
Pinch of freshly ground white
  pepper
Pinch of celery salt
1 scoop crushed ice

Mix all ingredients in a mixing glass. Stir well and pour into a chilled old-fashioned glass.

## Coffee Cooler

1½ ounces vodka
1 ounce coffee liqueur
1 ounce heavy cream
4 ounces iced coffee
1 scoop crushed ice
1 scoop coffee ice cream

In a shaker, mix the first five ingredients. Pour the mixture into a chilled double old-fashioned glass. Top off the drink with the coffee ice cream.

## Cossack Charge

1½ ounces vodka
½ ounce cognac
½ ounce cherry brandy
1 scoop crushed ice

In a shaker, mix all ingredients. Pour the mixture into a chilled cocktail glass.

## Creamy Screwdriver

2 to 3 ounces vodka
1 egg yolk
6 ounces orange juice
2 teaspoons sugar
1 scoop crushed ice

Mix all ingredients in a shaker. Pour the mixture into a chilled collins glass.

## Egghead

1½ ounces vodka
4 ounces orange juice
1 egg
Crushed ice

Mix all ingredients in a blender and blend until smooth. Pour the blend into a chilled old-fashioned glass.

## Eiffel Tower

1 ounce vodka
1 ounce cognac
½ ounce anisette
½ ounce triple sec

Mix all ingredients in a shaker with ice. Strain the mixture into a chilled cocktail glass.

## Emerald Bay

1½ ounces vodka
3 ounces pineapple juice
Juice of 1 lime
½ teaspoon sugar syrup
1 scoop crushed ice
½ ounce green crème de menthe
Pineapple spear

Mix the first five ingredients in a shaker. Pour the mixture into a chilled hurricane glass. Top off the drink with a float of the crème de menthe and garnish with the pineapple spear.

## Georgia Peach

1½ ounces vodka
¾ ounce peach-flavored brandy
1 teaspoon peach preserves
1 teaspoon lemon juice
1 slice canned or fresh peach,
    peeled and chopped
1 scoop crushed ice

Combine all ingredients in a blender. Blend until smooth. Pour the blend into a chilled double old-fashioned glass.

# Gingersnap

3 ounces vodka
1 ounce ginger wine
Club soda

Combine vodka and ginger wine in a double old-fashioned glass. Add several ice cubes and top off with the soda. Stir gently.

# Ginza Mary

1½ ounces vodka
1½ ounces tomato juice cocktail
1½ ounces sake
½ ounce lemon juice
Several dashes of Tabasco
Dash of soy sauce
Pinch of freshly ground white
   pepper

Mix all ingredients with ice in a mixing glass. Pour the mixture into a chilled old-fashioned glass.

# Green Fly

1½ ounces vodka
½ ounce green crème de menthe
½ ounce white crème de menthe
1 scoop crushed ice

Mix all ingredients in a shaker. Pour the mixture into a chilled collins glass.

# Green Spider

1½ ounces vodka
½ ounce green crème de menthe

Pour both ingredients into an old-fashioned glass over ice.

# Hot Vodka

1½ ounces pepper vodka
3 ounces tomato juice

In a shaker with crushed ice, mix both ingredients. Strain the mixture into an old-fashioned glass with fresh ice cubes.

# Ice Pick

1½ ounces vodka
Iced tea
Lemon wedge

Fill a highball or collins glass with several ice cubes. Add the vodka to the glass, then top it off with iced tea. Squeeze the lemon over the drink and drop it in.

## Iceberg

1 ounce peppermint schnapps
1 ounce vodka
1 scoop crushed ice

In a mixing glass, stir together the schnapps, the vodka, and several ice cubes. Strain the mixture into a brandy snifter over crushed ice.

## Jessica's Blue

2 ounces vodka
1 ounce blue curaçao
Several dashes of kirsch
1 scoop crushed ice

In a shaker, mix all ingredients. Strain the mixture into a chilled cocktail glass.

## Jungle Joe

1 ounce vodka
1 ounce crème de banana
1 ounce milk
1 scoop crushed ice

In a shaker, mix all ingredients. Pour the mixture into a chilled old-fashioned glass.

## Kangaroo

1½ ounces vodka
¾ ounce dry vermouth
Lemon peel twist

In a mixing glass with ice, stir the vodka and vermouth. Strain the mixture into a cocktail glass or over ice in an old-fashioned glass. Garnish with the lemon twist.

## Kempinsky Fizz

1½ ounces vodka
½ ounce crème de cassis
1 teaspoon lemon juice
Cold ginger ale, bitter lemon
    soda, or club soda

Pour the first three ingredients into a chilled highball glass with ice. Top off with the soda and stir gently.

## The Kremlin

1 ounce coffee liqueur
1 ounce vodka
1 ounce half-and-half
1 scoop crushed ice

In a blender, combine all ingredients. Blend until smooth. Pour the blend into a chilled cocktail glass.

## La Banane

1 ounce vodka
1 ounce crème de banane
1 ounce cream

Mix all ingredients in a shaker with ice. Strain the mixture into a chilled cocktail glass.

## Lieutenant Bill

1 ounce vodka
1 ounce apricot liqueur
1 ounce orange juice

Mix all ingredients in a shaker with ice. Strain the mixture into a chilled cocktail glass.

## Loose Lips Lemon Drop

1 lemon wedge
Sugar
1 shot of vodka

Saturate a wedge of lemon with granulated sugar by pressing the wedge into a bowl of sugar. Bite into the sugar-coated wedge, but do not swallow. With the pulp still in your mouth, quickly drink a shot of vodka.

## Moscow Milk Toddy

1½ ounces vodka
½ ounce grenadine
4 ounces milk
1 scoop crushed ice
Powdered cinnamon

In a shaker, mix the first four ingredients. Pour the mixture into a chilled old-fashioned glass. Sprinkle the cinnamon on top before serving.

## Olympic Circle

1 ounce vodka
1 ounce curaçao
½ ounce lime juice
½ ounce lemon juice
4 ounces orange juice
1 scoop crushed ice
Orange slice

Mix the first six ingredients in a shaker. Pour this mixture into a chilled old-fashioned glass. Garnish with the orange slice.

## Petit Zinc

1 ounce vodka
½ ounce Cointreau
½ ounce sweet vermouth
½ ounce orange juice
Squeeze of lemon juice
1 orange wedge

Shake all ingredients with crushed ice. Strain into a chilled cocktail glass and garnish with a wedge of orange.

## Polynesian Pepper Pot

1½ ounces vodka
¾ ounce gold rum
4 ounces pineapple juice
½ ounce orgeat or sugar syrup
½ teaspoon lemon juice
1 tablespoon cream
Several dashes of Tabasco
¼ teaspoon cayenne pepper
1 scoop crushed ice
Curry powder

Mix all ingredients, except the curry powder, in a shaker. Pour the mixture into a chilled double old-fashioned glass. Sprinkle lightly with the curry powder.

## Red Snapper

2 dashes of salt
2 dashes of black pepper
2 dashes of cayenne pepper
3 dashes of Worcestershire sauce
1 dash of lemon juice
1½ ounces vodka
2 ounces tomato juice
1 celery stalk

Combine the salt, pepper, Worcestershire sauce, and lemon juice in a shaker glass. Add ice, vodka, and tomato juice. Shake and pour the drink into a highball glass. Garnish with the celery stalk.

## Rich Babe

1 ounce vodka
1 ounce crème de cacao
½ ounce lemon juice
½ teaspoon grenadine

In a shaker, mix all ingredients with ice. Strain the mixture into a chilled cocktail glass.

## Rudolf Nureyev

1 ounce vodka
1 ounce apricot liqueur
½ ounce lemon juice
4 ounces orange juice
1 scoop crushed ice
Orange slice

In a shaker, mix the first five ingredients. Pour the mixture into a chilled wineglass. Garnish with the orange slice.

## Russian Bear

1 ounce vodka
1 ounce dark crème de cacao
1 ounce heavy cream
1 scoop crushed ice

Mix all ingredients in a shaker. Strain the mixture into a chilled cocktail glass.

## Russian Cocktail

1 ounce vodka
1 ounce gin
1 ounce white crème de cacao

Mix all ingredients in a shaker with ice. Strain the mixture into a chilled cocktail glass.

## Russian Coffee

½ ounce vodka
1½ ounces coffee liqueur
1 ounce heavy cream
1 scoop crushed ice

Mix all ingredients in a blender. Pour the blend into a chilled brandy snifter.

## Russian Rose

2 ounces vodka
½ ounce grenadine
Dash of orange bitters

Combine all ingredients in a mixing glass with ice. Stir well and strain into a chilled cocktail glass.

## Salty Dog II

1 lime wedge
Sugar
Salt
2 ounces vodka
4 ounces grapefruit juice

Moisten the rim of an old-fashioned glass with the lime wedge, then dip the glass in a mixture of equal parts sugar and salt. Pour vodka and grapefruit juice into an ice-filled shaker. Shake, then strain into the glass. Garnish with the lime wedge.

## Sea Breeze II

1½ ounces vodka
4 ounces grapefruit juice
1 ounce cranberry liqueur
1 scoop crushed ice
Orange slice

Mix the first four ingredients in a shaker. Pour into a chilled highball glass. Garnish with the orange slice.

## Sparkler

¾ ounce Chambord
¾ ounce vodka
2½ ounces sparkling spring water
Orange slice

Mix first three ingredients gently. Serve over ice in a highball glass. Garnish with the orange slice.

## St. Lawrence Cooler

1½ ounces vodka
3 ounces grapefruit juice
½ ounce crème de cassis
1 scoop crushed ice
Cold ginger ale
Mint sprig
Orange slice

In a shaker, mix the first four ingredients. Pour the mixture into a chilled collins glass. Top off with the ginger ale. Garnish with the mint sprig and orange slice.

## St. Petersburg

2 ounces vodka
¼ teaspoon orange bitters
1 orange wedge

Combine vodka and bitters in a mixing glass with several ice cubes. Stir and pour into a chilled old-fashioned glass. Garnish with the orange wedge.

## Unified Team

1½ ounces vodka
½ ounce light rum
½ ounce curaçao
¼ ounce lime juice
1 teaspoon sugar syrup, or to
taste

Mix all ingredients with ice in a shaker. Strain this mixture into a chilled cocktail glass.

## Vodka Cooler

1½ ounces vodka
½ ounce sweet vermouth
½ ounce lemon juice
½ ounce sugar syrup
1 scoop crushed ice
Cold club soda

Mix the first five ingredients in a shaker. Pour the mixture into a chilled collins glass and top off with the club soda.

## Vodka Grand Marnier

1½ ounces vodka
½ ounce Grand Marnier
½ ounce lime juice
1 scoop crushed ice
Orange slice

Mix the first four ingredients in a shaker. Pour this mixture into a chilled cocktail glass. Garnish with the orange slice.

## Vodka Grasshopper

½ ounce vodka
¾ ounce green crème de menthe
¾ ounce white crème de cacao

Mix all ingredients in a shaker with ice. Strain into a chilled cocktail glass.

## Vodka Stinger

1 scoop crushed ice
1½ ounces vodka
1 ounce white crème de menthe

In a mixing glass, stir the ice, vodka, and crème de menthe. Strain into a chilled cocktail glass.

## Vulgar Boatman

1 scoop crushed ice
1½ ounces vodka
¾ ounce cherry liqueur
¼ ounce dry vermouth
½ ounce lemon juice
¼ teaspoon kirsch
Dash of orange bitters
1 scoop crushed ice

Mix all ingredients in a shaker. Strain the mixture into a chilled cocktail glass.

## Warsaw

1½ ounces vodka
½ ounce blackberry liqueur
½ ounce dry vermouth
1 teaspoon lemon juice
Crushed ice
Lemon peel

Mix the first five ingredients in a shaker. Strain the mixture into a chilled cocktail glass. Twist the lemon peel over the drink and drop it in.

## West Coast Samba

½ cup fresh fruit (bananas, straw-
    berries, oranges, pineapple,
    etc., as desired)
Root beer
1½ ounces vodka
1 scoop orange sherbet

Place the fruit on the bottom of a very tall glass. Fill the glass three-quarters full with root beer. Add the vodka to the glass and stir. Finally, add the orange sherbet and garnish with more fresh fruit.

## White Wim

1½ ounces vodka
1½ ounces lemon juice
1 ounce pineapple juice
Cold club soda

Mix the first three ingredients in a shaker. Pour the mixture into a collins glass and top off with the soda. Stir gently.

## Yorsh

1½ ounces vodka
12-ounce mug of beer

Drink one shot of vodka and follow it with a mug of beer, or add the vodka to the mug of beer and drink them together.

# Signature Drinks

## *Algonquin Bloody Mary*

CREATED BY BARTENDER JIMMY FOX,
BLUE BAR, ALGONQUIN HOTEL,
NEW YORK CITY

1½ ounces vodka
4 ounces tomato juice
Salt and freshly ground black
    pepper to taste
Juice of half a lime
1 teaspoon of Worcestershire
    sauce
4 to 6 dashes of Tabasco
1 lime wedge

Combine all ingredients, except the lime wedge, in a shaker filled with ice. Using the glass and metal container, shake quickly, 9 or 10 times. Strain into a fresh glass and drop in the lime wedge.

## *Bix Bloody Mary*

BIX, SAN FRANCISCO

1½ ounces vodka
Tomato juice
Juice of one whole lemon
Dash of Worcestershire sauce
Dash of salt and pepper
1 thinly sliced lemon wheel

Fill a shaker with ice and add all ingredients. Shake vigorously and strain into a stemmed 6- to 8-ounce glass. Garnish with the lemon wheel.

NOTE: No Tabasco, no ice in drink, no celery, no gimmicks.

## *The Blue Suite*

THOM, NEW YORK CITY

4 ounces Stoli Vanil
Splash of triple sec
2½ tablespoons pureed
    blueberries
Splash of fresh lime juice
Splash of orange juice
Splash of sugar syrup

Shake and serve over ice in a highball glass. Garnish with a slice of orange.

NOTE: To make simple sugar syrup, mix together 4 tablespoons sugar and 4 tablespoons water in a small saucepan. Slowly bring to a boil, stirring constantly to dissolve sugar. Boil for 1 minute without stirring. Allow to cool.

## Bolshoi Punch

RUSSIAN TEA ROOM, NEW YORK CITY

1 ounce vodka
¼ ounce light rum
¼ ounce crème de cassis
Juice of 1 lemon
1 to 2 teaspoons sugar syrup to
   taste
1 scoop crushed ice

Combine all ingredients in a shaker. Mix well and strain into a chilled cocktail glass.

## Bravo

BRAVO, DALLAS

1 ounce vodka
4 ounces pink lemonade
1 ounce triple sec
Splash of lime juice
4 ounces grapefruit juice
1 scoop crushed ice

Blend all ingredients until frothy. Pour this blend into a large wineglass.

## Cary Grant Cocktail

"21" CLUB, NEW YORK CITY

2 ounces vodka
½ ounce dry sherry
½ ounce lime juice
Lime twist

Combine all ingredients, except the lime twist, in a mixing glass. Stir well and pour into a champagne flute. Garnish with the lime twist.

## Cement Mixer

BALBOA CAFE, SAN FRANCISCO

1 ounce vodka
½ ounce cranberry juice
½ ounce Irish cream

Pour the vodka and cranberry juice into a shot glass. Float the Irish cream on top. The Irish cream will cause the drink to congeal and thicken. By the time it reaches your throat, it feels like cottage cheese.

## Dazzling Dina

Yow Bar, Le Passage, Chicago

2 ounces vodka
1½ ounces club soda
¾ ounce cranberry juice
¾ ounce lemon juice
¾ ounce pineapple juice
Splash of lemon-lime soda

Flash-blend all ingredients with crushed ice. Serve over ice in a highball glass.

## En Demi L'Un

Plaza Athénée Hotel, Paris

½ ounce Liqueur de Manzana Verde (sour apple liqueur)
1 ounce fresh apple juice
1 ounce vodka
Dash of grenadine
Champagne

Add first four ingredients to a cocktail shaker, along with a scoop of ice. Shake to blend. Strain into a chilled cocktail glass. Finish with a splash of champagne.

## Essex Lemonbreeze

Griswold Inn, Essex, Connecticut

1½ ounces lemon-flavored vodka
Lemonade
Splash of cranberry juice

In a tall glass filled with ice, pour in the vodka, lemonade, and cranberry juice.

## Fuzzy Navel

Pat O'Shea's Mad Hatter, San Francisco

1 ounce vodka
½ ounce peach schnapps
6 ounces orange juice
1 scoop crushed ice
Orange slice

Combine all ingredients, except the orange slice, in a shaker. Shake well and pour into a chilled collins glass. Garnish with the orange slice.

## Gazpacho Fizz

WESTIN ST. FRANCIS, SAN FRANCISCO

1½ ounces vodka
2 ounces Bloody Mary mix
2 slices fresh tomato
1 scoop crushed ice
Cold club soda
Salt and freshly ground pepper
½ stick green onion
½ stick celery
Cherry tomato

Blend the first four ingredients. Pour the blend into an all-purpose tulip glass. Top off with the soda. Season to taste. Garnish with the stick of green onion, the celery, and the cherry tomato.

## Green Eye-Opener

SIGN OF THE DOVE, NEW YORK CITY

1 ounce vodka
2 ounces fresh lime juice
3 ounces orange juice
5 to 6 drops blue curaçao
½ ounce triple sec
1 celery stalk

In a shaker, mix all ingredients, except the celery stalk, with ice. Pour into a tall glass. This drink is green because, as you remember from art class, that is what you get when you mix blue and yellow. Garnish with the celery.

## Hawaiian Vacation

BALBOA CAFE, SAN FRANCISCO

½ ounce vodka
½ ounce amaretto
½ ounce Southern Comfort
1 ounce orange juice
1 ounce pineapple juice
Splash of lime juice

Pour all ingredients into a shaker with crushed ice. Mix well and strain into an old-fashioned glass.

## Hot Sand

CHEF ALLEN'S, MIAMI

1 ounce hazelnut liqueur
4 ounces cream
1 ounce vodka
Fresh ginger

Combine all ingredients, except the ginger, in a shaker. Add ice to the mixture and shake until frothy. Strain into a rocks glass and top with a slice of the ginger.

## The Kiss

GRAND HYATT HOTEL, NEW YORK CITY

1½ ounces vodka
¾ ounce chocolate-cherry liqueur
¾ ounce heavy cream
½ fresh strawberry

Mix the first three ingredients in a shaker with ice. Strain into a chilled cocktail glass and garnish with the strawberry.

## La Playa

EL DORADO CANTINA,
BRENTWOOD, CALIFORNIA

½ ounce Chambord
1½ ounce Absolut Kurant
Club soda
Cherry

In a 9-ounce rocks glass, add ice, Chambord, vodka, and soda. The drink will layer slightly. Garnish with a cherry.

## Lemon Lambada

CHEF ALLEN'S, MIAMI

1 scoop crushed ice
Juice of 1 fresh lemon
1½ ounces vodka
2 ounces sour mix
3 ounces 7 UP soda
1 lemon wheel

Fill a tall 10-ounce glass three-quarters full with ice. Pour the lemon juice into the glass. Top with the vodka, sour mix, and 7 UP. Stir well and garnish with the lemon wheel.

## Long Island Iced Tea

BALBOA CAFE, SAN FRANCISCO

½ ounce vodka
½ ounce gin
½ ounce tequila
½ ounce white rum
½ ounce triple sec
1 ounce sweet 'n' sour mix
6 ounces cola

Pour all ingredients into a tall collins glass filled with ice cubes. Stir well before serving.

## Magnolia Twist

FOUR SEASONS HOTEL, BOSTON

1 ounce lemon vodka
1 ounce blackberry liqueur
Dash of grenadine
1 scoop crushed ice
Orange twist

Mix all ingredients, except the orange twist, in a blender. Pour the mixture into a martini glass and garnish with the orange twist.

## Manny's All-the-Time Drink

CREATED BY MANNY AGUIRRE,
MUSSO & FRANK GRILL, HOLLYWOOD

1½ ounces vodka
2 ounces cranberry juice
½ ounce fresh squeezed
   lemonade
¼ ounce Rose's lime juice
¼ ounce triple sec

Add all ingredients to a mixing glass, along with a scoop of ice. Stir several times to mix well. Strain into chilled cocktail glass. Garnish with a cherry or an orange slice.

## Mazatlán

EL DORADO CANTINA,
BRENTWOOD, CALIFORNIA

1½ ounces citrus vodka
3 ounces cream of coconut
1 ounce pineapple juice
½ ounce blue curaçao
1 ounce frozen mango puree
Cherry

Add all ingredients, except the cherry, to a blender. Puree until thoroughly mixed. Pour into a cocktail glass. Garnish with the cherry.

## Mazetto

MAZETTO-BRENNER'S PARK-HOTEL
& SPA, BADEN-BADEN, GERMANY

1 ounce vodka
1 ounce Cointreau
1 ounce grapefruit juice
2 dashes of grenadine
Sparkling wine (preferably
   German)
Orange slice
Cherry

Mix all ingredients, except the sparkling wine and the fruit, over ice. Strain into a champagne flute and fill with chilled sparkling wine, preferably German. Garnish with the slice of orange and the cherry.

## Melon Breeze

MICKEY'S PLACE,
BALDWIN, NEW YORK

1 ounce vodka
¾ ounce melon liqueur
1½ ounces pineapple juice
1½ ounces cranberry juice
Pineapple wedge
Watermelon wedge

Mix the vodka and melon liqueur over ice in a highball glass. Add the juices. Garnish with the fruit wedges on a stick.

## Miami Mango

CHEF ALLEN'S, MIAMI

1 scoop crushed ice
1½ ounces fresh mango juice
2½ ounces freshly squeezed
   orange juice
½ ounce orange liqueur
1½ ounces vodka
1 slice fresh mango or orange

Fill a large margarita glasse three-quarters full with crushed ice. Top off the glass with the next four ingredients. Garnish with the fresh mango or orange slice.

## Nuts and Berries

BALBOA CAFE, SAN FRANCISCO

½ ounce vodka
½ ounce Irish cream
½ ounce hazelnut liqueur
½ ounce blackberry liqueur

In a shaker with crushed ice, mix all of the ingredients. Strain the mixture into a shot glass.

## Peppered Bloody Mary

REDWOOD ROOM,
CLIFT HOTEL, SAN FRANCISCO

1¼ ounces pepper-flavored vodka
3 ounces Bloody Mary mix
1 lime wedge
1 celery stick

NOTE: If Bloody Mary mix isn't available, try using the Sangrita mix on page 107.

Pour the vodka, followed by Bloody Mary mix, over ice into a highball glass. Garnish with the lime wedge and the celery stick.

## Pink Lemonade

CHIP PYRON, SAM'S ANCHOR CAFE,
SAN FRANCISCO

1½ ounces lemon-flavored vodka
1 ounce 7 UP
1 ounce sweet 'n' sour mix
½ ounce fresh lemon juice
1½ ounces cranberry juice
Lemon peel twist

In a tall glass filled with ice, pour in
the ingredients in the order listed.
Do not stir before serving. Garnish
with the lemon twist.

## Portofino

PORTOBELLO YACHT CLUB,
LAKE BUENA VISTA, FLORIDA

1¼ ounce Ketel One Citroen
¾ ounce Chambord
2 ounces sour mix
¼ ounce soda (just a splash)
Lime wheel

Add all ingredients, except the
lime wheel, to a mixing glass, along
with a scoop of ice. Stir until
chilled. Strain into a chilled cocktail
glass. Garnish with the lime wheel.

## The Pink Thing

CYPRESS CLUB, SAN FRANCISCO

1 ¼ ounces vodka
1 teaspoon orange juice
1 teaspoon cranberry juice
½ ounce blueberry schnapps

Combine all ingredients in a shaker
with crushed ice. Mix well and
strain into a shot glass.

## Prickly Pear Paradise

WESTCOURT IN THE BUTTES,
TEMPE, ARIZONA

2 ounces vodka
8 to 10 each of fresh raspberries,
    blueberries, and blackberries
2 medium scoops raspberry
    sorbet
1 tablespoon prickly pear
    marmalade
1 ounce cranberry juice
1 ounce sweet 'n' sour mix
2 packets sugar
Splash of 7 UP
1 scoop crushed ice
Pear wedge

In a mixer, blend all ingredients,
except the pear wedge, until the

consistency is thick and frothy. Pour this blend into a large wineglass and garnish with the pear wedge.

## Pterodactyl

JULIE'S SUPPER CLUB, SAN FRANCISCO

1¼ ounces lemon-flavored vodka
¼ ounce triple sec
Dash of sweet 'n' sour mix
Dash of pineapple juice
Lemon twist garnish

Pour all ingredients, except the lemon twist, over ice into a large mixing glass. Stir and strain into a chilled martini glass. Garnish with the lemon twist.

## Purple Hooter

BALBOA CAFE, SAN FRANCISCO

¾ ounce vodka
¾ ounce sweet 'n' sour mix
½ ounce blackberry liqueur
Splash of 7 UP

In a shaker with crushed ice, mix the first three ingredients. Strain the mixture into a shot glass and add the splash of 7 UP.

## Red Rock Canyon

CAESARS PALACE, LAS VEGAS

1½ ounces vodka
¼ ounce crème de cassis
¼ ounce peach brandy
¼ ounce triple sec
Several dashes of Campari
1 maraschino cherry
Orange slice

Mix the first four ingredients in a blender with ice. Pour into a chilled collins glass. Top with a Campari float. Garnish with the cherry and orange slice.

## Russian Apple

BALBOA CAFE, SAN FRANCISCO

1 ounce vodka
½ ounce cranberry juice
½ ounce pineapple juice

Mix all ingredients in a shaker with crushed ice. Strain the mixture into a shot glass.

## Russian Quaalude

BALBOA CAFE, SAN FRANCISCO

½ ounce vodka
½ ounce Irish cream
½ ounce coffee liqueur
½ ounce half-and-half

In a shaker with crushed ice, mix all ingredients. Strain the mixture into a shot glass.

## San Francisco Blues

WESTIN ST. FRANCIS, SAN FRANCISCO

1 ounce vodka
¼ ounce blue curaçao
6 ounces pineapple juice
Splash of soda
Pineapple wedge

Pour the first four ingredients over ice into a mixing glass. Stir and strain into an all-purpose tulip glass. Garnish with the pineapple wedge.

## Sex on the Beach

BALBOA CAFE, SAN FRANCISCO

¾ ounce vodka
¾ ounce peach schnapps
1 ounce pineapple juice
1 ounce cranberry juice
Splash of blackberry liqueur

This drink can be served as a shot or as a cocktail. As a shot, add all ingredients to a shaker with crushed ice. Mix and strain into a shot glass. As a cocktail, pour all of the ingredients directly into a cocktail glass with several ice cubes.

## Sir John's Folly

FOX AND HOUNDS PUB, ST. LOUIS

½ ounce vodka
½ ounce rum
1 ounce sweet 'n' sour mix
2 ounces orange juice
¼ ounce blue curaçao
1 scoop crushed ice
Orange slice

In a shaker, mix the first five ingredients. Serve in a snifter over the crushed ice. Garnish with the orange slice.

## Southampton Stinger

FOX AND HOUNDS PUB, ST. LOUIS

1 ounce vodka
½ ounce Galliano
½ ounce apricot brandy
1 scoop crushed ice

Mix all ingredients in a blender with the crushed ice. Strain over ice in a brandy snifter.

## Southside

"21" CLUB, NEW YORK CITY

2 ounces vodka
Juice of ½ lemon
1½ teaspoons powdered sugar
6 fresh mint sprigs

Put aside 2 mint sprigs. Combine the rest of the ingredients in a shaker with ice. Strain into a cocktail glass. Garnish with the 2 fresh mint sprigs.

## Spiked Lemonade

FULTON'S CRAB HOUSE,
LAKE BUENA VISTA, FLORIDA

1 ¼ ounce raspberry-flavored
   vodka
¾ ounce Chambord
6 ounces freshly squeezed
   lemonade
Lemon wedge

Stir all ingredients, except the lemon wedge, together. Serve in a collins glass over ice. Garnish with the lemon wedge.

## Stars Russian

STARS, SAN FRANCISCO

2 ounces frozen vodka
1 ounce Moka liqueur

Pour the vodka into a frosted stem glass. Add the liqueur and stir gently.

## Summer Aid

PUMP ROOM, CHICAGO

1½ ounces vodka
Juice of 2 oranges, 1 lemon, and
   1 lime
Splash of cranberry juice
Sugar syrup to taste
1 scoop crushed ice

In a shaker, mix all ingredients. Strain into a chilled highball glass.

## Tahoe Julius

HARRAH'S HOTEL AND CASINO,
LAKE TAHOE, NEVADA

1½ ounces vodka
3 ounces orange juice
1 ounce heavy cream
1 egg
1 teaspoon sugar syrup
1 cup ice cubes

Combine all ingredients in a blender and blend until smooth. Pour into a chilled wineglass.

## Visitor

JASPER'S, BOSTON

1½ ounces vodka
½ ounce triple sec
¼ ounce Grand Marnier
½ ounce orange juice
1 teaspoon crème de banana

Combine all ingredients in a shaker with crushed ice. Mix well and pour into a martini glass or wineglass.

## Watermelon Shooter

BALBOA CAFE, SAN FRANCISCO

½ ounce sloe gin
½ ounce vodka
½ ounce melon liqueur
1 ounce pineapple juice
1 scoop crushed ice

Combine all ingredients in a shaker. Mix well and strain into an old-fashioned glass.

## Woo Woo

JULIE'S SUPPER CLUB, SAN FRANCISCO

1¼ ounces vodka
½ ounce peach schnapps
Splash of cranberry juice

Pour all ingredients over ice into a large mixing glass. Stir and strain into a chilled martini glass.

## Zarisian

THE ECCENTRIC, CHICAGO

1½ ounces vodka
¼ ounce white vermouth
¼ ounce blackberry liqueur
Champagne or sparkling wine
1 raspberry

Shake the first three ingredients with ice and strain into a martini glass. Top off with the champagne and garnish with the raspberry.

# Tropical Drinks

## *Chi-Chi*

1½ ounces vodka
2 ounces pineapple juice
1 ounce coconut cream
1 cup ice

Combine all ingredients in a blender. Blend until smooth and pour into a saucer-shaped champagne glass.

## *Volcano*

1 ounce vodka
½ ounce crème de almond
2 ounces coconut cream
1 scoop vanilla ice cream

Combine all ingredients in a blender and blend until smooth. Pour the mixture into a chilled parfait glass.

## *Tropic Moc-Olada*

*Makes 4 servings*

4 ounces vodka
¼ cup lemon-flavored instant tea
   mix, sweetened
1 cup cold water
1 cup light cream, or half-and-half
1 8-ounce can crushed pineapple
   in natural juice
2 teaspoons coconut extract
1½ teaspoons lime juice
½ medium banana

Combine all ingredients in a blender. Slowly add two cups of ice cubes while blending at high speed. Blend until frothy and serve in wineglasses.

## *Waikiki Comber*

1½ ounces vodka
6 ounces guava juice
½ ounce fresh lime juice
1 scoop crushed ice
½ ounce black raspberry liqueur

Mix the first four ingredients in a shaker. Pour the mixture into a chilled collins glass. Over the back of a spoon, float the raspberry liqueur.

# GIN

London dry gins such as Tanqueray, Beefeater, Gordon's, and Gilbey's start with a grain formula that is three-quarters corn and one-quarter barley malt and other grains. This mixture is combined with water and "mashed," then cooked, and finally fermented. The procedure is virtually identical to the early stages of the production of whiskey.

The resulting liquid is distilled to 180 proof (90 percent alcohol) in a column still, a device invented by Dubliner Aeneas Coffey in 1830. The result is a strong and pure spirit that retains a hint of malty, whiskeylike flavor. It is then cut to 120 proof by the addition of distilled water. This slightly diluted spirit is next placed in a modified pot still—called, appropriately, a "gin still"—and redistilled in the presence of flavorings, primarily juniper berries. The gin still was developed by James Burrough, founder of the Beefeater distillery, in the late 19th century.

One can't help but be impressed with the cleanliness and order of the big gin distilleries. Unlike wineries, they have no wooden barrels or damp cellars, just rows and rows of pipes and ranks of shiny stills. There is no season for gin—it is made throughout the year—nor is it aged for any appreciable amount of time. Clean water flows into the distillery from artesian wells and two weeks later it leaves, already bottled and ready for market. Another characteristic of a gin distillery is the seductive aroma of juniper and herbs that perfumes the air.

The juniper comes from northern Italy and Yugoslavia. In addition, distillers use many other herbs and botanicals, including cassia bark, calamus, cardamom, bitter almonds, orris root, licorice, anise, cocoa nibs, lemon peel, caraway, and orange peel. It is the small amounts of these ingredients that give each gin its individual brand distinction.

London is not the only place gin is made. Unlike scotch whisky, which is produced only in Scotland, gin can be made anywhere there is a still, some grain, and the requisite flavoring ingredients. A number of stateside distillers have gotten into the act, with great success, but American gins differ slightly from their English counterparts.

In America, laws require that gin be made from 100 percent neutral spirits. This means that the best domestic gins, such as Gilbey's and Gordon's, are crisper and cleaner-tasting. They do not have the extra complexity of that slight hint of malt that can be found in true London gins. American-made gin makes up for this difference by being quite a bit less expensive than the English product.

The first gin was made in Holland about 1650 and was a much more aromatic spirit than either the London or American versions that are so prevalent today. The Dutch continue to make gin in this same assertive style.

Dr. Sylvius was a respected Dutch physician and scientist in the mid-17th century. He lectured and conducted chemical experiments at the University of Leiden. One of the substances that occupied his attention was oil of juniper, a popular diuretic. He sought to discover an easy way to administer this medicine to patients.

Eventually, he hit upon the idea of blending juniper waters with neutral distilled spirits. He called his concoction "genever" from the French word for juniper, *genièvre*. Within a few months the good doctor's "medicine" was the rage of Holland. Not long afterward, the enterprising Bols firm in Amsterdam was marketing a commercial version.

Soon enough, English soldiers, returning from adventures in faraway places, passed through Holland and discovered what they called "Dutch courage." They triumphantly transported it back home, where it soon became known as "gin," a corruption of genever. When Prince William of Orange, a Dutch grandson of the English Stuart kings, ascended to the British throne as King William III, gin became the stylish drink at the Court of St. James.

Gin was an instant hit in England, especially around the port cities of Bristol, Plymouth, and Portsmouth. It soon became known as the "spirit of the masses," as opposed to the upscale and expensive ports and brandies that had been the darlings of the upper crust.

Over the next century or more, until the onset of the industrial revolution, gin was the engine that drove British society. Its use pervaded every level of English life, and by the mid-18th century a population of 6 million was imbibing more than 20 million gallons a year. London dry gin was being exported to all corners of the Empire.

Meanwhile, back in Holland, the original style of gin continued to be made—and is made to this day. What causes this drink to be different is the fact that it is made from equal parts of barley, corn, and rye and distilled to a much lower proof than London gin. This leaves it with an intense whiskey flavor.

Riding a surge of cocktail popularity, gin seems to be gaining appeal for a younger generation. Historically the base of the very dry martini, gin is also being incorporated into more racy drinks. There has recently been a proliferation of "ultrapremium" gins, which offer delicate flavor nuances and slick packaging in exchange for an often hefty price tag. Of these newcomers, I like Citadelle, a smooth French import with layers of spicy floral flavors; Damrak, a Bols-made product from Holland, the birthplace of gin; and, best of all, Tanqueray No. 10, the perfect martini gin. Among the standbys, there are Beefeater, Gilbey's, Booth's, Boodles, and the elegant Plymouth, which is made with smooth, soft water. Bombay Sapphire, in its distinctive blue glass bottle is also a good bet. Mix these gins into your favorite cocktail or pour them over ice and let your taste buds seek out myriad flavors of licorice, pepper, lemon peel, the sweet violet whisper of orris root, and the tang of juniper.

# Classics

## Bronx Cocktail

1½ ounces gin
½ ounce dry vermouth
½ ounce sweet vermouth
1 ounce orange juice
1 scoop crushed ice

Combine all ingredients in a shaker. Mix well and strain into a chilled cocktail glass.

NOTE: For a dry Bronx cocktail, omit sweet vermouth.

## Gimlet I

2 ounces gin
¼ ounce lime juice
1 scoop crushed ice
Lime slice

Mix all ingredients, except the lime slice, in a shaker. Pour the mixture into a chilled old-fashioned glass and garnish with the lime slice.

## Gimlet II

2 ounces gin
½ ounce fresh lime juice
1 scoop crushed ice
Lime peel

Mix gin, lime juice, and ice in a mixing glass. Pour the mixture into a chilled old-fashioned glass. Twist the lime peel over the drink and drop it in before serving.

## Gin and Bitters (Pink Gin)

2 to 3 ounces gin
½ teaspoon bitters

Mix gin and bitters in a glass with ice cubes until chilled. Strain the mixture into a chilled old-fashioned glass without ice.

## Gin and Tonic

2 ounces gin
Tonic water
Lime wedge

Pour gin into a chilled collins glass with several ice cubes. Top off with tonic water. Squeeze the lime wedge over the drink and drop it in.

## Gin Cobbler

2 ounces gin
1 teaspoon orgeat or sugar syrup
Club soda
Orange slice

Mix gin and syrup in a double old-fashioned glass with ice. Top off with cold club soda. Stir gently. Garnish with the orange slice.

## Gin Daisy

2 to 3 ounces gin
1 ounce lemon juice
¼ ounce raspberry syrup or
    grenadine
½ ounce teaspoon sugar syrup, or
    to taste
1 scoop crushed ice
Club soda
Orange slice or mint sprigs

Mix the first five ingredients in a blender. Pour the mixture into a chilled highball glass. Top off the glass with cold soda and garnish with the orange slice.

## Gin Fizz

2 to 3 ounces gin
½ ounce sugar syrup
Juice of ½ lemon
Juice of ½ lime
Club soda
Maraschino cherry

Mix the first four ingredients in a shaker or blender. Pour the mixture into a chilled highball glass. Top off with cold club soda and garnish with the maraschino cherry.

## Gin Sling

2 to 3 ounces gin
1 ounce lemon juice
½ ounce orgeat or sugar syrup, or
    to taste
1 scoop crushed ice
Club soda or water

Mix gin, lemon juice, and syrup with crushed ice in a double old-fashioned glass. Top off with cold club soda or water. Stir well and serve.

## Gin Sour

2 to 3 ounces gin
1 ounce lemon juice
1 teaspoon sugar syrup
1 scoop crushed ice
Orange slice
Maraschino cherry

Mix the first three ingredients in a shaker with crushed ice. Strain the mixture into a chilled whiskey sour glass. Garnish with the orange slice and maraschino cherry.

## Martini

2 ounces gin
½ teaspoon dry vermouth, or to
    taste
Olive or lemon twist

Stir gin and vermouth in a mixing
glass with plenty of ice. Strain the
mixture into a chilled cocktail
glass. Garnish with the olive or
lemon twist.

## Melon Ball

1½ ounces gin
¾ ounce melon liqueur
½ ounce triple sec
½ ounce lemon juice
1 scoop crushed ice

Mix all ingredients in a shaker.
Strain the mixture into a chilled
cocktail glass.

## Negroni

2 ounces gin
½ ounce sweet vermouth
¾ ounce Campari
1 scoop crushed ice
Orange peel

Stir all ingredients, except the
orange peel, in a mixing glass.

Strain the mixture into a chilled
cocktail glass. Twist the orange
peel over the drink, then use it as a
garnish.

## Orange Blossom

1½ ounces gin
1 ounce orange juice
1 scoop crushed ice
Orange slice

Mix gin and orange juice in a
shaker with the crushed ice. Strain
the mixture into a chilled cocktail
glass. Decorate with the orange
slice.

## Pink Lady

*Makes 2 servings*

3 ounces gin
3 ounces applejack or calvados
2 ounces lemon juice
2 teaspoons sugar syrup
2 teaspoons grenadine
1 egg white
Crushed ice

Mix all ingredients in a shaker.
Strain the mixture into chilled
cocktail glasses.

## Singapore Sling

2 ounces gin
1 ounce cherry brandy
Juice of ½ lemon
Dash of Benedictine
1 scoop crushed ice
Club soda
Lemon slice
Mint sprig (optional)

Mix the first five ingredients, with a splash of soda or water, in a shaker or blender. Strain the mixture into a chilled 12-ounce collins glass. Add ice cubes and top off the glass with cold club soda. Stir gently. Garnish with the lemon slice and mint sprig.

## Tom Collins

2 to 3 ounces gin
1½ ounces lemon juice
½ ounce sugar syrup, or to taste
Club soda
Maraschino cherry

Mix the gin, lemon juice, and sugar syrup in a tall collins glass with ice. Top off the glass with club soda and garnish with the cherry.

# Creative Concoctions

## Admiral Growney

2 ounces gin
1 ounce dry vermouth
½ ounce lime juice
1 maraschino cherry (optional)

Combine gin, vermouth, and lime juice in a mixing glass with several ice cubes. Stir to mix ingredients. Strain the mixture into a chilled old-fashioned glass and garnish with the maraschino cherry.

## Alaska

2 ounces dry gin
½ ounce green Chartreuse
½ ounce dry sherry (optional)
Lemon twist

Stir together all ingredients, except the lemon twist, in a mixing glass with ice. Strain the mixture into a cocktail glass and garnish with the lemon twist.

## Alberto Tomba

1½ ounces gin
½ ounce plum brandy
½ ounce orange juice
½ ounce lemon juice
1 scoop crushed ice
Brandied cherry

Combine all ingredients, except the cherry, in a shaker. Mix well and pour into a chilled cocktail glass. Garnish with the cherry.

## Alexander

1 ounce gin
1 ounce crème de cacao
1 ounce heavy cream
1 scoop crushed ice

Combine all ingredients in a shaker. Mix well and strain into a chilled cocktail glass.

## Alexander's Sister

1½ ounces gin
½ ounce white or green crème de menthe
¾ ounce heavy cream
1 scoop crushed ice

Mix all ingredients in a shaker. Strain the mixture into a chilled cocktail glass.

## Annapolis Fizz

1½ ounces gin
½ ounce lemon juice
1 teaspoon raspberry syrup
Several dashes of raspberry schnapps
1 scoop crushed ice
Club soda

Mix all ingredients, except the soda, in a shaker. Pour the mixture into a chilled highball glass. Top off the glass with ice cubes and the soda.

## Anthony's Spur

1½ ounces gin
½ ounce dry vermouth
½ ounce sweet vermouth
1 ounce orange juice
1 egg yolk
1 scoop crushed ice

Combine all ingredients in a shaker. Mix well and strain into a chilled cocktail glass.

## Antibes

1½ ounces dry gin
½ ounce Benedictine
2 ounces grapefruit juice
1 scoop crushed ice
Orange slice

Mix all ingredients, except the orange slice, in a shaker. Pour the mixture into a chilled old-fashioned glass and garnish with the orange slice.

## Aruba

*Makes 2 servings*

3 ounces gin
1 ounce curaçao
2 ounces lemon juice
1 egg white
2 teaspoons orgeat or Falernum
　　syrup
Crushed ice

Combine all ingredients in a shaker. Mix well and strain into a chilled cocktail glass.

## Avalanche

1½ ounces gin
1 ounce white crème de cacao
1 ounce heavy cream
1 scoop crushed ice

Combine all ingredients in a shaker. Mix well and strain into a chilled cocktail glass.

## Aviation

1½ ounces gin
½ ounce lemon juice
½ teaspoon maraschino liqueur
½ teaspoon apricot brandy
1 scoop crushed ice

Combine all ingredients in a shaker. Mix well and strain into a chilled cocktail glass.

## Barbary Coast

1 ounce gin
½ ounce dark rum
½ ounce light rum
½ ounce tequila
½ ounce scotch
1 ounce crème de cacao
1 ounce light cream
1 scoop ice

Combine all ingredients, except the scoop of ice, in a cocktail shaker. Add the ice. Shake vigorously to mix. Strain into a chilled cocktail glass.

## Bay Bridge Cooler

2 ounces gin
3 ounces pineapple juice
½ ounce lime juice
1 teaspoon maraschino liqueur
Club soda, lemon-lime soda, or
    ginger ale
1 scoop crushed ice

Combine all ingredients in a shaker. Mix well and pour into a chilled double old-fashioned glass.

## Beauty Mark

1 ounce gin
½ ounce sweet vermouth
½ ounce dry vermouth
1 teaspoon orange juice
Dash of grenadine
Cherry (optional)

In a shaker with a scoop of ice, shake the first four ingredients. Splash grenadine in the bottom of a cocktail glass. Strain the other ingredients into glass. Garnish with the cherry if desired.

## Belmont

2 ounces gin
¾ ounce light cream
1 teaspoon raspberry syrup
1 raspberry

Combine all ingredients in a shaker along with a scoop of ice. Shake to blend. Strain into a chilled cocktail glass. Garnish with the fresh raspberry.

## Bermuda Bouquet

1½ ounce gin
1 ounce apricot brandy
½ teaspoon triple sec
1 teaspoon grenadine
Juice of ½ orange
Juice of ½ lemon
1 scoop ice

Add all ingredients to a cocktail shaker. Shake vigorously to mix. Put some ice in a highball glass and strain the mixture over it.

## Bermuda Highball

1 ounce gin
1 ounce brandy
1 ounce dry vermouth
Club soda or ginger ale

Pour the gin, brandy, and vermouth into a chilled highball glass with several ice cubes. Top off the glass with the club soda or ginger ale.

Mix all ingredients, except soda and fruit, in a shaker. Strain the mixture into a chilled highball glass. Top off the glass with the soda and stir gently. Garnish with the raspberries.

## Bermuda Triangle

1½ ounces gin
1 ounce apricot brandy
½ ounce lime juice
1 teaspoon sugar syrup
Dash of grenadine
1 scoop crushed ice
Orange peel
½ teaspoon curaçao

Mix the first six ingredients in a shaker. Pour the mixture into a chilled old-fashioned glass. Twist the orange peel over the drink and drop it in. Top with a float of curaçao.

## Berry Fizz

2 ounces gin
½ ounce maraschino liqueur
1 ounce lemon juice
1 teaspoon raspberry syrup
Crushed ice
Club soda
2 raspberries

## Big Kahuna

1½ ounces gin
½ ounce curaçao
2 ounces pineapple juice
1 teaspoon sweet vermouth
1 scoop crushed ice

Combine all ingredients in a shaker. Mix well and strain into a chilled cocktail glass.

## Blue Canary

¾ ounce gin
1 tablespoon blue curaçao
3 tablespoons grapefruit juice
Mint sprig

Add the first three ingredients to a mixing glass. Stir gently to combine. Fill a cocktail glass with ice. Strain the mixture over the ice. Garnish with a mint sprig.

## Blue Devil

1½ ounces mescal tequila
1 ounce Madeira wine
1 egg yolk
1 scoop crushed ice

Combine all ingredients in a blender. Blend well and pour into an iced cocktail glass.

## Bonnie Prince

1½ ounces gin
½ ounce white aperitif wine
¼ ounce Drambuie
1 scoop crushed ice
Orange peel

Mix all ingredients, except the orange peel, in a shaker. Strain the mixture into a chilled cocktail glass. Twist the orange peel over the drink and drop it in.

## Bridgehampton Fizz

1 ounce gin
1 ounce brandy
1 ounce dry vermouth
1 scoop crushed ice
Club soda
Lemon peel

Mix the first four ingredients in a shaker. Pour the mixture into a chilled highball glass and top with the soda. Twist the lemon peel over the drink and drop it in.

## Bulldog Cafe

½ ounce gin
½ ounce rye whiskey
½ ounce sweet vermouth
½ ounce brandy
Several dashes of triple sec or
    orange bitters
1 scoop crushed ice

Combine all ingredients in a shaker. Mix well and strain into a chilled glass.

## Bumblebee

1½ ounces gin
1 teaspoon honey
1 scoop crushed ice
Several dashes of lemon juice

Mix the first three ingredients in a shaker or blender. Strain the mixture into a chilled cocktail glass. Add the lemon juice to taste.

## Burberry

1½ ounces gin
Several dashes of maraschino
  liqueur
Several dashes of orange bitters
Several dashes of sugar syrup
1 scoop crushed ice

Combine all ingredients in a shaker. Mix well and strain into a chilled cocktail glass.

## Cabaret

1½ ounces gin
1½ ounces Dubonnet rouge
Several dashes of bitters
Several dashes of Pernod
1 scoop crushed ice
1 maraschino cherry

Mix the first five ingredients in a shaker. Strain the mixture into a chilled cocktail glass and garnish with the maraschino cherry.

## Cablecar

1½ ounces gin
¾ ounce triple sec
1 ounce lemon juice
1 scoop crushed ice

Combine all ingredients in a shaker. Mix well and pour into a chilled old-fashioned glass.

## Call of the Wild

1½ ounces gin
¾ ounces yellow Chartreuse
2 dashes of orange bitters
1 scoop ice
Lemon twist

Add all ingredients, except the lemon twist, to a mixing glass. Stir gently to mix. Strain into a cocktail glass. Garnish with the twist of lemon.

## Casino

1¼ ounces gin
¼ ounce maraschino liqueur
2 dashes of orange bitters
1¼ ounces sour mix
1 scoop ice
1 orange slice

Combine all ingredients in a cocktail shaker. Shake to mix. Strain into a cocktail glass. Garnish with the orange slice.

## Claridge Cocktail

1½ ounces gin
1 ounce dry vermouth
½ ounce apricot brandy
½ ounce triple sec
1 scoop crushed ice

Mix all ingredients in a shaker. Strain the mixture into a chilled cocktail glass.

## Clover Club

*Makes 2 servings*

3 ounces gin
2 ounces lime juice
1 ounce grenadine
1 egg white
2 scoops crushed ice

Add all ingredients to a shaker. Mix well and strain into chilled cocktail glasses.

## Coco Chanel

1 ounce gin
1 ounce coffee liqueur
1 ounce heavy cream
1 scoop crushed ice

Combine all ingredients in a shaker. Mix well and strain into a chilled cocktail glass.

## Colony Club

1½ ounces gin
1 teaspoon anisette
Several dashes of orange bitters
1 scoop crushed ice

Mix all ingredients in a shaker. Strain the mixture into a chilled cocktail glass.

## Company 19

1 ounce gin
½ ounce dry vermouth
½ ounce apricot brandy
1 teaspoon lemon juice
1 scoop crushed ice

Add all ingredients to a shaker. Mix well and pour into a chilled old-fashioned glass.

## Cool Toby

1½ ounces gin
6 mint leaves
½ ounce peppermint schnapps
½ ounce lemon juice
½ ounce sugar syrup
Lemon slice
Mint sprig

Muddle the gin, mint leaves, schnapps, lemon juice, and sugar syrup in a double old-fashioned glass with a little water. Add ice cubes and stir well. Garnish with the lemon slice and mint sprig.

## Daily Bruin

1 ounce gin
½ ounce apple brandy
½ ounce sweet vermouth
½ ounce lemon juice
Several dashes of grenadine
1 scoop crushed ice

Combine all ingredients in a shaker. Mix well and strain into a chilled cocktail glass.

## Deep Sea

1 ounce gin
1 ounce dry vermouth
¼ teaspoon anisette
Dash of orange bitters
Orange twist

Pour the first four ingredients into a mixing glass. Stir gently to combine. Strain into a chilled cocktail glass. Garnish with the orange twist.

## Delmonico

2 ounces gin
½ ounce dry vermouth
½ ounce sweet vermouth
1 ounce brandy
Dash of orange bitters
1 scoop ice
Lemon twist

Combine the first six ingredients in a cocktail shaker. Shake to mix. Strain into a chilled cocktail glass. Garnish with the twist of lemon.

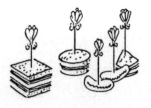

## Dempsey

1 ounce gin
1 ounce applejack or calvados
1 teaspoon sugar syrup
2 dashes of Pernod
2 dashes of grenadine
1 scoop crushed ice

Mix all ingredients in a shaker. Pour the mixture into a chilled old-fashioned glass.

## Devil's Advocate

1½ ounces gin
½ ounce applejack
¼ ounce lime juice
Several dashes of grenadine
1 scoop crushed ice

Mix all ingredients in a shaker. Pour the mixture into a chilled cocktail glass.

## Diamond Head

*Makes 2 servings*

4 ounces gin
1½ ounces apricot brandy
2 ounces lemon juice
2 teaspoons sugar syrup
1 egg white
2 scoops crushed ice

Combine all ingredients in a shaker. Mix well and strain into chilled cocktail glasses.

## Douglas Fairbanks

*Makes 2 servings*

4 ounces gin
1½ ounces apricot brandy
2 ounces lemon juice
2 teaspoons sugar syrup
1 egg white
Crushed ice

Mix all ingredients in a shaker. Strain the mixture into chilled cocktail glasses.

## Drake Gin Sour

*Makes 2 servings*

4 ounces gin
2 teaspoons lemon juice
2 teaspoons orgeat or sugar syrup
1 egg white
Crushed ice

Mix all ingredients in a shaker. Strain the mixture into a chilled whiskey sour glass.

## Dutch Treat

*Makes 2 servings*

3 ounces gin
1 ounce aquavit
1 ounce lemon juice
2 teaspoons sugar syrup
2 teaspoons heavy cream
1 egg white
Crushed ice

Mix all ingredients in a shaker. Pour the mixture into chilled old-fashioned glasses.

## Everybody's Irish

2 to 3 ounces cork gin
1 teaspoon green crème de menthe
2 to 3 dashes of green Pomeranz or Angostura bitters
Green cherry

In a shaker with crushed ice, mix together cork gin, crème de menthe, and bitters. Strain the mixture into a chilled cocktail glass and garnish with the green cherry.

## Flipper

2 ounces gin
¾ ounce amaretto
½ ounce dry vermouth
½ ounce Campari
1 scoop crushed ice
Orange peel

Stir all ingredients, except the orange peel, in a mixing glass. Pour the mixture into a chilled cocktail glass and garnish with the orange peel.

## Georgetown

1 ounce gin
¾ ounce Dubonnet blanc
½ ounce apricot brandy
Dash of lemon juice
1 scoop crushed ice
Maraschino cherry

Combine all ingredients, except the cherry, in a shaker. Strain the mixture into a chilled cocktail glass and garnish with the cherry.

## Gin and Ginger

1½ ounces gin
Lemon peel
Ginger ale

Pour gin into a chilled highball glass with several ice cubes. Twist the lemon peel over the drink and drop it in. Top off the glass with the ginger ale and stir gently.

## Gin and Sin

1¼ ounces gin
¾ ounce orange juice
½ teaspoon grenadine
¾ ounce lemon juice
1 scoop ice

Combine all ingredients in a cocktail shaker and shake to mix. Strain into a chilled cocktail glass.

## Gin Cassis

1½ ounces gin
½ ounce lemon juice
½ ounce crème de cassis
1 scoop crushed ice

Mix all ingredients in a shaker. Pour the mixture into a chilled old-fashioned glass.

## Gin Milk Punch

1½ ounces gin
5 ounces milk
1 teaspoon sugar syrup
1 scoop crushed ice
Pinch of ground nutmeg

Mix all ingredients, except the nutmeg, in a shaker. Pour the mixture into a chilled highball glass. Sprinkle with the nutmeg.

## Gin Rickey

1½ ounces gin
Club soda
Juice of ½ lime

Pour gin into a chilled highball glass with several ice cubes. Top off with the club soda and lime juice and stir gently.

## Golden Fizz

2 to 3 ounces gin
1 ounce lemon or lime juice
1 teaspoon sugar syrup
1 egg yolk
1 scoop crushed ice
Club soda
Lemon or lime slice

Mix all ingredients, except the soda and fruit slice, in a shaker. Pour the mixture into a chilled collins glass. Top off with the cold club soda and stir gently. Garnish with the fruit slice.

## Golden Rooster

1 ounce gin
½ ounce dry vermouth
½ ounce triple sec
½ ounce apricot brandy
1 scoop crushed ice
Maraschino cherry

Mix the first five ingredients in a shaker. Pour the mixture into a chilled old-fashioned glass. Decorate with the cherry.

## Gradeal Special

1½ ounces gin
¾ ounce light rum
¾ ounce apricot brandy or liqueur
1 scoop crushed ice

Combine all ingredients in a shaker. Mix well and strain into a chilled cocktail glass.

## Grand Passion

2 ounces gin
1 ounce dry vermouth
1 ounce passion fruit liqueur
1 scoop crushed ice
Orange peel

Mix the gin, vermouth, liqueur, and crushed ice in a shaker. Strain the mixture into a chilled cocktail glass. Twist the orange peel over the drink and drop it in.

## Green Jade

*Makes 2 servings*

2 ounces gin
1 ounce green crème de menthe
1 egg white
2 ounces heavy cream
Green cherries
Mint sprigs

In a shaker with crushed ice, mix together the gin, crème de menthe, egg white, and cream. Pour the mixture into cocktail glasses and garnish with the cherries and mint sprigs.

## Guggenheim

1 ounce gin
1 ounce brandy
1 ounce triple sec
1 scoop crushed ice

Combine all ingredients in a shaker. Mix well and strain into a chilled cocktail glass.

## Harlem Cocktail

1½ ounces gin
1 ounce pineapple juice
1 teaspoon maraschino liqueur
1 tablespoon diced canned
   pineapple
1 scoop crushed ice

Mix all ingredients in a shaker. Pour the mixture into a chilled old-fashioned glass.

## Harvard Yard

1 ounce gin
¾ ounce peppermint schnapps
½ ounce cranberry liqueur
Dash of triple sec
Orange slice

Mix the first four ingredients in a shaker with ice. Strain the mixture into a chilled cocktail glass and garnish with the orange slice.

## Hawaiian

*Makes 2 servings*

3 ounces gin
2 ounces pineapple juice
1 egg white
Several dashes of orange bitters
2 scoops crushed ice

Mix all ingredients in a shaker. Strain the mixture into chilled cocktail glasses.

## Hokkaido

1½ ounces gin
½ ounce triple sec
1 ounce sake
1 scoop ice

Add all ingredients to a cocktail shaker. Shake well. Strain into a chilled cocktail glass.

## Ivy Club

1½ ounces gin
½ ounce amaretto
½ ounce lime juice
Dash of grenadine
1 scoop crushed ice

Mix all ingredients in a shaker. Strain the mixture into a chilled cocktail glass.

## Jamaica Glow

1½ ounces gin
½ ounce dry red wine
¼ ounce dark Jamaican rum
½ ounce orange juice
1 scoop crushed ice
Lime slice

Mix all ingredients, except the lime slice, in a shaker. Strain the mixture into a chilled cocktail glass. Garnish with the lime slice.

## Jasmine

1½ ounces gin
¾ ounce Campari
1 ounce Cointreau
½ ounce lemon juice
1 scoop ice

Add all ingredients to a shaker. Shake vigorously to mix. Strain into a chilled cocktail glass.

## Judge, Jr.

1 ounce gin
1 ounce light rum
½ ounce lemon juice
1 teaspoon grenadine
1 scoop crushed ice

Mix all ingredients in a shaker. Strain the mixture into a chilled cocktail glass.

## Jupiter Cocktail

1½ ounces gin
¾ ounce dry vermouth
1 teaspoon Parfait Amour or
　　crème de violette
1 teaspoon orange juice
1 scoop crushed ice

Mix all ingredients in a shaker or blender. Strain the mixture into a chilled cocktail glass.

## Key Club Cocktail

1½ ounces gin
½ ounce dark rum
½ ounce Falernum
½ ounce lime juice
1 scoop crushed ice
Pineapple stick

Mix the first five ingredients in a shaker. Strain the mixture into a chilled cocktail glass. Decorate with the pineapple stick.

## Kyoto Cocktail

1½ ounces gin
½ ounce dry vermouth
½ ounce melon liqueur
Dash of lemon juice
1 scoop crushed ice

Mix all ingredients in a shaker or blender. Strain the mixture into a chilled cocktail glass.

## Leapfrog

1½ ounces gin
½ ounce lemon juice
1 scoop crushed ice
Ginger ale

Mix the gin, lemon juice, and crushed ice in a tall highball glass. Top off the glass with the cold ginger ale.

## Little Devil

1 ounce gin
1 ounce golden rum
½ ounce triple sec
½ ounce lemon juice
1 scoop crushed ice

In a shaker, mix all ingredients. Strain the mixture into a chilled cocktail glass.

## London French "75"

1½ ounces gin
Juice of ½ lemon
1 teaspoon sugar syrup
1 scoop crushed ice
Brut champagne

Mix all ingredients, except the champagne, in a shaker. Pour the mixture into a chilled collins glass. Top off the glass with the cold champagne.

## London Royal

1½ ounces gin
¾ ounce triple sec
½ ounce lemon juice
1 scoop crushed ice

Mix all ingredients in a shaker. Pour the mixture into a chilled cocktail glass.

## Maiden's Blush

2½ ounces gin
¾ ounce Pernod
½ teaspoon grenadine
1 scoop crushed ice

Mix all ingredients in a shaker. Strain the mixture into a chilled cocktail glass.

## Maiden's Prayer I

1½ ounces gin
¾ ounce triple sec
¼ ounce orange juice
¼ ounce lemon juice
1 scoop crushed ice

Mix all ingredients in a shaker. Strain the mixture into a chilled cocktail glass.

## Maiden's Prayer II

1½ ounces gin
½ ounce Lillet blanc
¼ ounce lemon juice
¼ ounce orange juice
1 scoop crushed ice

Mix all ingredients in a shaker. Strain the mixture into a chilled cocktail glass.

## Maple Tree

2 ounces gin
½ ounce light or gold rum
½ ounce lemon juice
½ ounce maple syrup
Crushed ice

Mix all ingredients in a shaker or blender. Strain the mixture into a chilled cocktail glass.

## Marmalade Cocktail

2 ounces gin
1 ounce lemon juice
1 tablespoon orange marmalade
1 scoop crushed ice

Mix all ingredients in a shaker. Pour the mixture into a chilled cocktail glass.

## Martha's Vineyard

2 ounces gin
1 ounce lemon juice
1 ounce lime juice
1 scoop vanilla ice cream
1 scoop crushed ice
Club soda

Mix all ingredients, except the soda, in a blender. Shake or blend until the mixture is smooth. Pour the blend into a chilled double old-fashioned glass. Top off the glass with the soda and stir gently.

## Martini Mint

2 ounces gin or vodka
1 ounce peppermint schnapps

Combine both ingredients in a mixing glass with ice cubes. Stir and strain into a chilled cocktail glass.

## Mia's Gingerini

*Makes 2 servings*

1 tablespoon peeled and chopped fresh ginger root
3 ounces plus 1 tablespoon fresh lime juice (4 to 6 limes)
9 ounces gin
2 tablespoons sugar
2 lime slices

Place the peeled and chopped ginger in a cocktail shaker and add 1 tablespoon of lime juice. Mash the ginger and lime juice together for about 15 seconds, then fill the shaker with ice. Add the gin, remaining 3 ounces of lime juice, and 1 tablespoon of sugar. Shake vigorously. Spread the remaining tablespoon of sugar on a saucer. Coat rims of 2 martini glasses with lime juice and dip the glasses into the sugar to coat the rims. Strain the drink into the glasses and garnish with the lime slices.

## Midnight Rendezvous

1½ ounces gin
½ ounce kirsch
½ ounce Campari
1 scoop crushed ice
Lemon peel

Mix all ingredients, except the lemon peel, in a shaker. Strain the mixture into a chilled cocktail glass. Twist the lemon peel over the drink and drop it in.

### Mint Collins

2 ounces gin
½ ounce lemon juice
1 teaspoon white crème de menthe
1 teaspoon sugar syrup
1 scoop crushed ice
Club soda
Mint sprigs

Mix all ingredients, except the soda and mint sprigs, in a blender. Pour the mixture into a chilled collins glass. Top off the glass with the cold soda and stir gently. Garnish with the mint sprigs.

### Moll Cocktail

1 ounce gin
1 ounce sloe gin
1 ounce dry vermouth
Dash of orange bitters
1 scoop crushed ice

Mix all ingredients in a shaker. Strain the mixture into a chilled cocktail glass.

### Mule's Hind Leg

¾ ounce gin
¾ ounce apple brandy
¾ ounce Benedictine
¾ ounce apricot brandy
¾ ounce maple syrup, or to taste
1 scoop crushed ice

Mix all ingredients in a shaker. Pour the mixture into a chilled cocktail glass.

### Nantucket Red

1½ ounces gin
¾ ounce apricot liqueur
½ ounce lemon juice
1 teaspoon grenadine
Dash of bitters
1 scoop crushed ice

Mix all ingredients in a shaker. Strain the mixture into a chilled cocktail glass.

## Newport Cooler

1½ ounces gin
½ ounce brandy
½ ounce peach liqueur
Several dashes of lime juice
Ginger ale or lemon-lime soda

Mix the first four ingredients in a chilled collins glass with ice cubes. Top off the glass with the ginger ale or lemon-lime soda.

## Night Train

2 ounces gin
1 ounce Cointreau
Dash kirsch
½ ounce lemon juice
1 scoop ice
Lemon twist

Add all ingredients to a cocktail shaker. Shake well to mix. Strain into a chilled cocktail glass. Garnish with the lemon twist.

## Normandy Cocktail

1½ ounces gin
¾ ounce calvados or applejack
½ ounce apricot brandy
Several dashes of lemon juice
1 scoop crushed ice

Mix all ingredients in a shaker. Pour the mixture into a chilled cocktail glass.

## Opera

1½ ounces gin
¾ ounces Dubonnet rouge
½ ounces maraschino liqueur
1 scoop crushed ice
Orange peel

Mix all ingredients, except the orange peel, in a shaker. Strain the mixture into a chilled cocktail glass. Twist the orange peel over the drink and drop it in.

## Our Home

*Makes 2 servings*

2 ounces gin
2 ounces peach brandy
1 ounce dry vermouth
Dash of lemon juice
1 egg white
Crushed ice

Mix all ingredients in a shaker. Strain the mixture into chilled cocktail glasses.

## Panda

1 ounce gin
1 ounce calvados or applejack
1 ounce slivovitz
1 ounce orange juice
Dash of sugar or sugar syrup
1 scoop crushed ice

Mix all ingredients in a shaker or blender. Strain the mixture into a chilled cocktail glass.

## Passion Cup

2 ounces gin
2 ounces orange juice
1 ounce passion fruit juice
1 ounce piña colada mix or equal
    parts of pineapple juice and
    coconut milk
1 scoop crushed ice
1 maraschino cherry

Mix all ingredients, except the cherry, in a shaker. Pour the mixture into a chilled wine goblet and garnish with the cherry.

## Peach Blow Fizz

2 to 3 ounces gin
1 ounce lemon juice
1 ounce heavy cream
1 teaspoon sugar syrup, or to
    taste
4 mashed strawberries
1 scoop crushed ice
Club soda

Mix all ingredients, except the soda, in a shaker. Pour the mixture into a chilled highball glass. Top off the glass with the soda and stir gently.

## Pedro

1 ounce gin
1 ounce apple brandy
1 ounce lemon juice
1 teaspoon sugar syrup
¼ teaspoon curaçao
1 scoop crushed ice

Mix all ingredients in a shaker or blender. Strain the mixture into a chilled wine goblet.

## Pegu Cocktail Club

1½ ounces gin
¾ ounce orange curaçao
1 teaspoon lime juice
Dash of bitters
Dash of orange bitters
1 scoop crushed ice

Mix all ingredients in a shaker. Strain the mixture into a chilled cocktail glass.

## Pendennis Club Cocktail

1½ ounces gin
¾ ounce apricot brandy
½ ounce lime juice
1 teaspoon sugar syrup
Several dashes of bitters
1 scoop crushed ice

Mix all ingredients in a shaker. Strain the mixture into a chilled cocktail glass.

## Pink Gin

2 to 3 ounces gin
Bitters to taste
Ice cubes

In a mixing glass, stir the gin, bitters, and ice cubes. Strain the mixture into a chilled cocktail glass.

## Pink Panther

*Makes 2 servings*

3 ounces gin
1½ ounces dry vermouth
1 ounce crème de cassis
2 ounces orange juice
1 egg white
Crushed ice

Combine all ingredients in a shaker. Mix well and strain into chilled cocktail glasses.

## Pink Rose

1½ ounces gin
1 teaspoon lemon juice
1 teaspoon heavy cream
1 egg white
Several dashes of grenadine
1 scoop crushed ice

Mix all ingredients in a shaker. Strain the mixture into a chilled cocktail glass.

## Polish Sidecar

1 ounce gin
¾ ounce blackberry liqueur or
   blackberry brandy
¾ ounce lemon juice
1 scoop crushed ice
4 fresh blackberries (optional)

Mix the gin, brandy, lemon juice, and crushed ice in a shaker. Pour the mixture into a chilled glass. Garnish with the blackberries.

## Pré Catalan Cocktail

1½ ounces gin
1 ounce Parfait Amour
Several dashes of lemon juice
1 scoop crushed ice

Mix all ingredients in a shaker. Strain the mixture into a chilled cocktail glass.

## Princeton

1½ ounces gin
¾ ounce port
Several dashes of orange bitters
1 scoop crushed ice
Lemon peel

Mix all ingredients, except the lemon peel, in a shaker. Strain the mixture into a chilled cocktail glass. Twist the lemon peel over the drink and drop it in.

## Red Bluff

1 ounce gin
1 ounce cherry brandy
½ ounce dry vermouth
½ ounce lemon juice
Several dashes of orange bitters
1 scoop crushed ice

Mix all ingredients in a shaker. Pour the mixture into a chilled old-fashioned glass.

## Red Lion Cocktail

1 ounce gin
1 ounce orange liqueur
½ ounce orange juice
½ ounce lemon juice
1 scoop crushed ice

Mix all ingredients in a shaker. Strain the mixture into a chilled cocktail glass.

## Road Runner

1½ ounces gin
½ ounce dry vermouth
½ teaspoon grenadine
Several dashes of Pernod
1 scoop crushed ice

Mix all ingredients in a shaker. Strain the mixture into a chilled cocktail glass.

## Roma

¾ ounce gin
¾ ounce grappa
½ ounce Sambuca
½ ounce dry vermouth
1 scoop crushed ice
Green olive

Mix all ingredients, except the olive, in a shaker or blender. Strain the mixture into a chilled cocktail glass and garnish with the olive.

## Royal Gin Fizz

1½ ounces gin
½ ounce orange liqueur
1 ounce lemon juice
½ ounce sugar syrup
1 egg
1 scoop crushed ice
Club soda
Maraschino cherry

Mix all ingredients, except the soda and cherry, in a shaker. Pour the mixture into a chilled collins glass. Top off the glass with the cold soda and garnish with the cherry.

## Santa Barbara Sunset

2 ounces gin
¾ ounce apricot liqueur
2 ounces orange juice
Juice of ½ lime
Dash of grenadine or raspberry
    syrup
1 scoop crushed ice

Mix all ingredients in a shaker. Strain the mixture into a chilled cocktail glass.

## Savoy Hotel Special

1 ounce gin
½ ounce dry vermouth
2 dashes of grenadine
1 dash of Pernod
1 lemon peel

Combine all ingredients in a mixing glass with ice. Stir and strain into a chilled cocktail glass. Garnish with the twist of lemon peel.

## Scarlet Letter

2 ounces gin
½ ounce lemon juice
1 teaspoon grenadine
1 scoop crushed ice
1 ounce port

Mix all ingredients, except the port, in a blender. Pour the mixture into a chilled highball glass and top with a float of port.

## Scooter

1½ ounces gin
½ ounce ginger-flavored brandy
½ ounce lemon juice
1 teaspoon sugar syrup
1 scoop crushed ice
Small section of preserved ginger

Mix all ingredients, except the ginger, in a shaker. Strain the mixture into a chilled cocktail glass. Garnish with the ginger.

## Sea Ray

2 ounces gin
1 ounce light rum
3 ounces orange juice
1 ounce lemon juice
1 teaspoon orgeat or sugar syrup
Several dashes of maraschino
    liqueur
1 scoop crushed ice

Mix all ingredients in a shaker. Pour the mixture into a chilled double old-fashioned glass.

## Seville

1½ ounces gin
½ ounce fino sherry
½ ounce orange juice
½ ounce lemon juice
½ ounce sugar syrup
1 scoop crushed ice

Mix all ingredients in a shaker or blender. Pour the mixture into a chilled old-fashioned glass.

## Shady Glade

1½ ounces gin
1 teaspoon powdered sugar
Juice of ½ lemon
Ginger beer

In a cocktail shaker, shake the first three ingredients with a scoop of ice. Fill a highball halfway with more ice. Strain the mixed cocktail over the ice and top off with the ginger beer.

## Shepard's Suffering Bastard

Bitters
1½ ounces gin
1½ ounces brandy
1 teaspoon lime juice
Ice cubes
Ginger beer
Mint sprig
Cucumber slice
Orange or lemon slice

Swirl the bitters around a chilled double old-fashioned glass so that the glass is thoroughly coated. Discard excess bitters. Add the gin, brandy, lime juice, and ice cubes to the glass and mix well. Top off the glass with the cold ginger beer and stir gently. Garnish with the mint, cucumber, and fruit slice.

## Sloe Ball

1½ ounces sloe gin
½ ounce gin
½ ounce vodka
1 ounce orange juice
½ ounce lemon juice
1 teaspoon grenadine
1 scoop crushed ice

Combine all ingredients in a shaker. Mix well and strain into a highball glass over ice cubes.

## Socrates

1½ ounces gin
½ ounce dry vermouth
½ ounce sweet vermouth
1 ounce orange juice
1 egg white
1 scoop crushed ice

Mix all ingredients in a shaker. Strain the mixture into a chilled cocktail glass.

## Spanish Gold

1½ ounces gin
½ ounce dry red wine
¼ ounce dark rum
½ ounce orange juice
1 scoop crushed ice
Lime slice

Mix all ingredients, except the lime slice, in a shaker. Strain the mixture into a chilled cocktail glass and decorate with the lime slice.

## Stanford Cocktail

1½ ounces gin
1 ounce strawberry liqueur
½ ounce lemon juice
Dash of triple sec
1 scoop crushed ice
Club soda
Lemon peel
1 whole strawberry

Mix the first five ingredients in a shaker. Strain the mixture into a chilled collins glass. Top off the glass with the soda, then twist the lemon peel and drop it in. Garnish with the strawberry.

## Steamboat

1½ ounces gin
¼ ounce crème de cassis
¼ ounce lemon juice
1 scoop crushed ice

Mix all ingredients in a shaker. Pour the mixture into a chilled old-fashioned glass.

## Stinson Beach Cooler

1½ ounces gin
3 ounces orange juice
Ginger ale

Pour gin and orange juice into a chilled highball glass with ice cubes. Top off the glass with the cold ginger ale and stir gently.

## Sweet Jessica

1 ounce gin
1 ounce apricot brandy
1 teaspoon lemon juice
½ teaspoon sugar syrup
½ teaspoon grenadine
1 scoop crushed ice

Mix all ingredients in a shaker. Strain the mixture into a chilled cocktail glass.

## Tangier

1 ounce gin
1 ounce triple sec
1 ounce Mandarin Napoleon
1 scoop crushed ice
Orange peel

Mix all ingredients, except the orange peel, in a shaker. Strain the mixture into a chilled cocktail glass. Garnish with the orange peel.

## Tinsley Island

1½ ounces gin
¾ ounce gold rum
3 ounces orange juice
½ ounce lemon juice
1 scoop crushed ice

Mix all ingredients in a shaker. Pour the mixture into a chilled old-fashioned glass.

## Tutti-Frutti

3 ounces gin
1 ounce maraschino liqueur
1 ounce amaretto
2 ounces diced apples
2 ounces diced pears
2 ounces diced peaches
1 scoop crushed ice

Mix all ingredients in a blender. Blend until smooth, then pour the mixture into a chilled highball glass.

## Ulanda

1½ ounces gin
¾ ounces triple sec
Several dashes of Pernod
1 scoop crushed ice

Mix all ingredients in a shaker. Pour the mixture into a chilled cocktail glass.

## Valencia Cocktail

1½ ounces gin
1 ounce dry sherry
Lemon peel

Pour the gin and sherry into a mixing glass with several ice cubes. Stir well and strain into a chilled cocktail glass. Twist the lemon peel over the drink and drop it in.

## Verona Cocktail

1 ounce gin
½ ounce sweet vermouth
1 ounce amaretto
Dash or two of lemon juice
1 scoop crushed ice
Orange slice

Mix all ingredients, except the orange slice, in a shaker. Pour the mixture into a chilled old-fashioned glass. Garnish with the orange slice.

## Warday's Cocktail

1 ounce gin
1 ounce sweet vermouth
1 ounce calvados or applejack
1 teaspoon yellow Chartreuse
1 scoop crushed ice

Mix all ingredients in a shaker or blender. Strain the mixture into a chilled cocktail glass.

## Wedding Belle

1 ounce gin
1 ounce Dubonnet rouge
½ ounce cherry brandy
1 ounce orange juice
1 scoop crushed ice

Mix all ingredients in a shaker. Pour the mixture into a chilled cocktail glass.

## White Baby

1 ounce gin
1 ounce triple sec
1 ounce heavy cream
1 scoop crushed ice

Mix all ingredients in a shaker. Strain the mixture into a chilled cocktail glass.

## White Cargo I

2½ ounces gin
½ ounce maraschino liqueur
Dash of dry white wine
1 scoop vanilla ice cream

Mix all ingredients in a blender until smooth. Pour the blend into a chilled wine goblet.

## White Cargo II

2 ounces gin
Several dashes of cream sherry
¼ cup vanilla ice cream
Maraschino cherry

Mix the gin, sherry, and ice cream in a blender until smooth. Pour the blend into a chilled parfait glass. Garnish with the cherry.

## White Lady

1½ ounces gin
¾ ounce triple sec
¾ ounce lemon juice
Crushed ice

Combine all ingredients in a shaker. Mix well and strain into a chilled cocktail glass.

## White Lie

*Makes 2 servings*

3 ounces gin
1½ ounces maraschino liqueur
4 ounces orange juice
1 ounce lime juice
2 teaspoons sugar syrup
1 egg white
Crushed ice

Mix all ingredients in a shaker. Strain the mixture into chilled cocktail glasses.

## Will Rogers

1½ ounces gin
1 tablespoon orange juice
Dash of triple sec
½ ounce dry vermouth
1 scoop ice

Add all ingredients to a cocktail shaker. Shake to blend. Strain into a chilled cocktail glass.

## Xanadu

1 ounce gin
1 ounce cherry brandy
1 ounce yellow Chartreuse
1 scoop crushed ice

Mix all ingredients in a shaker. Pour the mixture into a chilled cocktail glass.

## Yale

1 ounce gin
1 ounce curaçao
1 ounce grapefruit juice
1 scoop crushed ice

Mix all ingredients in a shaker or blender. Strain the mix into a chilled cocktail glass.

## Youngblood

1½ ounces gin
½ ounce sweet vermouth
½ ounce dry vermouth
1 teaspoon strawberry liqueur
Several whole strawberries
1 scoop crushed ice

Mix all ingredients in a blender. When it is frosty, pour the blend into a chilled cocktail glass.

# Signature Drinks

## Blond Bombshell

GORDON RESTAURANT, CHICAGO

1 ounce gin
1 ounce Lillet blanc
1 orange slice

Combine the gin and Lillet blanc in a cocktail shaker. Chill well. Pour the mixture into a martini glass and garnish with the orange slice.

## Bronx Cocktail (the original)

WALDORF-ASTORIA, NEW YORK CITY

1½ ounces gin
½ ounce orange juice
Dash of dry vermouth
Dash of sweet vermouth
1 scoop crushed ice

Combine all ingredients in a shaker. Mix well and strain into a chilled cocktail glass.

## Charles de Gaulle Cocktail

BISTRO TOUJOURS, PARK CITY, UTAH

1 teaspoon finely minced orange zest
1 tablespoon sugar
1 ounce Citadelle gin
¾ ounce Amaretto Disaronno
Crushed ice
1 ounce pineapple juice
1 thinly sliced blood orange wheel

Rim a martini glass with the combined finely minced orange zest and sugar. In a shaker, combine the gin, amaretto, ice, and pineapple juice. Shake well. Strain into a prepared martini glass. Garnish with the blood orange wheel.

## Cole Porter

WALDORF-ASTORIA, NEW YORK CITY

1½ ounces gin
3 to 4 small plum tomatoes, cooked and chilled
Dash of Angostura bitters
Dash of Worcestershire sauce
Dash of lemon juice
Crushed ice

Combine all ingredients in a blender. Blend until smooth. Pour the blend into a chilled old fashioned glass.

## Putting Green

COLONNADE HOTEL, BOSTON

¾ ounce gin
1 ounce melon liqueur
1½ ounces orange juice
1½ ounces lemon juice
Crushed ice
Green cherry
Orange slice

Mix all ingredients, except the cherry and orange slice, in a shaker or blender. Pour the mixture into a frosted collins glass. Garnish with the cherry and orange slice.

## Ramos Gin Fizz

BALBOA CAFE, SAN FRANCISCO

1 ounce gin
2 teaspoons sugar
2 ounces half-and-half
1 splash orange juice
2 squirts of orange flower water
1 egg white
6 ice cubes
1 teaspoon vanilla extract
Splash of club soda
Dash of ground nutmeg
Orange slice

Blend all ingredients, except the soda, nutmeg, and orange slice, at low speed. Pour the mixture into a tall collins glass, with the splash of club soda in the bottom of the glass. Sprinkle the freshly ground nutmeg on top and garnish with the slice of orange.

## Silver Kris Sling

SINGAPORE AIRLINES

1 ounce gin
1 ounce Cointreau
1 ounce orange juice
1 ounce pineapple juice
½ ounce champagne

Stir the gin, Cointreau, and juices with ice cubes. Strain into a stemmed glass. Float the champagne on top.

## Small Dinger

LA FLORIDA BAR, HAVANA, FLORIDA

½ ounce gin
¼ ounce rum
¼ ounce grenadine
¼ ounce lemon juice
Crushed ice

Combine all ingredients in a blender. Shake well and pour into a chilled cocktail glass.

## South Camp Special

SOUTH CAMP ROAD HOTEL,
KINGSTON, JAMAICA

¼ ounce dry gin
¼ ounce rum
¼ ounce scotch
Dash of lime juice
Dash of sweet vermouth
Dash of cherry brandy
1 scoop crushed ice
Maraschino cherry

Combine all ingredients, except the cherry, in a shaker. Shake well and strain into a cocktail glass. Garnish with the cherry.

# Tropical Drinks

## Bali Hai

1 ounce gin
1 ounce light rum
1 ounce okolehao (optional)
1 ounce lemon juice
3 ounces lime juice
1 teaspoon orgeat or sugar syrup
1 scoop crushed ice
Chilled champagne

Mix all ingredients, except the champagne, in a shaker. Pour the mixture into a chilled collins glass and top off with champagne.

## Blue Whale

1 ounce gin
¾ ounce curaçao
1 ounce cream of coconut
1 cup ice

Combine all ingredients in a blender and blend until smooth. Pour the mixture into a chilled parfait glass.

# THE MARTINI

Graceful as Fred Astaire, elegant as a transatlantic journey on the RMS *Queen Elizabeth,* simple, smooth, and icy cold, the martini has been called the quintessential American cocktail. In his memoir, *My Last Sigh,* filmmaker Luis Bunuel muses, "To provoke, or sustain a reverie in a bar, you have to drink English gin, especially in the form of a martini." But where did this reverie-inducing potion begin? Legends abound.

Some place the origin of the martini in the Gold Rush history of California, while others focus on the pre–World War I elegance of New York. John Doxat, a British journalist who has made an exhaustive study of martini history, asserts that the first martini was mixed at the old Knickerbocker Hotel on an evening in 1910. The inventor was the head bartender, a Martini di Arma di Taggia, and the first to taste his concoction was none other than oil magnate John D. Rockefeller.

Soon enough, the Knickerbocker's bar became renowned for this new drink, and serious imbibers flocked there to taste Martini's cocktail. Not to be outdone, other bartenders began featuring the drink, adding their own modifications. And so began the evolutionary process that has made the dry martini both the most satisfying and the most exasperating of cocktails.

The drink W. C. Fields referred to as "angel's milk" and that has prompted poetic tributes from the likes of Dorothy Parker, Ogden Nash, and Bernard De Voto is traditionally made with gin and only gin. Aficionados are quick to point out that there is no such thing as a "vodka martini." What many would agree is an unnecessary modification of this cocktail is properly called a "Vodkatini." For me, there is no substitute for the exquisite synergism of the juniper berry flavor of the gin and the nutlike herbs of dry vermouth. To mix a martini with vodka is simply to miss the point.

While there is little disagreement as to the ingredients of a martini, there is no end of discussion as to their proportions. That first martini poured at the Knickerbocker was equal parts gin and vermouth, making it an extremely "wet" drink. A "dry" trend started just prior to World War II and shifted the ingredients to 2 parts gin to 1 part vermouth. After the war, the formula changed again. My father's dry martini was 4 to 1. By the 1960s, the proportions had jumped to 6 to 1, and in the 1970s 8 to 1 was common. Current bar trends indicate that the "new" martini is made with a ratio of 5 to 1.

There are those who choose to forget the vermouth altogether. These are hard-core types who while mixing lean over their drink and whisper the word "vermouth" or let the shadow of the unopened vermouth bottle fall across the glass. Winston Churchill used to simply bow in the direction of France as he made his martini. While this is all quite amusing, these individuals seem to be confusing an elegant cocktail with a straight shot of gin. True martini aficionados would never stoop to such foolishness.

Most bartenders agree that despite the predilections of one Mr. James Bond, the perfect dry martini should be stirred and not shaken. Purists will tell you that shaking "bruises the gin" and causes too much dilution from melting ice. Additionally, too much shaking can cloud the hallmark clarity of the martini. But then there are those who welcome the initial cloudiness of a shaken martini (it quickly clarifies as the ice crystals melt).

When we speak of clarity, we should touch on the garnish. Be it an olive or a twist of lemon, it should sit neatly on the lip of the glass, where it will not compromise the drink's purity. A dropped olive or spiraling twist creates a little oil slick on the surface of the drink. The "Dirty Martini" is purposely polluted with olive juice, making it sharper, saltier, and not nearly as lovely to behold.

As you learn the rules of the martini, so will you learn to break them. If we look at current trends, bartenders across the country are determined to "one-up" Martini di Arma di Taggia. Throwing caution to the wind, they've come up with an entirely new class of "martinis." What do these crayon-colored drinks have in common with the original? Usually very little, save the shape of the glass.

There is something about the martini glass that sparks the imagination. Top-heavy yet delicate, it has the seductive wobble of Marilyn Monroe in *Some Like It Hot*. It is iconic—emblazoned on napkins and matchbooks, blazing in neon and metal sculpture. Fill the glass with the classic martini or shock the purists and fill it with one of the other recipes below. The gin may be absent, but when you hold the glass, the classic spirit of the martini remains.

# Classics

## Martini

2 ounces good-quality gin
½ teaspoon dry vermouth, or to
taste

Combine the ingredients in a shaker and stir gently. Strain into a chilled martini glass and garnish with an olive or a twist of lemon.

## Vodka Martini ("Vodkatini")

2 ounces vodka
1 ounce dry vermouth

Combine the ingredients in a cocktail shaker and stir gently. Strain into a chilled martini glass and garnish with an olive or a twist of lemon.

## Vesper (adapted from James Bond's martini as described in Casino Royale)

3 ounces Gordon's gin
1 ounce vodka
½ ounce Lillet blanc
1 slice of lemon peel

Fill a mixing glass with ice. Pour the first three ingredients over the ice and shake very well until they're ice-cold, strain the mixture into a large champagne glass, and add the large, thin slice of lemon peel.

## The Martini Against Which All Others Must Be Judged

MUSSO & FRANK GRILL, HOLLYWOOD

Splash of vermouth
2½ ounces gin

Fill a mixing glass with ice. Pour the vermouth over the ice and stir three times. Strain the vermouth. Add the gin to the ice and stir no fewer than 25 times. Strain into a 3-ounce martini glass over 2 skewered jumbo olives. Traditionally, the bartenders of Musso & Frank do not fill the martini glass to the rim, but serve the rest of the martini in a small carafe on the side.

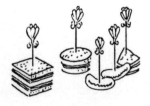

# Specialty Martinis

## Alaskan Martini

ASTA, SAN FRANCISCO

1½ ounces Alaskan vodka
3 drops crème de menthe
1 small candy cane

Pour the vodka and crème de menthe into a shaker with ice. Stir with a bar spoon for about 10 seconds. Strain the mixture into a chilled cocktail glass. Serve with the candy cane hooked onto the side of the glass.

## B9 Martini

BUTTERFIELD 9, WASHINGTON, D.C.

2½ ounces orange vodka
½ ounce peach schnapps
Splash of champagne
Orange twist

Combine the vodka and schnapps in a cocktail shaker along with a scoop of ice and shake to blend. Strain into a chilled martini glass. Add the splash of champagne and garnish with the orange twist.

## Apple Martini

REIGN, BEVERLY HILLS, CALIFORNIA

2 ounces Finlandia vodka
2 ounces Apple Pucker
1 ounce triple sec
Splash of sweet 'n' sour mix
Splash of 7 UP
Apple slice

Shake all ingredients together along with a scoop of ice. Strain into a chilled martini glass. Garnish with a thin slice of apple.

## Bellini Martini

FIFTYSEVENFIFTYSEVEN BAR,
FOUR SEASONS HOTEL, NEW YORK CITY

2 ounces peach vodka
1 ounce peach nectar
Splash of peach schnapps

Mix all ingredients over a scoop of ice in a cocktail shaker. Shake well to blend. Serve straight up or on the rocks in a chilled martini glass.

## Big Apple Martini

FiftySevenFiftySeven Bar,
Four Seasons Hotel, New York City

2 ounces vodka
½ ounce sour mix
½ ounce apple schnapps

Add all ingredients to a cocktail shaker along with a scoop of ice. Shake well until blended. Strain and serve straight up or on the rocks in a chilled martini glass.

## BIN 36 Martini

BIN 36, Chicago

2 ounces Mezzaluna vodka
2 ounces Hatsukuru plum wine
Lemon twist

Add the vodka and plum wine to a cocktail shaker along with a scoop of ice. Shake vigorously. Strain into a chilled martini glass. Garnish with a lemon twist.

## Black Forest Martini

1½ ounces vodka
¾ ounces cherry brandy
¾ ounce crème de cacao
Cherry

Add the vodka, brandy, and crème de cacao to a cocktail shaker along with a scoop of ice. Shake. Strain into a chilled martini glass. Garnish with the cherry.

## Brasserie Martini

Brasserie, New York City

3½ ounces Grey Goose vodka
3 sprays Tio Pepe
Olive stuffed with blue cheese

In a mixing glass filled with ice, add the vodka and stir 40 times. Spray a martini glass 3 times with Tio Pepe. Strain the vodka into the glass and garnish with the skewered olive.

## Caramel Apple Martini

Created by Fred McKibbin,
Grace Bar and Restaurant,
New York City

2 ounces vodka
½ ounce dark crème de cacao
2 ounces Berentzen Apfel Korn
Apple wedge

Place the vodka, dark crème de cacao, and Berentzen Apfel Korn in a cocktail shaker with ice and shake until mixed. Strain into a chilled martini glass. Garnish with the apple wedge.

## Chocolat

HOTEL CASA DEL MAR,
SANTA MONICA, CALIFORNIA

1½ ounces Stolichnaya Vanil
   vodka
1½ ounces crème de cacao
1½ ounces Godiva white
   chocolate liqueur
Powdered bitter dark chocolate

Combine the vodka, crème de cacao, and liqueur with ice in a martini shaker and shake. Strain into a martini glass with the rim dusted with the powdered bitter dark chocolate.

## Cosmopolitan

JULIE'S SUPPER CLUB, SAN FRANCISCO

1¼ ounces vodka
¼ ounce triple sec
¼ ounce lime juice
Splash cranberry juice
Lime wedge

Pour the first four ingredients over ice in a large mixing glass. Stir and strain into a chilled martini glass. Squeeze and garnish with the lime.

## Creole Martini

1½ to 2 ounces vodka
Dash of dry vermouth, or to taste
Large jalapeño pepper

Mix the vodka and vermouth in a shaker with ice. Strain the drink into a chilled cocktail glass. Garnish with the pepper.

## Eccentric Martini

THE ECCENTRIC, CHICAGO

2 ounces vodka
Splash of vermouth
Olive

In a shaker, mix the vodka and vermouth with ice. Strain the mixture into a 3-ounce beaker. Pour the mixture into a chilled martini glass and garnish with the olive.

## Edible Pansy Martini

BISTRO 110, CHICAGO

2 ounces Absolut Kurant vodka
Splash of Chambord
Squeeze of fresh lime
Pansy flower

Add all ingredients to a cocktail shaker. Shake until chilled. Strain into a chilled martini glass and garnish with the pansy flower.

## French Martini

2 ounces pineapple juice
1 ounce vodka
½ ounce Chambord
Pineapple wedge

Add the pineapple juice, vodka, and Chambord to a mixing glass along with a scoop of ice and stir until blended. Strain into a chilled martini glass. Garnish with the wedge of pineapple.

## Key Lime Pie

CREATED BY TODD BELLUCCI, BLUE ON BLUE, AVALON HOTEL, BEVERLY HILLS

1 ounce vodka
2½ ounces Licor 43
1½ ounces fresh sweetened lime juice (sour mix)
1 ounce whipped cream
1 lime wedge

Shake the first three ingredients and strain into a martini glass with a graham cracker crust rim. Garnish with a spritz of the whipped cream on the edge of the glass, then the lime.

## Liam Seide's Cantaloupe Martini

HAL'S BAR & GRILL, VENICE, CALIFORNIA

1 ounce vodka
1¾ ounce Marie Brizard watermelon liqueur
¼ ounce fresh lime juice
2 ounces fresh orange juice
2 melon balls

Combine the vodka, liqueur, lime juice, and orange juice in a cocktail shaker along with a scoop of ice. Shake until thoroughly chilled. Strain into a martini glass. Garnish with the 2 melon balls, spindled like olives on a toothpick. If melon is not in season, simply drop a cherry into the glass.

## The Long Division

SX137, NEW YORK CITY

3 parts Absolut Mandarin
1 part blue curaçao
1 part lime juice
Splash of orange juice
⅔ ounce fresh lime juice
Rock candy stick

Mix all ingredients, except the rock candy stick, in a shaker with ice. Strain the mixture into a chilled martini glass. Garnish with the rock candy stick.

## Magnificent Mile

WHISKEY BLUE, CHICAGO

2½ ounces Tanqueray No. 10 gin
1 ounce Cointreau
1 ounce orange juice
Juice of 4 lemon wedges
Kiwi slice

Shake the first four ingredients with a scoop of ice. Strain into a chilled martini glass. Garnish with the floating kiwi slice.

## Martini Thyme

BRASSERIE, NEW YORK CITY

3 ounces Belvedere vodka
¼ ounce green Chartreuse
Fresh thyme

In a shaker glass, combine the vodka, Chartreuse, and ice. Shake vigorously. Strain into a chilled martini glass. Garnish with the sprigs of thyme.

## Nine Ghostini

NINE, CHICAGO

3 ounces Absolut vodka
1½ ounces Midori
½ ounce sour mix
Cherry

Shake the first three ingredients together with a scoop of ice. Strain into a chilled martini glass. Garnish with a cherry and a glow-in-the-dark-ghost swizzle stick.

## Parisian

BISTRO 110, CHICAGO

2 ounces Grey Goose vodka
Splash of Lillet blanc
Lemon twist

Add the first two ingredients to a cocktail shaker along with a scoop of ice. Shake until chilled. Strain into a martini glass. Garnish with the lemon twist.

## Plumtini

THOM, NEW YORK CITY

2 ounces Absolut vodka
2 ounces plum sake
2 ounces coconut water
Splash of sugar syrup
Blueberries

Shake the first four ingredients with a scoop of ice. Strain into a chilled martini glass. Drop a few of the fresh blueberries to the bottom of the glass for garnish.

## Pump Martini

THE PUMP ROOM, CHICAGO

Olives, lemon twist, or onions
B&B
1½ ounces vodka
Splash of dry vermouth

In one mixing glass, marinate the olives, a lemon twist, or onions in B&B. In a second mixing glass, combine vodka, vermouth, and several ice cubes. Stir and strain into a chilled martini glass. Garnish with the marinated olives, lemon twist, or onions.

## Purple Haze

CREATED BY FRED McKIBBIN, GRACE BAR AND RESTAURANT, NEW YORK CITY

3 ounces Hendrick's rose and cucumber–infused gin
¼ ounce crème de cassis
¼ ounce fresh lemon juice
Dash of sugar syrup
Sprigs of mint
Slice of cucumber

Add a scoop of ice to a cocktail shaker and shake the gin, crème de cassis, lemon juice, sugar syrup, and mint as hard as you can. (Fred recommends shaking until it feels like your arm will fall off.) Strain into a chilled martini glass and garnish with the cucumber slice.

## Purple People Eater

CREATED BY TODD BELLUCCI,
BLUE ON BLUE, AVALON HOTEL,
BEVERLY HILLS, CALIFORNIA

2 ounces vodka
½ ounce Parfait Amour
2 ounces grape Kool-Aid

Shake all ingredients and strain into a martini glass with a Kool-Aid powder rim.

## Raspberry Ridge

SX137, NEW YORK CITY

1½ ounces Razberi Stolichnaya
¼ ounce Chambord
¼ ounce pineapple juice
¼ ounce Citrus Loco
2 bar spoons of raspberry puree
Sprig of mint

Shake the first five ingredients with ice. Strain into a chilled martini glass. Garnish with the sprig of mint.

## Sal's Wife

EL DORADO CANTINA,
BRENTWOOD, CALIFORNIA

1¾ ounces Stoli Vanil
½ ounce triple sec
Splash of pineapple juice
Splash of lime juice
Pineapple wedge

Combine the first four ingredients
in a mixing cup along with a scoop
of ice. Shake well and strain into a
martini glass with a sugared rim.
Garnish with the small wedge of
pineapple.

## Sub-Lime

CREATED BY TODD BELLUCCI,
BLUE ON BLUE, AVALON HOTEL,
BEVERLY HILLS, CALIFORNIA

2 ounces Charbay Key Lime
    vodka
2 ounces fresh sweetened lime
    juice (sour mix)
Lime

Shake the vodka and lime juice and
strain into a martini glass with a
sugar rim. Garnish with the lime.

## Sugar Lip Peach Martini with Costa Rican Pineapple

JIRAFFE, SANTA MONICA, CALIFORNIA

2 ounces premium vodka, infused
    with Costa Rican pineapple
1 ounce Cointreau
2 ounces Fresh Sugar Lip Peach
    Puree
Splash of fresh lime juice
Pineapple wedge

Shake the first four ingredients
with ice. Strain into a chilled martini glass. Garnish with the wedge
of pineapple.

## Thin Man Martini

BUTTERFIELD 9, WASHINGTON, D.C.

2½ ounces Boodles gin
Splash of sherry
Smoked salmon–stuffed olives

Combine gin and sherry in a cocktail shaker with a scoop of ice. Stir
gently to combine. Strain into a
chilled martini glass. Garnish with
the olives.

## Thom

THOM, NEW YORK CITY

4 ounces Skyy Citrus
2½ ounces fresh lime juice
2½ ounces simple syrup
4 to 6 sprigs of crushed mint

Shake all ingredients, including mint sprigs, with ice and strain into a chilled martini glass.

## Willet Watermelon Martini

SX137, NEW YORK CITY

1½ ounces vodka
½ ounce watermelon-flavored
  schnapps
⅛ of a lime squeezed
Chunk of watermelon
1 scoop crushed ice
½ ounce Midori
Watermelon slice

Mix the first five ingredients in a shaker. Pour the Midori into a chilled martini glass. Strain the mixture into the glass. Garnish with the watermelon slice.

# TEQUILA

Once labeled "the drink of the trenches," tequila has a history rooted in revolution. Made in Mexico for hundreds of years, this fiery spirit has been seen alternately as a gift from the gods and an instrument of the devil. Tequila is currently the fastest-growing segment in the alcoholic beverage industry, and its revolutionary spirit remains strong. The margarita, a legendary cocktail, has become the most popular mixed drink in America. In addition, a surge of premium tequilas have taken the market by storm and helped to move the spirit from the shot glass to the snifter. Leaving behind images of war, the new tequila seems to be the 21st century's definition of "play."

Tequila is sold at 80 proof, the same alcohol level as gin and less than some vodkas and whiskies. It has a delicious spicy, peppery flavor and falls into four categories according to age. The first, "blanco," sold in the U.S. as "silver," is bottled directly from the still. "Joven Abocado," roughly translated, means "bottled when young." This tequila is sold in the U.S. as "gold" and will have a slight amber color as a result of its resting in wooden barrels for a maximum of 60 days. Caramel coloring is often added to increase these amber tones. By law, "reposado," or "rested" tequila, ages in wooden vats or barrels for over 60 days, but not for more than one year. The color of the reposado is deeper and the flavors smoother than those of its younger cousins. "Añejo" denotes tequila that has aged for over a year. This deep amber spirit can be comparable to that of a fine cognac, brandy, or scotch.

Tequila is made in the Mexican state of Jalisco and named for the small town of Tequila. The highway into the town of Tequila winds through acres of sugarcane and silver-blue fields of agave (ah-GA-vay) plants, the raw materials of tequila. A large plant with distinctive spiky leaves, the agave is a member of the lily family. It takes more than 8 years to reach maturity and grows to a height of 7 feet, with a core weighing as much as 150 pounds. Throughout the growing process, the sharp leaves are pruned at the base in order to create the largest possible heart.

The tequila-growing area is delimited by the government, and of its many varieties only the blue agave may be used for distillation. There are over 100,000 acres of blue agave in the states of Jalisco, Michoacán, and Nayarit. In spite of these acres of agave fields, distillers are currently facing a shortage. The spike in tequila popularity coupled with the long growing season of the agave plant means that demand will eventually exceed supply. Although growers have been quick to sow more agave, fields planted today will not mature for 8 to 10 years. In addition, a blight is endangering mature agave plants and contributing to an overall rise in tequila prices. True to its reputation, this feisty spirit seems to be one part celebration and one part disappointment.

During harvest, *jimadors* wielding sharp hoelike implements called *coas* cut the mature agave off its root and trim it down to its heart. This heavy *piña*, so-called because of its resemblance to a large pineapple, is then transported to the factory to be cooked and distilled.

The agave is cooked in order to yield the sugar that is needed for fermentation. To accomplish this, the *piñas* are steamed for 48 hours in large furnaces or cooked in autoclaves (giant pressure cookers), after which they cool for 8 hours. After cooling, the *piñas* are transported by conveyor belt to a machine that shreds and crushes them to extract their juice (called *aguamiel*, or "honey water"). The juice is then pumped into large stainless steel fermentation vats.

At this point, the sugarcane can be added. According to regulations, alcohol bearing the name "tequila" must contain at least 60 percent pure blue agave. The remaining 40 percent is often a hangover-inducing solution of nonagave sugars. These tequilas are often referred to as *mixtos*. The difference between 100 percent agave tequilas and those that use cane sugar is similar to the comparison between single-malt and blended scotch whiskies; one is more assertively flavored and the other is softer and smoother.

The juice is fermented to 16 proof and then distilled. Unlike rum and gin, which are made in continuous column stills, tequila is made in copper pot stills, like the ones used in the making of cognac and single malts. The clear liquor is double-distilled to 150 proof, which means that the final product is extremely pure and clean.

In a market barraged with premium tequila, a trip to the liquor store can be a bit confusing. A few names to keep in mind are Herradura, a distillery producing only 100 percent blue agave tequila; Patron; Porfidio; El Tesoro; Casa Noble; and Cabo Wabo, a delightfully smooth tequila created by rock star Sammy Hagar. The Jose Cuervo 1800 is a fine sipping tequila.

Tequila has been wicked and it has been good. These days, it's wickedly good. As you savor this delectable and magical spirit, it might just be a good time to raise your glass to the spirit of revolution.

# Classics

## Coco Loco

1 coconut, topped
1 scoop crushed ice
1 ounce tequila
1 ounce gin
1 ounce light rum
1 ounce pineapple juice
Simple syrup to taste
½ fresh lime

Open the fresh coconut by sawing off the top. Retain the coconut water in the husk; the coconut will be your cup. Add the crushed ice to the coconut and pour in all of the liquid ingredients. Squeeze the lime over the drink and drop it in. Stir well, adding a little additional ice if necessary.

## Frozen Margarita

Crushed ice
1½ ounces tequila
½ ounce triple sec
1 ounce lemon or lime juice
Lime slice
Coarse salt or sugar-and-salt
　mixture

Use 1½ to 2 scoops of crushed ice for each drink. Add ice, tequila, triple sec, and juice to blender. Blend until slushy, but not too watery. Moisten the rim of a large chilled cocktail glass or wineglass with the lime slice. Coat the rim with coarse salt or the sugar-and-salt mixture. Pour the contents of the blender into the prepared glass and garnish with the lime slice.

## Margarita

Lime slice
Coarse salt
1½ ounces tequila
1 ounce triple sec
1 ounce lime juice

Moisten the rim of a cocktail glass with the lime slice. Press the rim into the salt. In a shaker, combine the next three ingredients with ice. Mix and strain into the glass. Garnish with the lime slice.

## Matador

Coarse salt
1½ ounces tequila
½ ounce triple sec
Juice of ½ large or 1 small lime
1 scoop crushed ice

Moisten the rim of a chilled cocktail glass and press the rim into the coarse salt. Mix all other ingredients in a shaker. Strain the mixture into the prepared glass.

## Tequila Neat

Sprinkle of coarse salt
1½ ounces tequila
1 lime wedge

Lick the back of the left hand between the thumb and index finger and sprinkle this area with salt. Hold a shot glass of tequila in the same hand. Hold the wedge of lime in the right hand. In one quick sequence, lick the salt on the back of the hand, drink the tequila, and bite into the lime wedge.

## Tequila Sour

1½ ounces tequila
1 ounce lime or lemon juice
1 teaspoon confectioners' sugar
1 scoop crushed ice

In a shaker, mix all ingredients. Strain the mixture into a chilled cocktail glass.

## Tequila Sunrise I

1 scoop crushed ice
2 ounces tequila
¼ ounce grenadine
3 ounces orange juice

Fill a tall collins glass with the crushed ice. Add the tequila and grenadine. Slowly fill the glass with the orange juice and stir gently.

## Tequila Sunrise II

1½ ounces tequila
Juice of ½ lime
½ ounce crème de cassis
1 scoop crushed ice
Club soda
Generous dash of orange liqueur
Lime slice

In a tall collins glass, mix the first four ingredients. Top off with the soda and the dash of orange liqueur. Garnish with the lime slice and stir gently.

# Creative Concoctions

## Acapulco Clam Digger

1½ ounces tequila
3 ounces tomato juice
3 ounces clam juice
½ teaspoon horseradish
Several dashes of Tabasco
Several dashes of Worcestershire
    sauce
Dash of lemon juice
1 scoop crushed ice
Lemon slice

Pour all ingredients, except the lemon slice, into a double old-fashioned glass. Mix well and garnish with the lemon slice.

## Be Merry

1½ ounces tequila blanco
2 teaspoons lemon juice
1 tablespoon raspberry syrup
Dash of Grand Marnier
Orange slice

Combine the first three ingredients in a cocktail shaker. Shake well. Pour into a cocktail glass over ice. Pour the Grand Marnier over the top. Garnish with the orange slice.

## Bonanza

1½ ounces tequila
1 ounce applejack
½ ounce lemon juice
1 teaspoon simple or maple syrup
Generous dash of triple sec or
     curaçao
1 scoop crushed ice
Lemon slice

Mix all ingredients, except the lemon slice, in a shaker. Pour the mixture into a chilled old-fashioned glass and garnish with the lemon slice.

## Bunny

2 ounces gold tequila
½ ounce lemon juice
1 ounce apple brandy
¾ teaspoon maple syrup
3 dashes of triple sec
Lemon slice

Add all ingredients, except the lemon slice, to a cocktail shaker, along with a scoop of ice. Shake well and strain into an old-fashioned glass. Garnish with the lemon slice.

## Brave Bull

1 ounce tequila
1 ounce coffee liqueur
Whipped cream

Mix the tequila and coffee liqueur in a stirring glass with ice cubes. Strain the mixture into a sherry glass and top with a dollop of the whipped cream.

## Carabinieri

1 ounce tequila
¾ ounce Galliano
1 egg yolk
2 ¾ ounces orange juice
½ ounce lemon juice
1 scoop crushed ice

In a shaker, combine all ingredients. Mix well and pour into a highball glass.

## Changuirongo

1½ ounce tequila
Orange or lemon-lime soda or
    ginger ale
Lemon or lime wedge

In a tall highball or collins glass
with ice cubes, pour in the tequila
and soda. Stir gently and garnish
with the lemon or lime wedge.

## Charro

1 ounce tequila
1 ⅓ ounces evaporated milk
⅔ ounce strong coffee
1 scoop crushed ice

Combine all ingredients in a shaker
and shake vigorously. Strain the
mixture into a chilled old-fashioned glass and add ice cubes, if
necessary.

## Compadre

1 ounce tequila
⅓ ounce grenadine
4 drops maraschino liqueur
4 drops bitters
1 scoop crushed ice

Combine all ingredients in a
shaker. Shake vigorously and strain
into a chilled cocktail glass.

## Corcovado

1½ ounces tequila
1½ ounces Drambuie
1½ ounces blue curaçao
1 scoop crushed ice
Lemonade
Lemon or lime slice

In a shaker, mix the spirits with
ice cubes. Strain the mixture into a
highball glass filled with the
crushed ice. Top off with the
lemonade. Garnish with the lemon
or lime slice.

## Crazy Nun

1 scoop finely crushed ice
1½ ounces tequila
1½ ounces anisette

Fill an old-fashioned glass with the
finely crushed ice. Pour in the
tequila and anisette and stir. Use
less anisette for a drier drink.

## Dolores Del Rio

1½ ounces tequila añejo
½ ounce amaretto
Champagne
Orange peel
Cherry

Place first two ingredients in a champagne flute. Add the champagne to fill. Garnish with the twist of orange peel and the cherry.

## El Cid

1½ ounces tequila
1 ounce lemon or lime juice
½ ounce orgeat
1 scoop crushed ice
Tonic water
Grenadine
Lime slice

Pour the tequila, juice, and orgeat into a tall collins glass and mix well. Add the crushed ice and top off the glass with the tonic water and a dash or two of grenadine. Garnish with the lime slice.

## El Diablo

1 scoop crushed ice
½ lime
1¾ ounces tequila
¾ ounce crème de cassis
Ginger ale

Fill a highball glass half full with the crushed ice. Squeeze the lime over the ice and add the lime half to the glass. Pour in the tequila and crème de cassis. Top off with the ginger ale and stir.

## Frozen Matador

1¾ ounces tequila
¼ ounce triple sec
1 teaspoon sugar
Juice of ½ lime
1 scoop crushed ice
2 pineapple rings

In a shaker, mix all ingredients, except the pineapple rings. Pour the mixture into a highball glass. Garnish with the pieapple rings.

## Gentle Ben

1 ounce tequila
1 ounce vodka
1 ounce gin
3 ounces orange juice
1 teaspoon sloe gin (optional)
Orange slice

Mix the first four ingredients in a shaker or blender with crushed ice. Pour the mixture into a double old-fashioned glass. Float the sloe gin on top and garnish with the orange slice.

## Gentle Bull

1½ ounces tequila
¾ ounces coffee liqueur
1 ounce heavy cream
1 scoop crushed ice

Combine the tequila, liqueur, and cream in a shaker with ice cubes. Shake vigorously and strain into a chilled brandy snifter filled with crushed ice.

## Grapeshot

1½ ounces tequila
¾ ounce curaçao
1 ounce white grape juice
1 scoop crushed ice

Combine all ingredients in a shaker. Mix well and strain into a chilled cocktail glass.

## Gust of Wind

1 ounce tequila blanco
½ ounce D'Aristi Xtabentun
(sweet anise liqueur)
½ ounce green crème de menthe

Place all ingredients in a shot glass. Set it on fire. Serve with a long straw.

## Horny Bull

1½ ounces white tequila
4 to 6 ounces orange juice,
chilled

Pour the tequila into a glass filled with ice. Top off the glass with the orange juice and stir well.

## Jade

1½ ounces tequila blanco
2 ounces Midori
3½ ounces kiwi fruit puree
½ ounce lime juice
Kiwi slice

Combine all ingredients, except kiwi slice, in a blender. Add a scoop of ice and blend. Serve in a cocktail glass, garnished with the slice of kiwi fruit.

## Lemonaid

1 ounce tequila
5 ounces natural lemon-lime soda
1 tablespoon frozen lemonade
    concentrate
Lemon wedge

Fill a tall glass with ice. Add the tequila, soda, and lemonade concentrate to the glass. Stir well and garnish with the lemon wedge.

## Malcolm Lowry

Lime rind
Coarse salt
1 ounce mescal tequila
¾ ounce light rum
¾ ounce triple sec
¾ ounce lemon or lime juice
1 scoop crushed ice

Using a lime rind, moisten the rim of an iced cocktail glass. Dip the rim in coarse salt. Combine the remaining ingredients in a shaker. Mix well and pour into the prepared glass.

## Mexican Ruin

½ ounce tequila
1½ ounces coffee liqueur
1 scoop crushed ice

In a mixing glass, stir all ingredients. Pour the mixture into a chilled cocktail glass.

## Miguelito

1½ ounces tequila
Juice of 1 lime
1 teaspoon honey
Dash of bitters (optional)
1 scoop crushed ice

Mix all ingredients in a shaker. Strain the mixture into a chilled cocktail glass.

## Montezuma

1½ ounces mescal tequila
1 ounce Madeira wine
1 egg yolk
1 scoop crushed ice

Combine all ingredients in a blender. Blend well and pour into an iced cocktail glass.

## Montezuma's Revenge

1½ ounces tequila
1 ounce fino sherry
1 egg yolk
1 scoop crushed ice

Combine all ingredients in a shaker. Mix well and pour into a chilled cocktail glass.

## Premium Punch

*Makes 12 (4-ounce) servings*

16 ounces tequila
2 cups cranberry juice
1 can (6 ounces) frozen
   lemonade concentrate
16 ounces club soda

Prechill all ingredients. In a punch bowl, combine the tequila, cranberry juice, and lemonade concen-
trate. Mix in the club soda. Add ice
before serving.

## Rocky Point

1½ ounces tequila
2 to 3 ounces grapefruit juice
1 teaspoon almond extract
Dash of lime juice
Dash of triple sec or curaçao
1 scoop crushed ice
Mint sprigs

Mix all ingredients, except the mint, in a shaker or blender. Pour the mixture into a chilled wineglass and garnish with the mint.

## Royal Matador

*Makes 2 servings*

Whole pineapple
3 ounces gold tequila
1½ ounces raspberry liqueur
Juice of 1 lime
1 teaspoon orgeat or amaretto

Remove the top of the pineapple and set it aside. Scoop out the pineapple, keeping the shell intact. Place the pineapple chunks in a blender and extract as much juice as possible. Strain the pineapple juice and return to the blender. Add the tequila, liqueur, lime juice, syrup, and ice cubes. Mix well and pour into the pineapple shell, adding additional ice if needed. Replace the pineapple top and serve with straws.

## Sangrita

*Makes 14 (2-ounce) servings*

2 cups tomato juice
1 cup orange juice
2 ounces lime juice
1 to 2 teaspoons Tabasco, or to taste
2 teaspoons finely minced onion
1 to 2 teaspoons Worcestershire sauce
Several pinches of white pepper
Celery salt or seasoned salt to taste

In a large pitcher, blend all ingredients. Strain the blend into a fresh pitcher and chill in the refrigerator. Sangrita is used as a chaser for tequila shots. It can also be used for a VERY spicy Bloody Mary.

VARIATIONS AND ADDITIONS: Mix 3 ounces Sangrita mix with 1 ounce of tequila. Serve over ice in a highball glass.

## Silk Stockings

1 ounce tequila
1 ounce evaporated milk
1 ounce sweetened condensed milk
¼ ounce grenadine
1 scoop crushed ice
Powdered cinnamon

Blend all ingredients, except the cinnamon, until smooth. Pour the blend into a champagne glass and sprinkle with the cinnamon.

## Sneaky Pete

*Makes 2 servings*

4 ounces tequila
1 ounce white crème de menthe
1 ounce pineapple juice
1 ounce lime or lemon juice
1 scoop crushed ice
Lime slices

Mix all ingredients, except the lime slices, in a shaker. Strain the mixture into 2 chilled cocktail glasses. Garnish with the lime slices.

## Sno-Cap

2 ounces tequila
¼ cup canned cream of coconut
   (such as Coco Lopez)
3 tablespoons lime juice
Lime wedge

Add all ingredients, except the lime wedge, to a blender along with a scoop of ice and blend until smooth. Serve in a stemmed glass and garnish with the lime wedge.

## Sombrero

1½ ounces tequila reposado
¾ ounce cream
¾ ounce Kahlúa coffee liqueur

Place the tequila and cream in a blender and mix well. Serve together with the Kahlúa in an old-fashioned glass.

## Speedy Gonzalez

1½ ounces tequila
3 ounces grapefruit juice
1 teaspoon superfine sugar, or to taste
1 scoop crushed ice
Club soda

Mix all ingredients, except the soda, in a shaker. Pour the mixture into a tall highball glass and top off with the cold club soda.

## Submarino

1 large mug of beer
1 ounce tequila

Fill a mug with cold beer, leaving a few inches at the top. Drop a jigger of tequila into the mug. (Some prefer to drink the tequila straight and follow it with a beer chaser.)

## Tequila Collins

1½ ounces light tequila
1 ounce lemon juice
Sugar syrup to taste
Club soda
1 maraschino cherry

Add the tequila, lemon juice, sugar syrup, and several ice cubes to a 14-ounce collins glass. Stir well. Top off with the cold club soda, and garnish with the cherry.

## Tequila Fizz

1 ¾ ounces tequila
½ ounce sugar syrup
1 ounce lemon juice
1 scoop crushed ice
Club soda
Lemon slice or maraschino
   cherry

Combine the first four ingredients in a shaker. Mix well. Pour the mixture into a highball glass and top off with the cold club soda. Garnish with the lemon slice or maraschino cherry.

## Tequila Grapefruit

1½ ounces tequila
½ ounce dry vermouth
4 ounces grapefruit juice
½ teaspoon sugar syrup, or to
   taste
1 scoop crushed ice
Orange slice

Mix all ingredients, except the orange slice, in a shaker. Pour the mixture into a double old-fashioned glass. Garnish with the orange slice.

## Tequila Julep

4 mint sprigs
1 teaspoon superfine sugar
1½ ounces tequila
4 to 6 ounces club soda, chilled

Fill a glass with ice. In a dish, crush 3 of the mint sprigs with sugar and add this mixture to the glass. Add the tequila and stir. Top off with the soda. Stir gently until the glass is frosted. Garnish with the remaining mint sprig.

## Tequila Manhattan (sweet)

1½ ounces tequila
¾ ounce sweet vermouth
2 splashes of bitters
1 maraschino cherry

Mix the tequila, vermouth, and bitters in a stirring glass with ice. Strain the mixture into a chilled cocktail glass. Garnish with the cherry.

## Tequila Maria

1½ ounces tequila
4 ounces tomato juice
Juice of ¼ lime
½ teaspoon freshly grated
    horseradish
Generous dashes of
    Worcestershire sauce
Generous dashes of Tabasco
Generous pinch of white pepper
Generous pinch of celery salt or
    seed
Generous pinch of tarragon,
    oregano, or dill
1 scoop crushed ice

In a mixing glass, stir all ingredients. Pour the mixture into a chilled double old-fashioned glass.

## Tequila Mockingbird

1½ ounces tequila
½ ounce green crème de menthe
Juice of ½ lime
1 scoop crushed ice
Ice water or club soda

Mix the first four ingredients in a highball glass. Top off with the ice water or cold club soda and stir gently.

## TNT (Tequila 'n' Tonic)

2 ounces tequila
½ ounce lime or lemon juice
About 6 ounces tonic water,
    chilled
1 strip lime or lemon peel

Fill a highball glass three-quarters full with ice cubes. Add the tequila and lime or lemon juice. Top off the glass with the tonic water and stir. Twist the lemon or lime peel over the drink and drop it in.

## Toreador

1½ ounces tequila
½ ounce crème de cacao
2 tablespoons whipped cream
Whipped cream
Cocoa powder

Mix the tequila and crème de cacao in a shaker with ice. Strain the mixture into a chilled cocktail glass or wineglass. Top with a dollop of the whipped cream and sprinkle a little of the cocoa over the top.

## *Torridora Mexicano*

1½ ounces tequila
¾ ounces coffee-flavored brandy
Juice of ½ lime
1 scoop crushed ice

In a shaker, mix all ingredients. Strain the mixture into a chilled cocktail glass.

# Signature Drinks

## *Austin Grill Swirlie*

AUSTIN GRILL, WASHINGTON D.C.

*Makes 4 (10-ounce) servings*

20 ounces Frozen Lime
    Margarita
20 ounces Strawberry Margarita
Lime wedge

Fill half of a chilled margarita glass with the frozen lime margarita and top off the glass with the strawberry margarita. Garnish with the lime wedge.

NOTE: Austin Grill recipes for frozen lime and strawberry margaritas can be found on pages 112 and 114.

## *Bairro Alto*

ALFAMA, NEW YORK CITY

2 ounces Jose Cuervo Gold
1 ounce Grand Marnier
1½ ounces blackberry liqueur
1 ounce fresh lime juice
Splash of sour mix
Lime slice

In a shaker filled with ice, combine all ingredients, except the lime slice, and shake vigorously for about 25 seconds. Strain into a cocktail glass and garnish with the slice of lime.

## *Berta's Special*

BERTITA'S BAR, TAXCO, MEXICO

2 ounces tequila
Juice of 1 lime
1 teaspoon sugar syrup or honey
Several dashes of orange bitters
1 egg white
1 scoop crushed ice
Club soda
Lime slice

Mix the first six ingredients in a shaker. Pour this mixture into a 14-ounce collins glass. Top off with the cold club soda and stir gently. Garnish with the lime slice.

## Cactus Kicker

DESERT MOON, SAN FRANCISCO

½ ounce tequila
½ ounce margarita schnapps
½ ounce pineapple juice
½ ounce blackberry or blueberry
  schnapps

Mix all ingredients in a shaker with crushed ice. Strain the mixture into a shot glass.

## French Melon Margarita

JIRAFFE, SANTA MONICA, CALIFORNIA

2 ounces pure agave tequila añejo
1 ounce Cointreau
1½ ounces lime juice
2 ounces French melon puree
Melon wedge

Combine all ingredients, except the melon wedge, in a cocktail shaker. Add a scoop of ice. Shake until blended. Pour into an old-fashioned glass. Garnish with the melon wedge.

## Frozen Lime Margarita

AUSTIN GRILL, WASHINGTON, D.C.

*Makes 2 servings*

3 ounces gold tequila
1½ ounces triple sec
3 ounces freshly squeezed lime
  juice
1 ounce simple syrup
2½ cups ice
Lime wedge

Mix all ingredients, except the lime wedge, in a blender and blend until smooth. Pour the mixture into a chilled wineglass or margarita glass. Garnish with the lime wedge.

## Frozen Melon Head

SOUTHERN CULTURE,
CHARLOTTESVILLE, VIRGINIA

1½ ounces premium gold tequila
¾ ounce triple sec
1½ ounces melon liqueur
Juice of 1 lime
1 scoop crushed ice

Combine all ingredients in a blender. Blend until frothy. Pour the mixture into a margarita glass.

## Loho Loco

SX137, NEW YORK CITY

3 ounces Jose Cuervo
1 ounce Cointreau
2 ounces Loho Citrus
Juice from ½ lime
Lime wedge

Add all ingredients, except the lime wedge, to a cocktail shaker along with a scoop of ice. Shake to blend. Salt the rim of an old-fashioned glass. Add a scoop of ice and strain the cocktail into the glass. Garnish with the wedge of lime.

## Mango Gorilla

HARRY DENTON'S, SAN FRANCISCO

½ ounce tequila
½ ounce Grand Marnier
½ ounce pineapple juice
Splash of lime juice

Pour all ingredients into a shot glass.

## Prairie Dog

BALBOA CAFE, SAN FRANCISCO

1½ ounces tequila
3 squirts of Tabasco

Add both ingredients to a shot glass.

## Prickly Pear Margarita

FURNACE CREEK INN & RANCH RESORT, DEATH VALLEY, CALIFORNIA

1 ounce Jose Cuervo 1800
½ ounce Cointreau
1 teaspoon Fred Harvey Prickly
   Pear Cactus Jelly
Salt or sugar
Lime wedge

Add all ingredients, except salt or sugar and lime wedge, plus a scoop of ice to a blender. Blend until smooth. Salt or sugar the rim of a stemmed margarita glass. Pour in the cocktail and garnish with the wedge of lime.

## Spanish Fly

EL DORADO CANTINA, BRENTWOOD, CALIFORNIA

1½ ounces Herradura Silver
   tequila
½ ounce Alize passion fruit
   cognac
Splash of pineapple juice
Sugar
Lime wedge

Combine all ingredients, except the sugar and lime, in a cocktail shaker. Add a scoop of ice. Shake until frothy. Coat the rim of a martini glass with the sugar. Strain the cocktail into the glass and garnish with the lime wedge.

## Stargarita

STARS, SAN FRANCISCO

½ ounce premium gold tequila
½ ounce triple sec
½ ounce fresh lime juice
Splash of Campari
2 teaspoons superfine sugar
Coarse salt
Lime wheel

Combine all ingredients, except the lime and salt, in a shaker with ice. Shake well and strain into a salt-rimmed balloon glass. Garnish with the lime wheel.

## Strawberry Margarita

AUSTIN GRILL, WASHINGTON, D.C.

*Makes 2 servings*

Lime rind
Coarse salt or salt-sugar mixture
3 ounces gold tequila
1½ ounces triple sec
2 ounces freshly squeezed lime juice
2½ cups ice
½ ounce simple syrup
4 ounces pureed smooth strawberries (fresh or frozen)
2 fresh strawberries

Moisten the rim of 2 wineglasses with the lime rind and roll the rims in the coarse salt or salt-sugar mixture. Combine the other ingredients, except the strawberries, in a blender and blend until smooth. Pour the mixture into the prepared wineglasses. Garnish with the strawberries.

## Sunset

SU CASA RESTAURANT, CHICAGO

Sugar
1 ounce tequila
1½ ounces pineapple juice
1½ ounces orange juice

Moisten the rim of a chilled wineglass and press the rim into the sugar. Combine the other ingredients in a blender and blend until frothy. Pour the mixture into the prepared glass.

## Tequila Sunset

SU CASA RESTAURANT, CHICAGO

Sugar
1 ounce white or gold tequila
1½ ounces orange juice
1½ ounces pineapple juice
1 scoop crushed ice

Moisten the rim of a large wineglass and frost it with sugar. Com-
bine the other ingredients in a blender and blend at medium speed for about 30 seconds.

## Top-Shelf Margarita

CRESCENT COURT, DALLAS

1½ ounces gold tequila
2 ounces sweet 'n' sour mix
Splash of lime juice
Splash of Grand Marnier
Splash of triple sec
Splash of Drambuie

Pour all ingredients into a shaker with crushed ice. Shake and strain into a chilled collins glass over fresh ice.

# Tropical Drinks

## Cactus Banger

1½ ounces tequila
Orange juice
½ ounce Galliano

Pour the tequila into a tall collins glass. Fill the glass with ice and orange juice. Top off with a float of the Galliano.

## Desert Glow

1 ounce tequila
4 ounces orange juice
1 ounce peach schnapps
Orange slice

Fill an old-fashioned glass with ice. Pour in the tequila, orange juice, and schnapps. Stir well and garnish with the orange slice.

## Frozen Cran Razz

*Makes 5 (3-ounce) servings*

6 ounces tequila
1 can (6 ounces) frozen
    concentrate cranberry juice
3 ounces raspberry liqueur

Combine all ingredients in a blender. Add ice cubes and continue to blend until thick and slushy. Pour the mixture into chilled wineglasses.

## Gringo Swizzle

2 ounces tequila
½ ounce crème de cassis, or to
    taste
1 ounce lime juice
1 ounce pineapple juice
1 ounce orange juice
1 scoop crushed ice
Ginger ale

Mix the first six ingredients in a shaker or blender. Pour this mixture into a 14-ounce collins glass. Top off the glass with the cold ginger ale and add a few ice cubes, if necessary.

## Latin Lover

1½ ounces tequila
¾ ounce cachaca (spiced rum)
2 ounces pineapple juice
¾ ounce lime juice
¼ ounce lemon juice
2 scoops crushed ice
Pineapple slice
1 maraschino cherry

Mix the first five ingredients in a shaker with 1 scoop of crushed ice and shake vigorously. Strain the mixture into a highball glass half filled with crushed ice. Garnish with the pineapple slice and cherry.

## Mexicana

1¾ ounces tequila
Splash of grenadine
1½ ounces pineapple juice
¾ ounces lemon or lime juice
2 scoops crushed ice

Mix all ingredients in a shaker. Strain the mixture into a highball glass over fresh crushed ice.

## Mexicolada

1½ ounces tequila
¾ ounce coffee liqueur
2 ounces pineapple juice
¼ ounce cream of coconut
¾ ounce sweet cream
1 scoop crushed ice

Mix all ingredients in a shaker or blender. Pour the mixture into a highball glass.

## Pepe

1 ounce tequila
¾ ounce cachaca
Splash of triple sec
1½ ounces grapefruit juice
¼ ounce lemon or lime juice
2 scoops crushed ice

Mix the first five ingredients in a shaker with 1 scoop of crushed ice. Strain the mixture into a highball glass half filled with the other scoop of crushed ice.

## Piña

1½ ounces white tequila
3 ounces pineapple juice
1 ounce lime juice
1 teaspoon superfine sugar

Combine all ingredients with 3 or 4 ice cubes in a shaker. Shake vigorously and strain into a tall chilled collins glass. Add fresh ice cubes.

## Piñata I

1½ ounces tequila
Pineapple juice
Pineapple spear

Fill a short or stemmed glass with ice. Add the tequila and top with the juice. Stir well and garnish with the pineapple spear.

## Piñata II

1½ ounces white tequila
1 tablespoon banana liqueur
1 ounce lime juice
1 scoop crushed ice

Combine all ingredients in a blender and blend at medium speed until smooth. Pour the mixture into a chilled whiskey sour glass.

## Raspberry Margarita

1½ ounces tequila
1 ounce triple sec
1 ounce lime juice
½ cup frozen raspberries
Fresh raspberries

In a blender, combine all ingredients, except the fresh fruit, with half a cup of ice. Blend until frothy. Pour the mixture into a chilled highball glass and garnish with the raspberries.

NOTE: You can substitute strawberries or peaches for different flavors.
When using fresh fruit, add sugar to taste.

## Tequila Tropical

1 scoop crushed ice
1½ ounces tequila
½ ounce grenadine
3 ounces orange juice, chilled
1 teaspoon lemon juice
½ slice orange
1 maraschino cherry

Fill a highball glass three quarters full with crushed ice. Add the tequila, grenadine, and fruit juices and stir. Garnish with the orange slice and cherry.

# Hot Drinks

## Cranberry Lodge Toddy

1 ounce tequila
1 ounce triple sec
½ ounce apple schnapps
1 cup hot cranberry juice

Pour the first three ingredients into the mug of hot cranberry juice. Stir well before serving.

## Mexican Coffee

1½ ounces tequila
¾ ounce coffee liqueur
1 cup hot strong coffee or
    espresso
Whipped cream

Mix the tequila and coffee liqueur in a large mug. Add the hot coffee or espresso. Top off with a dollop of the whipped cream.

## Mountain Melter

1 ounce tequila
½ ounce triple sec
Dash of cinnamon schnapps
1 cup hot cocoa

Pour the tequila, triple sec, and schnapps into the cup of hot cocoa. Stir well.

## Tequila Tea

1½ ounces tequila
Hot tea
Sugar
Lemon slice

Pour the tequila into a large mug. Fill the rest of the mug with the hot tea and add the sugar to taste. Garnish with the lemon slice.

## Toe Warmer

½ ounce tequila
½ ounce cream-based whiskey
    liqueur
½ ounce coffee brandy
½ ounce hazelnut liqueur
Hot coffee

Pour the first four ingredients into a cocktail glass. Top with the hot coffee and serve.

# Punches

## Pitcher Peach Piñata

*Makes about 6 (6-ounce) servings*

4 ounces tequila
4 ounces peach schnapps
3 cups pineapple juice
Fresh pineapple spears

In a 2- to 3-quart pitcher, mix the first three ingredients. Add ice and garnish with the pineapple.

# AQUAVIT AND SCHNAPPS

A group of people are clustered around a table for a typical lunch that will include several courses and a clear, fiery drink. The host pours the ice-cold liquid into frosty, chilled, conical-shaped glasses. He raises his glass, at which point the diners turn to one another and make eye contact. "Skoal," calls out the host, and everyone takes a sip. Again there is eye contact, and then the glasses are set on the table, not to be lifted again until the host raises his. The liquid is aquavit, and the ritual is virtually the same throughout Scandinavia.

Aquavit is a distilled spirit that is much like vodka. What makes it different from that neutral spirit are the extracts of herbs and spices that are added to aquavit. There are versions that taste of cinnamon, Madeira, coriander, lemon, dill, and—most popular of all—caraway.

The development of aquavit is an example of how distilled spirits took very different courses in different countries. From similar beginnings, hundreds of spirits have evolved, their variances based mainly on the diversity of the local agriculture.

Distillation has been around since ancient times. "Sea water can be rendered potable by distillation," wrote the Greek philosopher Aristotle. His discovery was allegedly based on the simple observation that steam from hot food condenses on the inner surface of a cover placed over the dish.

Early civilizations learned how to create medicines, perfumes, and flavorings using simple distillation. Herbs, spices, and plants were cooked, macerated, or infused to make concentrates that were easy to use and store. The ancient Chinese created a unique spirit from rice and beer, and in the East Indies as long ago as 800 B.C. something called arrack was made with fermented sugarcane and rice.

## A MODERN HISTORY

Despite the long-standing awareness of the distillation effect, it was not until the early Middle Ages that the distillation of alcohol became a widespread practice and the modern history of this remarkable process began.

It was the Arabs who started it all. They even invented the word "alcohol." It seems that for centuries the Arabs had been (and, in fact, still are) making eye makeup using black powder that was liquefied, vaporized, and solidified again. They called it kohl. When wine was first distilled, the name of this cosmetic was used to describe the result—"al koh'l"—since the procedure was so similar.

In the Latin-speaking regions of Europe during the Middle Ages, the newly discovered spirit was called aqua vitae ("water of life"). The reason for this rather grandiose name was the fact that, at first, distilled spirits were used mostly by alchemists, and many of these scientists thought that they had finally found the elusive "elixir of life." In the 13th century, for example, the Majorcan chemist and philosopher Raymond Lully wrote that aqua vitae was "an emanation of the divinity, an element newly revealed to men, but hid from antiquity, because the human race was then too young to need this beverage destined to revive the energies of modern decrepitude."

As this knowledge of distillation spread, the Latin name was translated into the local language. In France, it became known as *eau-de-vie*, while on the Irish peat bogs it was Gaelicized into *visige beatha*, which eventually was corrupted into "whiskey." In Russia, "water of life" evolved into "vodka" from the Russian word for water, *voda*.

Only in Denmark, Sweden, and other Scandinavian countries did the original Latin name remain relatively unscathed. True, the phrase was shortened slightly, but the essence of the word remains—"aquavit."

## DISTILLATION CATCHES ON

Fifteenth-century Europe saw distillation take hold and spread like wildfire. It was completely unregulated, and anyone who understood how the process worked could build a primitive still and produce his own aquavit. For raw materials, these cottage distillers used whatever was inexpensive and in good, constant supply. In Ireland and Scotland, whiskey got its distinctive character from barley and a dose of smoky peat. In France, Spain, and Italy, wine was plentiful, and it formed the basis for locally made brandies. Barley, corn, and rye were the backbone of gin in Holland. Later, Caribbean sugarcane was made into rum and the Mexican century plant was used in tequila.

In Sweden, at first, aquavit (or sometimes "akavit" or "akevit") was made by distilling wine. The problem was that all the fruit had to be imported from more temperate countries because no grapes are grown in Sweden. This made the aquavit so expensive that it could only be consumed sparingly. Its use was limited almost entirely to medicinal purposes.

Later on, when the Swedes discovered how to produce the spirit from grain, aquavit became less costly and easier to obtain. But grain was not the ideal raw ingredient either. Because of the country's harsh weather, the crop was often cut short by the early arrival of winter. To avoid a grain shortage, the government occasionally had to prohibit the distilling of aquavit.

The Swedes had grown accustomed to their "snaps," so frequent interruptions in its supply were quite unacceptable. Distillers experimented with myriad substitutes for grain, but nothing seemed to yield satisfactory results. Finally, in the 18th century, it was discovered that the common potato was ideal for the purpose. It was plentiful, inexpensive, relatively unaffected by variances in weather, and consistent in quality. Most aquavit has been made from potatoes ever since.

## A LIVELY DISPUTE

The Swedes and the Danes like to dispute which country was the first to produce aquavit. Both countries have a good case; in fact, it is quite possible that distillation began independently in the two places at about the same time. The first Swedish license to sell aquavit was granted in Stockholm in 1498. Danish distilling can be traced back to sometime around 1400, and in 1555 King Christian III of Denmark established a royal distillery.

Today in Denmark, where aquavit is known as "schnapps," distilling is centered in Aalborg, a town of 160,000 in northern Jutland. There, Danish Distilleries Ltd. produces half the world's supply of aquavit. Twelve brands, each flavored with a different herb, are made in the same distillery, including the biggest seller, caraway-flavored Aalborg Taffel Akvavit, and another that is readily available in this country, dill-flavored Jubilaeums.

Most Swedish distilleries are located in the Southern province of Skane. The best-known Swedish brand is O.P. Anderson. Flavored with caraway seed, fennel seed, and aniseed, this aquavit was first released at the Gothenburg Expo in 1891. There is also a small industry in Norway.

The manufacture of aquavit is simple and straightforward. Potatoes are cleaned and then boiled. The resulting starch mass is combined with a grain malt, which helps the starch convert to sugar. Yeast is added and the sugar is fermented into alcohol. Then the spirit is rectified and distilled, after which a flavoring is added.

In Scandinavia, aquavit is often accompanied by a beer chaser. It is not unusual for a Dane or a Swede to drink 3 or 4 shots of this icy 90-proof liquor during the course of a meal. Using this spirit in mixed drinks requires some experience. Aquavit in a martini or combined with tonic might not be too well received, but a Bloody Mary made with either a dill, lemon, or caraway version is quite delicious. There is also no law that says aquavit cannot be served over ice. In fact, people who drink vodka on the rocks may find this an exciting new alternative to their usual. Everything considered, aquavit, no matter how you choose to drink it, is surely one of the most delightful of all distilled spirits.

Aquavit makes a delicious companion to gravlax, caviar, and Asian-spiced food. A few terrific aquavits to try are O.P. Anderson, Skane, and Herrgard from Sweden; Norway's Linie, and Aalborg which is considered the national drink of Denmark.

Flavored schnapps offer a twist on the traditional flavored aquavits. Clear and sweetened, these spirits are flavored with everything from cinnamon to "cheriberi." Often, the aromas call to mind a well-stocked candy counter. It is apple schnapps that plays such a strong role in the very popular Apple Martini, and peppermint schnapps that adds the sting to the Vodka Stinger. These very popular spirits are excellent for mixed drinks and will appeal to the most imaginative mixologist.

# Aquavit • Creative Concoctions

## Aquaman

1 ounce aquavit
1 ounce gin
Dash of dry vermouth
Olive

In a mixing glass with ice, stir together the aquavit, gin, and vermouth. Strain the mixture into a chilled cocktail glass and drop in the olive.

## Aquavit Clam

3 ounces aquavit
1½ ounces clam juice
1 teaspoon lemon juice
½ teaspoon Worcestershire sauce
Salt, black pepper, and cayenne

In a mixing glass with ice, stir all ingredients. Chill thoroughly. Strain into an old-fashioned glass containing fresh ice cubes.

## Aquapolitan

3 ounces orange-lemon aquavit
1 ounce Grand Marnier
Dash of orange juice
Splash of cranberry juice
Splash of sour mix
Lime wedge

Add all ingredients, except the lime wedge, to a shaker along with a scoop of ice. Shake to blend. Strain into a chilled cocktail glass. Garnish with the lime wedge.

## Danish Mary

1 ounce Aalborg Taffel Aquavit
1 ounce tomato juice
Dash of Tabasco
Minced fresh dill
Fresh pepper
Celery stalk

Add the aquavit, juice, and Tabasco to a mixing glass. Stir to combine. Pour into a highball glass over ice. Garnish with a sprinkle of the minced dill, a grind of the fresh pepper, and the celery stalk.

## Flaming Glogg

*Makes 15 servings*

1½ pints aquavit
1 bottle (750 ml.) red wine
1 cup orange juice
Cardamom seeds
Fresh, peeled ginger root
6 cloves
1 cinnamon stick
Dried fruits: apricots, peaches,
    plums, apples
Grated citrus rind
Sugar
½ grapefruit

Putting aside one cup of the aquavit, mix all the other ingredients, except the sugar and grapefruit, in a large saucepan. Bring the mixture to a simmer, but do not boil. Pour the heated mixture into a chafing dish. Scoop out the inside of the grapefruit half. Moisten the rim and the inside of the shell with aquavit and press the shell into the sugar. Float the shell on the glogg. Fill it with the remaining aquavit. Light the spirit and let it burn for a few minutes before overturning the shell into the glogg.

## Gerry Fjord

½ ounce aquavit
1 ounce brandy
1 ounce orange juice
½ ounce lime juice
1 teaspoon grenadine
1 scoop crushed ice

In a shaker, combine all ingredients. Mix well and strain into a chilled cocktail glass.

## Northern Exposure

1½ ounces aquavit
1 ounce grapefruit juice
½ ounce lemon juice
1 teaspoon sugar syrup, or to
    taste
Dash of grenadine
1 scoop crushed ice
Orange slice

Mix all ingredients, except the orange slice, in a shaker or blender. Pour the mixture into a chilled cocktail glass. Garnish with the orange slice.

## Viking

1½ ounces Swedish Punsch
1 ounce aquavit
1 ounce lime juice
1 scoop crushed ice

Mix all ingredients in a shaker. Strain the mixture into a chilled cocktail glass.

## Wonder Woman

2 ounces Midori
2 ounces peach schapps
3 ounces orange juice
1 ounce pineapple juice
2 ounces cranberry juice
1 cherry

Fill a hurricane glass with crushed ice. Add ingredients in the order in which they are listed. Don't stir. The drink should layer green, orange, and red. Garnish with the cherry.

# Schnapps • Creative Concoctions

## Apple Pie

1½ ounces apple schnapps
1½ ounces cinnamon schnapps
1 orange slice

Pour the apple and cinnamon schnapps into a chilled cocktail glass with ice cubes. Garnish the glass with the orange slice.

## Black and Blue

1¼ ounces blueberry schnapps
1¼ ounces blackberry brandy
1 ounce orange juice
1 ounce cranberry juice
Several blueberries

Add all ingredients, except the blueberries, to a cocktail shaker, along with a scoop of ice. Shake well to blend. Strain into a chilled cocktail glass. Drop the blueberries to the bottom of the glass for a garnish.

## Blue Cool

1½ ounces peppermint schnapps
¾ ounce blue curaçao
Lemon-lime soda
Lemon slice

In a chilled highball glass, stir together the schnapps, curaçao, and several ice cubes. Top off the glass with the cold soda and stir. Garnish with the lemon slice on the rim of the glass.

## Frozen Peachy Orange Colada

1½ ounces peach schnapps
2 ounces cream of coconut
2 ounces orange juice
½ ounce grenadine
1½ cups crushed ice

Combine all ingredients in a blender and blend until smooth. Pour the mixture into a chilled parfait glass.

## Galway Bay

¾ ounce peppermint schnapps
¾ ounce coffee liqueur
¾ ounce Irish cream
¾ ounce cream

Mix all ingredients in a blender and blend until smooth. Pour the mixture into a chilled wineglass with several ice cubes.

## Girl Scout Cookie

¾ ounce peppermint schnapps
¾ ounce Kahlúa
1½ ounces cream
Girl Scout cookie (optional)

Add all ingredients, except the cookie, to a cocktail shaker along with a scoop of ice. Shake to blend. Strain into a chilled cocktail glass. Garnish with a Girl Scout cookie if they're in season.

## Patagonia

1 ounce peppermint schnapps
¾ ounce coffee liqueur
½ ounce bourbon
½ ounce vodka

Combine all ingredients in a mixing glass half filled with ice cubes. Stir well and strain into a chilled cocktail glass.

## Peaches 'n' Cream

1½ ounces peach schnapps
2 ounces half-and-half or milk

In a shaker with crushed ice, mix together both of the ingredients. Strain the mixture over fresh ice cubes in an old-fashioned glass.

## Tropical Peach

1 ounce banana liqueur
1 ounce peach schnapps
1 ounce cream of coconut
1 scoop crushed ice
2 ounces orange juice

Combine all ingredients in a blender. Blend until smooth. Pour the mixture into a chilled wineglass.

# Schnapps • Signature Drinks

## Apple Juice Cooler

MICKEY'S PLACE, BALDWIN, NEW YORK

2 ounces apple schnapps
1 ounce vodka
2 ounces cranberry juice
Club soda
Apple wedge

Combine the apple schnapps, vodka, and cranberry juice over ice in a tall glass. Top off with the cold club soda and garnish with the apple wedge.

## Brain Hemmorhage

BALBOA CAFE, SAN FRANCISCO

1 ounce peach schnapps
½ ounce Irish cream
Splash of grenadine

Pour the peach schnapps into a shot glass. Add the Irish cream to the glass so that it clouds up. Finish with the healthy splash of grenadine. Do not stir. (The grenadine will simulate the drink's name.)

## Deathmint

JASPER'S, BOSTON

1½ ounces green Chartreuse
½ ounce Rumplemintz or
peppermint schnapps

Prechill both ingredients. Combine the Chartreuse and the Rumplemintz or schnapps in a shaker with crushed ice. Mix well and strain into a small wineglass.

## Ginger Peach

MICKEY'S PLACE, BALDWIN, NEW YORK

1½ ounces peach schnapps
1 ounce gin
Ginger ale
Peach wedge

In a highball glass filled with ice, mix together the schnapps and gin. Top off the glass with the ginger ale and garnish with the peach wedge.

## Frozen Peachtree Road Race

RITZ-CARLTON, ATLANTA

1¼ ounces peach schnapps
1¼ ounces vodka
2 ounces peach puree
2 ounces orange juice
2 cups crushed ice
Cranberry juice

Mix all ingredients, except the cranberry juice, in a blender. Blend at high speed for a few seconds. Pour the mixture into a chilled collins glass. Top off with the cranberry juice float.

## Smurf Berry

RED ARROW TAP,
BENTON HEIGHTS, MICHIGAN

1½ ounces blueberry schnapps
½ ounce triple sec
2 to 3 dashes of blue food
coloring
Cream
1 maraschino cherry

Pour the first three ingredients into a cocktail glass with ice. Top off the glass with the cream. Stir well and garnish with the cherry.

## Wild Thing

Desert Moon, San Francisco

½ ounce wildberry schnapps
½ ounce bourbon
½ ounce cranberry juice
½ ounce sweet 'n' sour

Mix all ingredients in a shaker with
crushed ice. Strain the mixture into
a shot glass.

# RUM

In 1492, Christopher Columbus concluded that "the Indies" he had discovered would be ideal for the cultivation of sugarcane. As a result, on his second voyage to the New World, he brought along some sugar experts and several hundred cane shoots from the Canary Islands. Commercial plantations were developed on what is now Haiti, Puerto Rico, Cuba, and Jamaica—islands that all were eventually to become important sources of rum.

Puerto Rico, the most important in terms of volume, is the home of the Bacardi Distillery. Called "the Cathedral of Rum," this facility is the largest of its kind in the world and produces over 100,000 gallons of rum per day. Along with Bacardi, other distillers add to a booming rum business which contributes millions of dollars to the Puerto Rican economy. But this is nothing new for this Caribbean island. Rum production in Puerto Rico goes back to well before the island was handed over to the United States by Spain in 1898, at the end of the Spanish-American War. In fact, even before there was rum the locals produced a crude distillate called *aguardiente* which achieved considerable popularity throughout the Spanish colonial empire.

The true foundations of rum were laid at the beginning of the 19th century. At that time a Spaniard named Don Sebastian Serralles emigrated from Catalonia to settle in Puerto Rico and work on a sugar plantation. After his death, his son, Juan, expanded the family estate his father had established and built a sugar factory. In 1865 he bought a French pot still and began making Puerto Rico's first commercial rum. He named it "Don Q," after his favorite figure in Spanish literature, Cervantes's Don Quixote. Today, yearly sales of Don Q range well over the 100 million-dollar mark.

In the late 1940s—after World War II had seriously curtailed the

American yen for rum—it looked as if the Puerto Rican distillery industry was on the verge of extinction. But the government took bold measures to improve the production of rum in order to save the island's most valuable product. First a strict "Mature Spirits Act" was passed which mandated that rum be aged for at least one year. The act went on to specify that after aging, all export rums must be blended to give them a smoother, more complex flavor.

The most important government decision, however, was the establishment of a Rum Pilot Plant as a branch of the University of Puerto Rico. Placed in charge of this project was Dr. Victor Rodriguez-Benitez, who immediately set to work defining the standards of what Puerto Rican rum should be. Until that point the rum of Puerto Rico had been syrupy, dark, and sweet. Dr. Rodriguez-Benitez and his staff determined that the American market wanted a lighter, drier rum. They also insisted that Puerto Rican rum be a pure product, free of harsh-tasting fusel oils and aldehydes that could cause hangovers and upset stomachs.

Over the 19 years of Dr. Rodriguez-Benitez's stewardship, every aspect of rum production was studied and important guidelines were provided, free of charge, to any rum producers in the world who were interested. Many took advantage of this generosity, and the quality of rum improved everywhere it was made.

\* \* \*

Centuries before advanced technology was developed in Puerto Rico, crude rum was produced wherever sugarcane was grown. The process that converts cane juice into sugar yields thick, sweet syrup as a by-product. After a period when this syrup was put to such undignified uses as fertilizer and cattle feed, one of Columbus's observant settlers noticed that the brown, sticky fluid—called "molasses" by the English—fermented when it was left out in the sun. A coarse, very sweet drink resulted.

It wasn't until the 17th century, however, that enterprising colonists used the process of distillation, newly fashionable in Europe, to make a spirit drink from the molasses. This libation quickly became so popular that some growers had to be firmly reminded by the government that their primary purpose was to produce sugar, not inebriants. Mr. W. Hughes wrote after a visit in 1672: "They make a sort of strong water they call Rumbullion, stronger than spirit of wine."* The name, a product of English country slang, was eventually shortened to "rum."

In 1655 the Royal Navy, after failing to capture the Spanish-held island of San Domingo, turned its attention to Jamaica rather than returning to England empty-handed. The attack was successful, Jamaica was annexed to the expanding British Empire, and the sailors were rewarded with a ration of the rum that was found on the island. Prior to this conquest, British Navy men on long sea voyages had depended on water or beer for refreshment. But these liquids had a tendency to deteriorate over time; the water would become brackish and the beer would turn flat and sour. Rum, on the other hand, remained stable for months. It became customary to give each British seaman a ration of a half pint of rum each day, a substantial amount by today's standards. Unfortunately, many sailors adopted the practice of bolting the whole half pint all at once, a routine that, as you might imagine, caused them to be a little unsteady on their feet.

The admiralty was at a loss as to the most effective way to deal with this problem. Discontinuing the rum ration might lead to a massive mutiny; there had to be a more moderate solution. The answer to this predicament eluded the Royal Navy until it was solved dramatically by Admiral Edward Vernon in 1740.

Admiral Vernon was a dapper and intelligent fellow who always wore a heavy waterproof boat-cloak made of a coarse fabric woven from silk, mohair, and wool. This material was called grogram and it earned Vernon the nickname "Old Grogram."

Vernon's solution to the rum problem was to issue a decree in 1740 that ordered all ships' captains to mix each sailor's daily rum ration with a quart of water. He also suggested the use of sugar and limes to make the mixture "more palatable to them."†

Almost immediately a name was coined by sailors for this concoction. In honor of Old Grogram, the new rum ration was called

---

*Rum Yesterday and Today* by Hugh Barty-King and Anton Massel (London: Heinemann, 1983), p. 12.

†349 order to Captains, August 21, 1740. See *Nelson's Blood* by James Pack (Havant, Hampshire: K. Mason, 1982), p. 22.

"grog." Later, after Lord Admiral Nelson's death at Trafalgar in 1805, the drink was also known as "Nelson's Blood."

In putting forth his ingenious recipe, Admiral Vernon had not only saved the Royal Navy, he had inadvertently invented the rum cocktail. From that time on, rum was often blended with other ingredients—most frequently with fruit juices.

Throughout the 18th century, the modish drink was "punch," a mixture that took many forms but which often contained rum. The name was an anglicization of the Hindustani *panch,* meaning "five." The classic punch was a combination of five ingredients: spirit, sugar, lime juice, spice, and water.

In 1896, one of the most dramatic inventions in the history of rum took place outside Santiago in Cuba. An American named Jennings Cox, who was working in copper mines not far from a village called Daiquiri, combined light rum and lime juice in a cocktail to honor some visiting friends. He called it the daiquiri. The rest is history.

*    *    *

The greatest rum drink inventor was born in San Francisco six years after the daiquiri was born. The charismatic Vic Bergeron opened his first restaurant in Oakland in 1934. Three years later he changed the name of the place from Hinky Dinks to Trader Vic's and adopted the world-famous "tropical paradise" theme.

One night in 1944, Vic was in the service bar of his Oakland restaurant thinking about creating a new drink. He took down a bottle of 17-year-old Jamaican rum. "The flavor of this great rum wasn't meant to be overpowered with heavy additions of fruit juices and flavorings," Vic wrote in 1970. "I took a fresh lime, added some orange curaçao from Holland, a dash of rock candy syrup, and a dollop of French orgeat, for its subtle almond flavor. A generous amount of shaved ice and vigorous shaking by hand produced the marriage I was after."*

Trader Vic garnished the new drink with a sprig of mint and gave a glass to a Tahitian friend who happened to be in the restaurant that night. She took one sip and said, *"Mai tai—roa ae,"* which means "out of this world—the best" in Tahitian.

---

*  *Let's Get the Record Straight on the Mai Tai!* by Victor J. Bergeron (San Francisco: Trader Vic's, 1970).

Many other great rum drinks have been invented over the centuries. Planter's Punch, Swizzle, Piña Colada, Scorpion, Bacardi, Cuba Libre, and the Zombie are just a few of the best-known. And to think we have Christopher Columbus to thank.

Over the last several years, aged rum has been gaining popularity among those who favor single-malt scotch, small-batch bourbon, and vintage Armagnac. Time spent in oak casks renders a deep, smooth spirit. These ultrapremium rums are best savored alone, as the addition of juice or other mixers dilutes the balance of lush, sultry flavor. Sample a variety of aged rums and you may taste vanilla, butterscotch, caramel, brown sugar, tobacco, molasses, and leather. Served in a snifter or on the rocks following a fine meal, this tropical spirit may conjure the subtle slap of waves upon a moonlit beach, the scent of salt in the air, and the delicate rustling of palm fronds overhead.

A few aged rums I'd recommend are the Diplomatico Reserva Exclusiva, a cognaclike spirit from Venezuela; the Gran Blason, a blended golden rum from Costa Rica; the stunning Angostura 1824 from Trinidad, and both Kaniche Guadeloupe and Kaniche Martinique, aged 10 and 15 years respectively.

* * *

I would be remiss if I let you leave the rum chapter without a brief discussion of cachaca. Also known as caxaca, caxa, or chacha, this Brazilian spirit is the key ingredient in the Caipirinha, which is one of the hottest drinks of the new century. In an age when bell-bottoms are returning to the runways and furniture from the 1950s is commanding a high tariff, it should come as no surprise that this new, hip drink is actually very old. The name, roughly translated, means "Farmer's Drink." Cachaca is a cousin of the molasses-based rum, but takes its distinctive flavor from the juice of unrefined sugarcane. This juice is allowed to ferment in wood or copper vats for 3 weeks, then boiled down 3 times to a thick concentrate. There are over 4,000 types of cachaca available in Brazil, where the spirit is second only to beer in popularity. Over the last 10 years, a number of tasty cachacas have been exported to the United States. The sweetness of the caxaca accents the intensity of lime zest in the Caipirinha, making it especially refreshing in the summer months. Margarita fans and anyone looking to drink on the cutting edge will be well served by seeking out cachaca.

# Classics

## Bacardi Cocktail

*Makes 1 or 2 servings*

3 ounces light rum
Juice of ½ lime
2 dashes of grenadine
1 scoop crushed ice

In a shaker, combine all ingredients and shake until frothy. Pour the mixture into a cocktail glass.

## Between the Sheets

¾ ounce light rum
¾ ounce brandy
¾ ounce triple sec
¾ ounce lemon juice

Combine all ingredients in a shaker with ice cubes. Shake well and pour into a chilled cocktail glass.

## Cuba Libre

1¾ ounces light rum
Cola to taste
¼ lime

Mix the rum and cola in a highball glass with a few ice cubes. Add the lime after giving it a light squeeze over the drink and stir well.

## Daiquiri, Frozen

1¾ ounces light rum
Juice of ½ lime
2 teaspoons sugar
1 scoop crushed ice

Combine all ingredients in a blender. Blend well. Pour the mixture into a cocktail glass or champagne flute.

NOTE: Various fruits can be added to the mixture, such as strawberries, raspberries, peaches, watermelon, or mango.

## Daiquiri, Strawberry

1¾ ounces light rum
5 large strawberries
Juice of ¼ lime
1 to 2 teaspoons sugar
1 scoop crushed ice

Mix all ingredients, except 1 strawberry, thoroughly in a blender. Pour the mixture into a large cocktail glass or champagne flute. Garnish with the extra strawberry.

## Louisiana Planter's Punch

1½ ounces golden rum
¾ ounce bourbon
¾ ounce cognac
½ ounce sugar syrup
1 ounce lemon juice
Several dashes of bitters
Several dashes of Pernod
1 scoop crushed ice
Club soda
1 lemon slice, seeded
1 orange slice, seeded

Mix the first eight ingredients in a shaker or blender. Pour the mixture into a chilled highball glass and top off with the cold club soda. Garnish with the fruit slices.

## Mai Tai

1 ounce Jamaican rum, preferably well aged
1 ounce Martinique rum
½ ounce curaçao
¼ ounce rock candy syrup
¼ ounce orgeat
1 scoop crushed ice
Lime peel
Mint sprig
Strip of fresh pineapple

Mix the first six ingredients in a shaker or blender. Pour the mixture into a chilled double old-fashioned glass. Garnish with the lime peel, mint sprig, and fresh pineapple.

## Navy Grog

1 ounce light rum
1 ounce dark rum
1 ounce 86-proof Demerara rum
½ ounce orange juice
½ ounce guava juice
½ ounce lime juice
½ ounce pineapple juice
½ ounce orgeat, or to taste
1 scoop crushed ice
1 lime slice, seeded
1 mint sprig

Mix all ingredients, except the lime slice and mint sprig, in a shaker or blender. Pour the mixture into a chilled double old-fashioned glass. Garnish with the lime slice and mint sprig.

## Piña Colada I

*Makes 6 servings*

⅔ cup light or dark rum
½ cup cream of coconut
1 cup pineapple juice, chilled
2 cups crushed ice
Thin slices of ripe pineapple, each speared to a maraschino cherry with a toothpick

Thoroughly chill 6 cocktail glasses. In an electric blender, combine all ingredient, except the fruit garnish. Blend at high speed for 30 seconds. Pour the mixture into the chilled glasses and garnish with the pineapple-cherry spears.

Mix the first five ingredients thoroughly in a shaker or blender. Pour the mixture into a tall collins glass and fill with the cold club soda. Top off with the float of port and the fruit garnish.

## Piña Colada II

1½ ounces light rum
2 ounces pineapple juice
1 ounce cream of coconut
1 scoop crushed ice

Combine and mix all ingredients in the blender until smooth. Pour the mixture into a chilled cocktail glass.

## Plantation Punch

1½ ounces dark rum
¾ ounce Southern Comfort
1 teaspoon brown sugar, or to
    taste
1 ounce lemon juice
1 scoop crushed ice
Club soda
1 teaspoon port
Orange slice, seeded
Lemon slice, seeded

## Planter's Punch I

1½ ounces light rum
1½ ounces dark rum
3 ounces fresh orange juice
¾ ounce fresh lime juice
Simple syrup to taste
Crushed ice
1 unpeeled orange slice, speared
    with a peeled strip of ripe
    pineapple and a maraschino
    cherry with a toothpick

Combine all ingredients, except the fruit spear, in a shaker. Shake well and pour into a tall, chilled collins glass. Garnish with the fruit spear and serve with straws.

## Planter's Punch II

2 ounces dark rum
2 ¾ ounces orange juice
¾ ounce lemon juice
¼ to ½ ounce grenadine
1 maraschino cherry
1 slice orange, seeded

Mix the rum, juices, and grenadine in a shaker. Pour the mixture into a highball glass with ice. Garnish with the cherry and orange slice.

## Planter's Punch III

2 ounces dark rum
1½ ounces pineapple juice
1½ ounces orange juice
¼ to ½ ounce grenadine
¾ ounce lemon juice
1 maraschino cherry
1 strip fresh pineapple, peeled

Mix the rum, juices, and grenadine in a shaker. Pour the mixture into a highball glass with ice. Garnish with the cherry and pineapple strip.

## Planter's Punch IV

1½ to 2 ounces dark rum
3 ounces orange juice
Juice of ½ lemon or lime
1 teaspoon superfine sugar
Dash of grenadine
1 scoop crushed ice
1 orange slice, seeded
1 maraschino cherry

Mix all ingredients, except the orange slice and cherry, in a shaker

or blender. Pour the mixture into a tall, chilled collins glass. Garnish with the orange slice and cherry.

## Planter's Punch V

2 ounces light rum
1 ounce dark rum
½ ounce sugar syrup to taste
1 ounce lime juice
Several dashes of bitters
1 scoop crushed ice
Club soda
Orange slice
Lemon slice

Mix all ingredients, except the soda and fruit slices, in a shaker. Pour the mixture into a chilled collins glass and top off with the cold club soda. Garnish with the orange and lemon slices.

VARIATIONS AND ADDITIONS: For the punch recipes above, you can add to taste: fresh juice, canned grapefruit juice, tamarind nectar, guava nectar, apple cider, or mango nectar.

## Rum Collins

1½ ounces light rum
1 ounce fresh lime juice
1 ounce simple syrup
1 scoop crushed ice
Club soda
1 maraschino cherry speared to a
    slice of unpeeled, seeded
    orange with a toothpick

In a cocktail shaker, combine the
first four ingredients. Shake vigorously and strain into a tall collins
glass. Add additional ice, if desired.
Top off with the club soda and garnish with the fruit spear.

## Rum Highball

1¾ ounces light or dark rum
Ginger ale, club soda, or lemon-
    lime soda to taste
Twist of lemon

Combine the rum and choice of
soda in a highball glass with ice
cubes. Stir well. Garnish with the
lemon twist.

## Rum Old-Fashioned

1¾ ounces light rum
1 cube of sugar, laced with 2 to 3
    splashes of bitters

Maraschino cherry
Wedge of lemon and/or orange
Ice water or club soda to taste

Mix together the rum and sugar
cube in an old-fashioned glass with
a few ice cubes. Add the cherry,
wedges of lemon and/or orange as
desired. Top off with the ice water
or soda water.

## Rum Swizzle

1 ounce light rum
½ ounce fresh lime juice
¼ ounce simple syrup
1 dash of bitters
1 scoop crushed ice
Club soda
Maraschino cherry (optional)

In a cocktail shaker, combine the
first five ingredients. Shake until
frothy, then immediately pour into
a highball glass. Top off the glass
with chilled club soda. If desired,
garnish with the maraschino
cherry.

## Scorpion

1½ ounces dark rum
¾ ounce light rum
¾ ounce brandy
¼ ounce triple sec

1½ ounces orange juice
Juice of ½ lemon or lime
1 scoop crushed ice
Maraschino cherry

Mix all ingredients, except the cherry, in a shaker with crushed ice. Strain the mixture into a highball glass half filled with freshly crushed ice. Garnish with the maraschino cherry.

## Rum Screwdriver

1 to 2 ounces white rum
4 to 6 ounces orange juice
1 scoop crushed ice
Orange slice

Add all ingredients, except the orange slice, to a tall highball glass. Stir well and garnish with the orange slice.

## Tom and Jerry I

1 egg, separated
1 teaspoon confectioners' sugar
½ ounce brandy
½ ounce rum
Splash of hot milk
Nutmeg

Beat the white and the yolk of the egg separately. Blend them together in a fresh glass. Add the teaspoon of sugar to the blend and beat again. Pour in the brandy and the rum. While stirring gently, top with the splash of hot milk and sprinkle with the nutmeg.

## Zombie

2 ounces light rum
1 ounce dark rum
½ ounce 151-proof Demerara
   rum
1 ounce curaçao
1 teaspoon Pernod
1 ounce lemon juice
1 ounce orange juice
1 ounce pineapple juice
½ ounce papaya or guava juice
   (optional)
¼ ounce grenadine
½ ounce orgeat or sugar syrup to
   taste
1 scoop crushed ice
Mint sprig
1 fresh pineapple strip

Mix all ingredients, except the mint and pineapple strip, in a blender. Pour the mixture into a tall, chilled collins or hurricane glass. Garnish with the mint sprig and pineapple strip.

# Creative Concoctions

## Admiral Vernon

1½ ounces light rum
½ ounce Grand Marnier
½ ounce lime juice
1 teaspoon orgeat
1 scoop crushed ice

Combine all ingredients in a shaker. Shake well and strain into a chilled cocktail glass.

## Andalusia

¾ ounce light rum
¾ ounce brandy
¾ ounce dry sherry
Several dashes of bitters

Combine all ingredients in a mixing glass with several ice cubes. Stir well and strain into a chilled cocktail glass.

## Apricot Pie

1½ ounces light rum
½ ounce sweet vermouth
1 ounce apricot brandy
1 teaspoon lemon juice
Dash of grenadine
1 scoop crushed ice

Combine all ingredients in a shaker. Mix well and pour into a chilled cocktail glass.

## Apricot Queen

*Makes 2 servings*

3 ounces light rum
2 ounces apricot-flavored brandy
    or apricot liqueur
1 ounce curaçao
1 ounce lime juice
1 egg white
Crushed ice
Orange slices

Mix all ingredients, except the orange slices, in a blender. Blend at low speed for 15 seconds. Pour the mixture into a chilled old-fashioned glasses and garnish with the orange slices.

## Aunt Mary

2 ounces white rum
3 ounces tomato juice
Pickapeppa or Worcestershire
    sauce to taste
Salt and black pepper to taste
1 or 2 dashes of Tabasco or hot
    pepper sauce (optional)
Wedge of fresh, seeded lime

Place ice cubes in a glass. Add the first four ingredients and, if desired, the Tabasco or hot pepper sauce. Stir gently and garnish with the lime on the rim of the glass.

## Banana Rum

½ ounce light rum
½ ounce banana liqueur
½ ounce orange juice
1 scoop crushed ice

Combine all ingredients in a shaker. Mix well and strain into a chilled cocktail glass.

## Bee's Kiss

1½ ounces light rum
1 teaspoon honey
1 teaspoon heavy cream
1 scoop crushed ice

Mix all ingredients in a shaker. Strain the mixture into a chilled cocktail glass.

## Bee's Knees

1½ ounces golden rum
½ ounce orange juice
½ ounce lime juice
1 teaspoon sugar syrup, or to taste
Several dashes of curaçao
1 scoop crushed ice
Orange peel twist

Combine all ingredients, except the orange peel, in a shaker. Mix thoroughly. Strain the mixture into a chilled cocktail glass and garnish with the orange peel.

## Bermuda Cocktail

1½ ounces golden rum
¾ ounce apricot brandy
½ ounce lime juice
½ ounce orgeat or sugar syrup to taste
Dash of grenadine

Combine all ingredients in a shaker. Mix well and strain into a chilled cocktail glass.

## Black Marie (cold)

¾ ounce dark rum
¾ ounce brandy
¼ ounce coffee liqueur
1 cup cold strong coffee
1 to 2 teaspoons sugar
2 scoops crushed ice

Combine the first four ingredients, 1 teaspoon of the sugar, and 1 scoop of the ice in a shaker. Shake vigorously. Strain the mixture into a highball glass and fill with the other scoop of crushed ice. Add more sugar if desired.

## Buccaneer Cocktail

1¾ ounces dark rum
1¾ ounces light rum
1¾ ounces coffee liqueur
6 ounces pineapple juice
1 scoop crushed ice
2 tablespoons heavy cream
Nutmeg

Combine the first four ingredients in a blender. Pour the mixture into a large wine goblet over the crushed ice. Top with the heavy cream and sprinkle the with the freshly grated nutmeg.

## Bolero

1½ ounces light rum
¾ ounce apple brandy or
    applejack
Several dashes of sweet vermouth
Twist of lemon peel

Combine all ingredients, except the lemon peel, in a mixing glass with ice. Stir thoroughly and strain into a chilled cocktail glass. Garnish with the lemon peel.

## Calypso Cocktail

1½ ounces golden rum
1 ounce pineapple juice
½ ounce lemon juice
1 teaspoon Falernum or sugar
    syrup to taste
Dash of bitters
1 scoop crushed ice
Pinch of grated nutmeg

Combine all ingredients, except the nutmeg, in a shaker. Mix well and strain into a chilled cocktail glass. Sprinkle the nutmeg on top.

## Cardinal

2 ounces light rum
½ ounce amaretto
½ ounce triple sec
1 ounce lime juice (fresh or
    bottled)
½ teaspoon grenadine
Lime slice

Mix the first five ingredients in a shaker with ice. Pour the mixture into a chilled old-fashioned glass and garnish with the lime slice.

## Centenario

1½ ounces golden rum
¾ ounce aged white rum
¼ ounce triple sec
¼ ounce coffee liqueur
¼ ounce grenadine
Juice of 1 lime
1 scoop crushed ice
Fresh mint sprig

Combine all ingredients, except the mint sprig, in a highball glass. Stir well. Garnish with the mint sprig.

## Creole

1¾ ounces light rum
3½ ounces beef bouillon
2 splashes of lemon juice
Pepper, salt, Tabasco, and
    Worcestershire sauce to taste

Mix the rum, bouillon, and lemon juice in a highball glass with several ice cubes. Flavor to taste with the combined seasonings.

## Cuban Manhattan (dry)

1½ ounces light rum
¾ ounce dry vermouth
1 splash of bitters
1 twist of lemon

Mix all ingredients, except the lemon twist, in a mixing glass with ice cubes. Strain the blend into a chilled cocktail glass and garnish with the lemon twist.

## Cuban Manhattan (sweet)

1½ ounces light rum
1 splash of bitters
¾ ounce sweet vermouth
Maraschino cherry

Mix the rum, bitters, and vermouth in a mixing glass with ice cubes. Strain the mixture into a chilled cocktail glass and garnish with the maraschino cherry.

## Curaçao Cooler

1 ounce dark rum
1 ounce curaçao
1 ounce lime juice
1 scoop crushed ice
Club soda
1 orange slice, seeded

Mix the first four ingredients in a shaker. Pour the mixture into a chilled highball glass and top off with the cold club soda. Garnish with the orange slice.

## Davis Cocktail

1½ ounces dark rum
¾ ounce dry vermouth
2 dashes of raspberry syrup
Juice of ½ lime
1 scoop crushed ice

In a shaker, mix together all ingredients. Strain the mixture into a cocktail glass.

## Derby Special

1½ ounces light rum
½ ounce triple sec
1 ounce orange juice
½ ounce lime juice
1 scoop crushed ice

Mix all ingredients in a blender until almost slushy. Pour the mixture into a chilled cocktail glass.

## Devil's Tail

1½ ounces golden rum
½ ounce vodka
½ ounce apricot liqueur
½ ounce lime juice
½ teaspoon grenadine
1 scoop crushed ice
Lime peel

Mix the first six ingredients thoroughly in a blender. Pour the mixture into a chilled cocktail glass. Twist the lime peel over the drink and drop it in.

## Doctor Bird Cocktail

1½ ounces light rum
1 teaspoon honey
1 teaspoon cream
1 or 2 dashes of grenadine
1 scoop crushed ice
Fresh flower

Combine all ingredients, except the flower, in a shaker and shake vigorously. Strain the mixture into a chilled champagne glass and garnish with a rinsed bougainvillea or other fresh flower.

## El Floridita

1½ ounces rum
½ ounce sweet vermouth
½ ounce lime juice
Splash of white crème de cacao
Splash of grenadine
Lime twist

Pour all ingredients, except the lime twist, into a cocktail shaker. Add a scoop of cracked ice. Shake to mix. Strain into a chilled cocktail glass. Garnish with the lime twist.

## Ernest Hemingway Special

1½ ounces light rum
Juice of ½ lime
¼ ounce grapefruit juice
¼ ounce maraschino liqueur
1 scoop crushed ice

Mix all ingredients thoroughly in a shaker. Pour the mixture into a chilled cocktail glass.

## Gilligan's Island

1½ ounces light rum
Juice of ½ lime
¼ ounce grapefruit juice
¼ ounce maraschino liqueur
1 scoop crushed ice

Mix all ingredients thoroughly in a shaker. Pour the mixture into a chilled cocktail glass.

## Goldie's Rum Fizz

3 ounces light rum
1 egg yolk
1 tablespoon powdered sugar
1½ ounces (or more) fresh lime
     juice
Dash of bitters
Crushed ice
Chilled club soda

Combine all ingredients, except the soda, in a shaker. Mix well and strain into a tall highball glass. Top off the glass with the chilled soda.

## Happy Apple

1½ ounces golden rum
3 ounces sweet apple cider
½ ounce lemon juice
1 scoop crushed ice
Twist of lime peel

Combine rum, cider, lemon juice, and ice in a shaker or blender. Mix well. Pour the mixture into a chilled old-fashioned glass and garnish with the lime peel.

## Harbour Street Cocktail

1½ to 2 ounces light rum
¾ ounce lime juice
Twist of lime peel

Pour the rum and lime juice into an old-fashioned glass with ice cubes. Stir gently and garnish with the lime peel.

## Hawaii Five-O

1 ounce dark rum
1 ounce gin
1 ounce dry red wine
1 ounce orange juice
1 scoop crushed ice
1 lime slice

Combine all ingredients, except the lime, in a shaker or blender. Mix briefly, just to combine. Pour the mixture into a chilled old-fashioned glass and garnish with the lime slice.

## Heavyweight Sailor

1½ ounces high-proof dark rum
1½ ounces dark rum
¾ ounce light rum
¼ ounce coffee liqueur
1½ ounces lime juice
Juice of ½ lime or lemon
Wedge of lime, seeded

Mix all ingredients, except the lime wedge, in a shaker with crushed ice. Pour the mixture into a highball glass. Garnish with the lime wedge.

## Honeybunch

2 ounces golden rum
Juice of one lime
1 teaspoon clear honey
    (preferably orange or lemon
    blossom)
Lemon twist

Add all ingredients, except the lemon twist, to a cocktail shaker along with 4 to 5 ice cubes. Shake vigorously. Strain into a chilled cocktail glass. Garnish with the lemon twist.

## Jamaica Cream

1½ ounces light rum
1 ounce gin
1 ounce light cream
1 teaspoon lemon juice
1 teaspoon sugar syrup, or to
    taste
1 scoop crushed ice
Chilled club soda

Mix all ingredients, except the soda, in a blender until thoroughly combined. Pour the mixture into a chilled highball glass and top off with the chilled club soda.

## Jamaica Blue

2 ounces light rum
½ ounce triple sec
½ ounce lemon juice
1 teaspoon blueberry syrup
1 scoop crushed ice
Club soda
Lemon wedge, seeded
Fresh blueberries (optional)

Mix the first five ingredients in a shaker. Pour the mixture into a chilled collins glass and top off with the club soda. Garnish with the lemon slice, plus the fresh blueberries if desired.

## Jamaican Martini

2 ounces light rum
¼ to ½ ounce dry sherry
1 scoop crushed ice
Lime peel or green olive

In a mixing glass, stir together the rum, sherry, and ice. Stir until well chilled, but do not allow the mixture to become diluted. Strain the mixture into a chilled martini glass. Garnish with the lime peel or green olive.

## Kathy Kocktail

1½ ounces light rum
Juice of ½ lime
1 teaspoon sugar
2 splashes of apricot brandy
2 splashes of triple sec
1 scoop crushed ice
Lime twist

Mix all ingredients, except the lime twist, in a shaker. Pour the mixture into a cocktail glass and garnish with the lime twist.

## Liberty Cocktail

1½ ounces light rum
¾ ounce applejack
Juice of ½ lime
1 scoop crushed ice
1 teaspoon superfine sugar
1 lime wedge, seeded (optional)

Combine all ingredients, except the lime wedge, in a shaker, adding the sugar last. Blend thoroughly. Pour the mixture into a chilled cocktail glass. Garnish with the lime, if desired.

## Lallah Rookh

1½ ounces light rum
¾ ounce cognac
½ ounce crème de vanille or
    vanilla extract
1 teaspoon sugar syrup, or to
    taste
1 scoop crushed ice
1 generous tablespoon whipped
    cream

Mix all ingredients, except the whipped cream, in a shaker or blender. Pour the mixture into a chilled wineglass and top off with the whipped cream.

## Lightweight Sailor

1 ounce dark rum
¾ ounce light rum
¼ ounce sugar syrup
¾ ounce lime juice
Juice of ½ lime or lemon
1 scoop crushed ice
1 lime wedge, seeded

Combine all ingredients, except the lime wedge, in a shaker and shake vigorously. Strain the mixture into an old-fashioned glass half filled with freshly crushed ice. Garnish with the lime wedge.

## Little Flower

1½ ounces orange curaçao
1½ ounces white rum
1½ ounces grapefruit juice
Orange peel

In a shaker, mix the curaçao, rum, and juice with ice. Strain the mixture into a cocktail glass and garnish with the orange peel.

## Mary Pickford

1½ ounces light rum
1½ ounces pineapple juice
1 splash of grenadine
1 scoop crushed ice
1 maraschino cherry

Combine all ingredients, except the cherry, in a shaker. Mix well and pour into a chilled cocktail glass. Garnish with the cherry.

## Maude's Downfall

2 ounces light rum
Canned or fresh grapefruit juice, well chilled
1 scoop crushed ice
Salt

In a tall highball glass filled with crushed ice, combine the rum and grapefruit juice. Add the salt to taste. Serve with a swizzle stick.

## Mojito

Juice of ½ lime
1 teaspoon superfine sugar
Mint leaves to taste
1 scoop crushed ice
2 ounces light rum
Club soda
Sprig of mint (optional)

Place the lime juice and sugar in a highball glass, then stir until the sugar is dissolved. Add a few of the mint leaves, pressing them to the inside of the glass. Fill the glass with the crushed ice and pour in the rum, stirring gently. Top off with the soda, then garnish with the sprig of mint if desired.

## Montego Tea

1 scoop crushed ice
¾ ounce light rum
¾ ounce dark rum
¾ ounce brandy
¾ ounce triple sec
¾ ounce orange juice
Juice of ½ lime
Cola to taste

Fill a tall drink glass with the scoop of ice. Pour in the next five ingredients. Stir well. Add the lime juice and top off with the cola.

## Naked Lady Cocktail

*Makes 3 servings*

4½ ounces light rum
3 ounces sweet vermouth
4 dashes of apricot brandy
2 dashes of grenadine
4 dashes of fresh lime or lemon
    juice
1 scoop crushed ice

Combine all ingredients in a shaker. Shake well and strain into 3 chilled cocktail glasses.

## Myrtle Bank Punch

1½ ounces 151-proof Demerara
    rum
Juice of ½ lime
1 teaspoon grenadine
1 teaspoon sugar syrup, or to
    taste
1 scoop crushed ice
½ ounce maraschino liqueur

Combine all ingredients, except the liqueur, in a shaker or blender. Mix well and pour into a chilled highball glass. Top off with a maraschino liqueur float.

## Pancho Villa

1 ounce light rum
1 ounce gin
1 ounce apricot liqueur or apricot
    brandy
1 teaspoon cherry brandy
1 teaspoon pineapple juice
1 scoop crushed ice

Combine and mix all ingredients in a shaker. Pour the mixture into a chilled cocktail glass.

## Pancho's Rum Fizz

*Makes 2 servings*

1½ ounces light rum
1½ ounces dark rum
1½ ounces apricot brandy
1½ ounces fresh lime juice
1 tablespoon (or more)
    granulated sugar
2 tablespoons heavy cream
1 scoop crushed ice
Chilled club soda

Combine all ingredients, except the soda, in a shaker. Mix until well blended. Strain the mixture into 2 chilled highball glasses and top off with the soda.

## Pirate's Julep

6 mint leaves
1 teaspoon sugar syrup
Several dashes of bitters
1 scoop crushed ice
2 to 3 ounces golden rum
1 teaspoon curaçao
Mint sprig
Confectioners' sugar

Muddle the mint leaves with the sugar syrup in a chilled old-fashioned glass. Add the bitters and fill the glass with crushed ice. Pour in the rum and swizzle the mixture until the glass frosts, adding more ice if necessary. Top with the curaçao and garnish with the mint sprig dusted with powdered sugar.

## Platinum Blonde Cocktail

1½ ounces light rum
1½ ounces triple sec
½ ounce cream
1 scoop crushed ice
Green maraschino cherry
    (optional)

Combine all ingredients, except the cherry, in a shaker. Shake well and strain into a cocktail glass. Garnish with the green maraschino cherry on a cocktail stick, if desired.

## Presidente Seco

1½ ounces light rum
¾ ounce dry vermouth
1 splash red curaçao
1 lemon twist

Mix the rum, vermouth, and curaçao in a mixing glass with 6 to 8 ice cubes. Pour the mixture into a chilled cocktail glass and garnish with the lemon twist.

## Riptide

1 ounce dark rum
1 ounce light rum
1 ounce 151-proof rum
1 ounce grapefruit juice
1 ounce orange juice
Several dashes of orange curaçao
Several dashes of Pernod
1 orange slice, seeded
1 maraschino cherry

Mix all ingredients, except the orange slice and cherry, in a shaker with ice. Pour the mixture into a chilled double old-fashioned glass and garnish with the fruit.

## Rum Alexander

1½ ounces light rum
¾ ounce brown crème de cacao
1 ounce cream
Freshly grated nutmeg

Combine all ingredients, except the nutmeg, in a shaker with a few ice cubes. Mix well and strain into a cocktail glass. Sprinkle the grated nutmeg on top.

## Rum Apple

1½ ounces light rum
¾ ounce sweet vermouth
½ ounce calvados or applejack
1 teaspoon lemon juice
Dash of grenadine
Dash of apricot brandy
1 scoop crushed ice

Combine all ingredients in a shaker and mix thoroughly. Strain the mixture into a chilled cocktail glass.

## Rum Beguine

1½ ounces Martinique or Haitian rum
2 ounces sauternes, chilled
2 ounces pineapple juice
1 ounce lemon juice
½ ounce sugar syrup or Falernum to taste
Several dashes of bitters
1 scoop crushed ice
1 slice fresh pineapple

Mix all ingredients, except the pineapple slice, in a shaker. Pour the mixture into a chilled collins glass. Garnish with the pineapple.

## Rum Martini

1 ¾ ounces light rum
¼ ounce dry vermouth
1 black olive

Mix the rum and vermouth in a stirring glass with 6 to 8 ice cubes. Strain the mixture into a chilled martini glass or a chilled small cocktail glass. Garnish with the olive.

## Rum Sour

1½ ounces light rum
¼ ounce golden rum
¾ ounce fresh lemon juice
¾ ounce sugar syrup
1 maraschino cherry

Combine all ingredients, except the cherry, in a shaker with ice cubes. Shake until frothy. Strain the mixture into a chilled sour glass and garnish with the cherry.

## Rum and Tonic

1 scoop crushed ice
1½ ounces light rum
Quinine water or tonic water
Wedge of lime, with seeds
    removed

In a tall highball glass filled with the crushed ice, combine the light rum with the quinine water or tonic to taste. Garnish with the lime wedge on the rim of the glass.

## Salome Cocktail

3 ounces dark rum
1½ ounces crème de banane
¾ ounce fresh lime juice
4 tablespoons simple sugar syrup
1 scoop crushed ice
Thick ripe banana slice speared to
    a maraschino cherry with a
    toothpick

In a shaker, combine all ingredients except the banana-cherry garnish. Shake vigorously and strain into a chilled champagne glass. Decorate with the banana-cherry garnish.

## September Sunrise

2 to 3 ounces light rum
½ ounce lime juice
1 teaspoon grenadine
1 egg white
1 scoop crushed ice

Mix all ingredients in a shaker until almost frothy. Strain the mixture into a chilled cocktail glass.

## Shingle Stain

1 ounce dark rum
½ ounce St. James Rhum or other
   ultradark rum
¼ ounce Pimento Dram
½ ounce lime
Dash of grenadine

Combine all ingredients in a shaker
with crushed ice. Shake and strain
into a 12-ounce chimney glass
with more freshly crushed ice.

## Sir Walter Cocktail

1 ounce golden rum
¾ ounce brandy
¼ ounce triple sec
1 splash of grenadine
Juice of ½ lime
1 scoop crushed ice

Mix all ingredients thoroughly in a
shaker with the crushed ice. Pour
the mixture into a chilled cocktail
glass and serve.

## Sledgehammer

¾ ounce golden rum
¾ ounce brandy
¾ ounce calvados or applejack
Dash of Pernod
1 scoop crushed ice

Mix all ingredients in a shaker.
Strain the mixture into a chilled
cocktail glass.

## Southern Skies

2 ounces dark rum
1 ounce Southern Comfort
Juice of ½ lime
Dash of sugar syrup
Slice of lime

Pour all ingredients, except the
lime slice, over ice in a cocktail
shaker. Shake until a frost forms.
Strain into a chilled cocktail glass.
Garnish with the slice of lime.

## Spanish Main Cocktail

2 ounces rum
½ ounce dry vermouth
½ ounce sweet vermouth
Dash of bitters
Maraschino cherry

Add the rum, vermouths, and bitters to an old-fashioned glass filled
with ice cubes. Stir well and garnish with the cherry speared onto a
cocktail stick.

## Sunsplash

1½ ounces light rum
½ ounce dry vermouth
½ ounce sweet vermouth

Combine all ingredients in a mixing glass with ice cubes and stir well. Strain the mixture into a chilled cocktail glass.

## Sweet Gold

1 ounce light rum
1 ounce triple sec
1 ounce heavy cream
1 scoop crushed ice

Mix all ingredients thoroughly in a blender. Strain the mixture into a chilled cocktail glass.

## Tobago Cays

1½ ounces golden rum
½ ounce lime juice
½ ounce sugar syrup
½ teaspoon maraschino liqueur
1 scoop crushed ice
½ teaspoon Pernod

Mix all ingredients, except the Pernod, in a blender until smooth.

Pour the mixture into a chilled wineglass. Top with the float of Pernod.

## Trade Winds

2 ounces golden rum
½ ounce slivovitz
½ ounce lime juice
½ ounce Falernum or orgeat
1 scoop crushed ice

Combine all ingredients in a blender and mix until smooth. Pour the mixture into a chilled cocktail glass.

## Watermelon Cooler

2 ounces light rum
½ ounce melon liqueur
½ ounce lime juice
½ ounce sugar syrup, or to taste
1 cup watermelon, seeded and diced
1 scoop crushed ice
1 lime slice, seeded

Mix all ingredients, except the lime slice, in a blender at low speed for 15 seconds. Pour the mixture into a chilled double old-fashioned glass. Garnish with the lime slice.

### White Witch

1 ounce white rum
½ ounce white crème de cacao
½ ounce Cointreau
Juice of ½ lime
Club soda
Orange, lime slices

Pour the first four ingredients into a cocktail shaker. Add a scoop of ice. Shake vigorously. Strain over ice into an old-fashioned glass. Top with the soda and stir to mix. Decorate with the slices of orange and lime.

# Signature Drinks

### Añejo Highball

DALE DeGROFF, THE RAINBOW ROOM, NEW YORK CITY

1¾ ounces aged rum
¾ ounce orange curaçao
¾ ounces fresh lime juice
Dash of bitters
Club soda
Ginger beer
Thin wheel of fresh lime
Slice of fresh orange, cut in half

Pour the first four ingredients into a highball glass with ice. Top off with a splash of the soda and a splash of the ginger beer. Garnish with the lime and orange slices.

### Barbados Cocktail

ASTA, SAN FRANCISCO

1½ ounces Barbados rum
½ ounce triple sec
Juice of 3 lime wedges
Lime slice

Fill a shaker with ice. Add all ingredients, except the lime slice, and shake with long sweeping motions 3 times. Strain the mixture into a chilled cocktail glass and garnish with the lime slice.

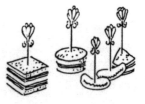

## Barbancourt Rum Cosmopolitan

CYPRESS CLUB, SAN FRANCISCO

1¼ ounces Barbancourt 15-year
   rum
½ ounce cranberry juice
½ teaspoon lime juice
½ teaspoon Cointreau or
   triple sec

Mix all ingredients in a shaker with crushed ice. Strain the mixture into a chilled martini glass.

## Big Kahuna (for two)

NEWPORT LANDING RESTAURANT,
NEWPORT BEACH, CALIFORNIA

1½ ounce Myers's rum
1½ ounces tequila
1½ ounces triple sec
1½ ounces brandy
Orange juice
Pineapple juice
Cranberry juice
Club soda
½ ounce Grand Marnier
1 wedge each of orange, lemon,
   lime, and pineapple
Cherry

Pour the first four ingredients into a 60-ounce schooner over ice. Fill the glass with equal parts orange juice, pineapple juice, and cranberry juice. Top with the soda and float the half ounce of Grand Marnier. Garnish with an orange wedge, a lemon wedge, a lime wedge, a pineapple wedge, a cherry, and an umbrella. Sip through jumbo straws.

## Bonga Cola

VARIOUS WEST COAST BARS

1½ ounces golden rum
1 ounce coffee liqueur
2 ounces pineapple juice
Dash of kirsch
Dash of lemon juice
1 scoop crushed ice
Cola
Maraschino cherry

Mix all ingredients, except the cola and cherry, in a shaker. Pour the mixture into a tall, chilled collins glass with fresh ice cubes. Top off the glass with the cold cola and stir gently. Garnish with the cherry.

## Caipirinha

CIUDAD, LOS ANGELES

2 small limes, cut into eighths
2 teaspoons superfine sugar
2 ounces cachaca

Place the lime sections in a muddler, sprinkle with the sugar, and muddle until the sugar dissolves. Place in a rocks glass and add ice. Top with the cachaca and add a stirring stick. The beauty of this drink is that the drinker will keep muddling with the stirrer, releasing more and more flavor as he or she drinks.

## Captain Cosmo

JULIE'S SUPPER CLUB, SAN FRANCISCO

1¼ ounces spiced rum
¼ ounce triple sec
¼ ounce lime juice
Splash of cranberry juice
Lime wedge

Pour all ingredients, except the lime wedge, into a large mixing glass filled with ice cubes. Stir well and strain into a chilled martini glass. Gently squeeze the lime wedge over the drink, then use it as garnish.

## Cancún

EL DORADO,
BRENTWOOD, CALIFORNIA

2 ounces spiced rum
3 ounces pineapple juice
1½ ounce cream of coconut
2 ounces strawberry puree

Add the rum, pineapple juice, cream of coconut, and a scoop of ice to a blender. Pour the strawberry puree into the bottom of a 12-ounce glass. Add the blended cocktail to the glass and let the strawberry puree swirl itself through the mixture.

## Caribe Piña Colada

CARIBE HILTON, SAN JUAN

*Makes 4 servings*

2 ounces dark rum
8 ounces light rum
2 ounces heavy cream
5 ounces cream of coconut
10 ounces pineapple juice
2 to 3 scoops crushed ice
4 fresh pineapple strips

Mix all ingredients, except the pineapple strips, in a blender for 10 seconds. Pour the mixture into chilled hurricane glass. Garnish with the pineapple strips.

## Chapultepec

HOTEL PRESIDENTE, MEXICO CITY

1¼ ounces golden rum
½ ounce brandy
¼ ounce sweet vermouth
¼ ounce tequila
1 teaspoon sugar syrup, or to
   taste
1 scoop crushed ice

Combine all ingredients in a shaker or blender. Mix well and pour the mixture into a chilled whisky sour glass.

## Dirty Banana

THE CAFE AT THE SIGN OF THE DOVE, NEW YORK CITY

1 ounce light rum
2 ounces sweet lemon mix
1 ounce banana liqueur
½ overripe banana
3 to 4 banana slices

Blend together all ingredients, except the banana slices, until well mixed. Pour the mixture into an old-fashioned glass with ice cubes and garnish with the banana slices.

TO MAKE SWEET LEMON MIX: Blend juice from 8 lemons with ¼ cup sugar and 1 egg white until well mixed. Yield: 16 ounces.

## Dr. Pepper

BALBOA CAFE, SAN FRANCISCO

½ ounce 151-rum
½ ounce amaretto
½ pint beer

Pour the rum and amaretto into a small shot glass. Light the shot glass on fire. Drop the flaming glass into a half-pint glass of beer.

## El Floridita's Hemingway Daiquiri

YOW BAR, LE PASSAGE, CHICAGO

1½ ounces Bacardi light rum
Juice of ⅛ grapefruit
Juice of 1 lime
Dash of marachino liqueur

Add all ingredients to a shaker with a scoop of ice. Shake well to mix. Strain into a chilled martini glass.

## Foreign Affair

THE ECCENTRIC, CHICAGO

1¼ ounces light rum
¼ ounce coffee liqueur
1 scoop (2 to 3 ounces) vanilla
   ice cream
Splash of milk
1 pirouette cookie (optional)

Combine all ingredients, except the cookie, in a blender and mix into a creamy consistency—do not overmix. Pour the mixture into a martini glass and garnish with the cookie.

## French Stinger

STARS, SAN FRANCISCO

3 ounces light rum
1 ounce green Chartreuse

Stir the rum and Chartreuse in a mixing glass with plenty of ice. Pour the mixture into a frozen stem glass.

## Golden Gloves

LA FLORIDA BAR, HAVANA

2 ounces rum
1 teaspoon Cointreau or triple sec
1 teaspoon sugar
Juice of ½ lemon
1 scoop crushed ice
Orange peel

In a blender, blend together all ingredients except the orange peel. Squeeze the peel into a chilled cocktail glass and rub it around the inside of the glass. Pour the mixture into the prepared glass.

## Green Eyes

"21" CLUB, NEW YORK CITY

1 ounce dark rum
¼ ounce melon liqueur
½ ounce lime juice
½ ounce cream of coconut
1½ ounces pineapple juice

Pour all ingredients into an old-fashioned glass containing several ice cubes. Stir gently.

## Green Lizard

BALBOA CAFE, SAN FRANCISCO

¾ ounce 151-proof light rum
¾ ounce green Chartreuse

Pour both ingredients into a shot glass.

## Griswold Inn Hot Buttered Rum

GRISWOLD INN, ESSEX, CONNECTICUT

Cinnamon stick
Lemon slice
Dash of ground cloves
Dash of bitters
Dash of superfine sugar
1½ ounces Myers's rum
Hot apple cider

Add all ingredients, except the rum and cider, to a small mug. Add the rum to the mug, then top off with the hot cider.

Combine all ingredients in a shaker. Mix well and strain into a large chilled cocktail glass.

## Harpoon

MOORS RESTAURANT, PROVINCETOWN, CAPE COD, MASSACHUSETTS

2 ounces rum
4 ounces cranberry juice
½ cling peach
½ ounce grenadine
1 scoop crushed ice
Orange slice
Cherry

In a blender, combine the rum, juice, cling peach, grenadine, and ice. Blend until frozen. Pour the mixture into a wineglass. Garnish with the orange slice and cherry.

## Havana Beach

LA FLORIDA BAR, HAVANA

1 ounce light rum
1 ounce pineapple juice
1 teaspoon sugar
1 scoop crushed ice

## Henry Morgan Cocktail

"21" CLUB, NEW YORK CITY

2 ounces light rum
3 ounces orange juice
Dash of grenadine
Club soda

Pour the rum, juice, and grenadine over ice into a collins glass. Stir gently. Top off the glass with the soda.

## Jamaican Dust

DORIAN'S RED HAND, NEW YORK CITY

*Makes 3 shots*

1 ounce coffee liqueur
2 ounces dark rum
4 ounces pineapple juice
1 scoop crushed ice

Combine all ingredients in a shaker. Mix well and strain into 3 shot glasses.

## Kohala Sunset

MAUNA LANI BAY HOTEL,
BIG ISLAND, HAWAII

2 ounces light rum
Dash of orange liqueur
Dash of grenadine
2 ounces orange juice
1 ounce freshly squeezed lemon
    juice
1 scoop crushed ice
¼ lime
1 maraschino cherry
1 pineapple wedge

Mix the first five ingredients in a blender with half the scoop of crushed ice, place the rest of the ice in a 14-ounce punch glass. Squeeze the lime and leave the shell in the glass. Fill the glass with the blended mixture. Garnish with the cherry and pineapple wedge.

## Kona

TRADER VIC'S, SAN FRANCISCO

½ lime
¼ ounce maraschino liqueur
1½ ounces light rum
½ ounce lemon juice

Squeeze the lime in a mixing glass with several ice cubes. Drop in the shell and add the liqueur, rum, and lemon juice. Stir well and strain into a chilled cocktail glass.

## Madison Mojita

SX137, NEW YORK CITY

5 lime wedges
Fresh mint
1½ ounces Bacardi Limon rum
1 ounce sugar water
Splash of club soda

In a rocks glass, muddle together the 5 lime wedges and 2 sprigs of the fresh mint. Discard the lime peel. Add the rum and the sugar water. Add ice and the splash of soda. Garnish with additional mint or a short stalk of sugarcane.

## Martian Tweetie

WESTIN PEACHTREE PLAZA, ATLANTA

½ ounce dark rum
½ ounce light rum
½ ounce passion fruit syrup
½ ounce Mai Tai mix
⅛ ounce or 1 teaspoon honey
2 teaspoons cream of coconut

Combine all ingredients in a blender with ice. Blend well. Pour the mixture over fresh ice cubes in a chilled collins glass.

## Mojito I

BRASSERIE, NEW YORK CITY

5 to 7 mint leaves
¼ ounce sugar syrup
¼ ounce lime juice
1 ounce Brugal white rum
1½ ounces Brugal añejo rum
Splash of club soda
Mint sprig

Place the mint leaves, sugar syrup, and lime juice in rocks glass. Muddle. Add ice and the rums, then shake. Splash with the soda and garnish with the sprig of mint.

## Mojito II

CIUDAD, LOS ANGELES

*Makes 2 servings*

½ cup freshly squeezed lime juice
⅓ cup sugar
½ cup packed fresh mint leaves
1 12-ounce bottle sparkling
    water, chilled
Ice cubes
2 tablespoons lime juice
    concentrate
4 ounces premium light rum
Lime slices and mint sprigs

Combine the lime juice, sugar, and mint leaves in a blender. Puree until smooth. Pour 2 tall glasses half full with ice cubes. Pour half of the lime juice concentrate, half of the puree, and 2 ounces of the rum into each. Top with the sparkling water. Garnish with the lime and the mint sprigs.

## The Oaxacan

EL DORADO CANTINA,
BRENTWOOD, CALIFORNIA

1 ounce Stoli Vanil
1½ ounces Malibu rum
½ ounce Apple Pucker schnapps
Splash of sweet 'n' sour mix
Lime wedge

Add all ingredients, except the lime, along with a scoop of ice to a mixing glass. Shake well and strain into a martini glass with a sugar rim. Garnish with the lime wedge, first squeezing it into the glass.

## Os Lusiadas

CREATED BY TARCISIO COSTA,
ALFAMA FINE PORTUGUESE CUISINE,
NEW YORK CITY

2 ounces Captain Morgan spiced
   rum
1 ounce crème de cassis
Splash of Malibu coconut rum
½ ounce fresh lime juice
Splash of pineapple juice
Mint leaf

Fill a shaker with ice. Add all ingredients, except the mint, and shake vigorously for about 20 seconds. Strain into a cocktail glass and garnish with the mint leaf.

## Pink Elephant

SALAMANDER, CHICAGO

⅛ ounce Malibu coconut rum
⅜ ounce cachaca
½ ounce coconut milk
½ ounce grenadine
Lemon twist

Pour the first four ingredients in order into a martini glass. Garnish with the twist of lemon.

## Prairie Fire

BALBOA CAFE, SAN FRANCISCO

1½ ounces 151-proof light rum
3 squirts of Tabasco

Add both ingredients to a shot glass. Carefully ignite the shot with a match. Blow out the flame before drinking!

## Rivington Punch

SX137, NEW YORK CITY

1½ ounces Myers's rum
½ ounce Malibu rum
½ ounce Mango Loco
½ ounce pineapple juice
Pineapple wedge

Mix all ingredients, except the pineapple, and serve over ice in a rocks glass. Garnish with the wedge of pineapple.

## Rum Keg (for two)

YOW BAR, LE PASSAGE, CHICAGO

1 ounce Jamaican rum
2½ ounces Bacardi light rum
½ ounce apricot liqueur
½ ounce rock candy syrup
2 ounces pineapple juice
2 ounces lemon juice
1 ounce passion fruit juice

Flash-blend all ingredients with crushed ice. Though the bar serves this drink in a ceramic "Volcano Bowl," it is just as tasty when sipped from a hurricane glass.

## Rum Punch Happy Jack

CREATED BY DOUG BIEDERBECK,
BIX, SAN FRANCISCO

2 ounces light rum
Juice of 1 lime
2 dashes of bitters
Splash of guava juice
1 scant teaspoon superfine sugar
Splash of grenadine
Freshly grated nutmeg

Combine all ingredients, except for the nutmeg, in a shaker with ice and mix thoroughly. Pour the mixture into a 10-ounce highball glass. Garnish with a small amount of the nutmeg.

## Sharkbite

BALBOA CAFE, SAN FRANCISCO

1 ounce dark rum
1 ounce orange juice
1 splash of grenadine

In a shaker with crushed ice, mix together the rum and orange juice.

Strain the mixture into a shot glass and top with the splash of grenadine.

## Shark's Tooth

TRADER VIC'S, SAN FRANCISCO

1 ounce 151-proof rum
Juice of ½ lime (save shell)
½ ounce lemon juice
Dash of grenadine
Dash of sugar syrup
1 scoop crushed ice
Club soda

Mix all ingredients, except the soda, in a shaker. Pour the mixture into a large pilsner glass and top off with the cold soda. Add the lime shell for garnish. Stir gently.

## Tahiti Bikini

DORIAN'S RED HAND, NEW YORK CITY

1 ounce rum
1 ounce vodka
1 ounce Malibu rum
1 ounce peach schnapps
1 ounce triple sec
1 ounce pineapple juice
1 ounce orange juice
1 thin slice of mango or tropical
   fruit (optional)

Pour all ingredients, except the fruit, into a collins glass containing several ice cubes. Stir thoroughly. Garnish with the fruit.

## Tahitian Honey Bee

TRADER VIC'S, SAN FRANCISCO

1 teaspoon honey
½ ounce lemon juice
1½ ounces rum
1 scoop crushed ice
Lemon peel twist

In a shaker, mix together the honey and lemon juice. Add the rum and crushed ice to the shaker. Shake well and strain into a chilled cocktail glass. Garnish with the lemon peel.

## Tamarind Treat

CHEF ALLEN'S, NORTH MIAMI

2 ounces spiced rum
4 ounces tamarind juice
1 slice star fruit (carambola)

Combine the rum and tamarind juice in a highball glass with ice. Stir and garnish with the star fruit.

## T.A.T.'s Mon Dude

T.A.T.'S, PALM BEACH, FLORIDA

½ ounce dark rum
½ ounce light rum
¼ ounce banana liqueur
¼ ounce Galliano
3 ounces orange juice
1 ounce piña colada mix
1 ounce pineapple juice
1 scoop crushed ice
1 fresh orange slice
1 maraschino cherry

In a shaker, mix all ingredients, except the orange slice and cherry, and mix until smooth. Pour the mixture into a chilled collins glass and garnish with the orange and cherry, skewered on a toothpick.

## Waikoloa Fizz

VARIOUS WAIKIKI BARS

1½ ounces Barbados rum
½ ounce Jamaica rum
3 ounces pineapple juice
½ ounce passion fruit juice
1 teaspoon coconut syrup
1 scoop crushed ice
Lemon-lime soda
Slice of fresh lime

Mix the first six ingredients in a shaker. Pour the mixture into a chilled collins glass and fill with the lemon-lime soda. Stir gently and garnish with the lime slice.

# Tropical Drinks

## *Acapulco*

1¾ ounces light rum
¼ ounce triple sec
1 egg white
1 teaspoon sugar or 2 splashes of
    sugar syrup
Juice of ½ lime
1 scoop crushed ice
1 wedge of lime, seeded

Mix all ingredients, except the lime wedge, in a shaker until well blended. Pour the mixture into a chilled cocktail glass and garnish with the lime wedge.

NOTE: Ice cubes may be used in place of crushed ice; the drink will no longer have a slushy consistency, but it will still be delicious.

## *Amanda's Mango Masterpiece*

*Make 10 servings*

1 cup peeled fresh mango
1 cup light rum
¼ cup strained fresh lime juice
¼ cup water
Sugar syrup to taste
1 scoop crushed ice

Have all ingredients well chilled prior to assembling this recipe. Puree the mango in a blender until smooth. Add the other ingredients and blend until smooth and very cold. Serve small portions in chilled stemmed cocktail glasses.

## *Angostura Scorpion*

3 tablespoons light rum
2 tablespoons sugar syrup
2 tablespoons strained fresh lime
    juice
Dash of bitters
1 scoop crushed ice

Combine all ingredients in a shaker. Mix well and strain into a chilled cocktail glass.

## *Banana Bliss*

1½ ounces white rum
1½ ounces crème de banane
1 ounce orange juice
Dash of bitters
1½ ounces heavy cream
2 dashes of grenadine
3 banana wheels

In a shaker, mix the first five ingredients with ice. Strain the mixture into an old-fashioned glass. Decorate with the grenadine and banana wheels.

## Banana Colada

1½ ounces rum
2 ounces cream of coconut
1 sliced banana
1 teaspoon lemon juice
1 cup ice

Combine all ingredients in a blender and blend until smooth. Pour the mixture into a chilled parfait glass.

## Bananarama

1½ ounces gold rum
1 ounce crème de banane
½ ounce 151-proof rum
4 ounces pineapple juice
1 ounce orange juice
½ ounce orgeat
½ ripe banana, peeled and sliced
1 scoop crushed ice
Lime slice

Mix all ingredients, except the lime slice, in a blender. Blend until smooth. Pour the mixture into a chilled collins glass and garnish with the lime slice.

## Barbados Planter's Punch

3 ounces golden rum
Juice of 1 lime
1 teaspoon sugar syrup
Dash of bitters
Club soda or water
1 scoop crushed ice
Ripe banana slice
Orange slices
Maraschino cherry
Pinch of ground nutmeg

Combine the first six ingredients in a shaker. Shake vigorously. Pour the mixture into a large, chilled collins glass. Garnish with the banana and orange slice, cherry, and a sprinkle of the ground nutmeg.

## Batida de Piña

2 to 3 ounces light rum
⅔ cup crushed pineapple (fresh or canned)
1 teaspoon sugar syrup
Mint sprig (optional)

Mix all ingredients, except the mint, in a blender with a few ice cubes. Blend until smooth. Pour the mixture into a chilled double old-fashioned glass and garnish with the mint sprig.

## Beachcomber

1½ ounces light rum
½ ounce triple sec
½ ounce lime juice
Several dashes of maraschino
  liqueur
1 scoop crushed ice

Mix all ingredients in a blender until smooth. Strain the mixture into a chilled cocktail glass.

## Blue Hawaiian

1 ounce white rum
½ ounce blue caraçao
2 ounces pineapple juice
1 ounce cream of coconut
Pineapple wedge

Add the first four ingredients to a blender along with a small scoop of crushed ice. Blend at high speed until frothy. Pour into a chilled cocktail glass and garnish with the pineapple wedge.

## Cantaloupe Cup

1½ ounces light rum
⅓ cup ripe cantaloupe, diced
½ ounce lime juice
½ ounce orange juice
½ teaspoon sugar syrup
1 scoop crushed ice
1 thin slice of cantaloupe

Mix all ingredients, except the cantaloupe slice, in a blender until smooth. Pour the mixture into a chilled old-fashioned glass and garnish with the cantaloupe slice.

## Chocolada

1½ ounces white rum
¼ ounce coffee liqueur
¼ ounce dark rum
¾ ounce chocolate syrup
¾ ounce cream of coconut
1 scoop crushed ice
Chocolate shavings

Mix all ingredients, except the chocolate shavings, in a blender. Pour the mixture into a highball glass and sprinkle the shavings on top.

## Daiquiri, Apple

1½ ounces light rum
½ ounce calvados or applejack
½ ounce lemon juice
1 teaspoon sugar syrup, or to
    taste
2 teaspoons apple juice
1 scoop of crushed ice
Apple wedge

Mix all ingredients, except the apple wedge, in a shaker. Strain the mixture into a chilled cocktail glass. Garnish with the apple wedge.

## Daiquiri, Banana

1 ¾ ounces white rum
½ banana
Juice of ¼ lime
1 teaspoon sugar
1 scoop crushed ice

Combine all ingredients in a blender. Blend until frothy. Pour the mixture into a large, chilled wineglass.

## Daiquiri, Coconut

1¼ ounces rum
4 ounces cream of coconut
1½ ounces lime juice
1½ cups ice

Combine all ingredients in a blender and blend until smooth. Pour the mixture into a chilled parfait glass.

## Daiquiri, Cool Lime

1½ ounces light rum
¾ ounce dark rum
¾ ounce triple sec
Juice of 1 lime
2 teaspoons sugar
1 scoop crushed ice
Lime twist

Mix all ingredients, except the lime twist, in a shaker. Pour the mixture into a large cocktail glass and garnish with the lime twist.

## Daiquiri, Derby Orange

1¾ ounces rum
Juice of 1 orange
Juice of ¼ lime
1 teaspoon sugar
1 scoop crushed ice

Mix all ingredients thoroughly in a blender. Pour the mixture into a large cocktail glass or champagne flute.

## Daiquiri, Florida

1¾ ounces light rum
Juice of ½ lime
2 teaspoons sugar
¼ ounce grapefruit juice
¼ ounce maraschino liqueur
1 scoop crushed ice

Mix all ingredients thoroughly in a shaker. Pour the mixture into a cocktail glass or champagne flute.

## Daiquiri, Frozen Guava

1½ ounces light rum
1 ounce guava nectar
½ ounce lime juice
1 teaspoon crème de banane
  (optional)
1 scoop crushed ice

Mix all ingredients in a blender until almost slushy. Pour the mixture into a chilled deep-saucer champagne glass.

## Daiquiri, Frozen Peach

1½ ounces light rum
½ ounce lime juice (fresh or
  bottled)
1 heaping teaspoon fresh,
  canned, or frozen peaches,
  diced
½ ounce syrup from canned or
  frozen peaches or sugar syrup
1 to 2 scoops crushed ice

Mix all ingredients in a blender until slushy; the peaches should be well incorporated into the mixture. Pour the mixture into a chilled deep-saucer champagne glass.

## Daiquiri, Mint

1¾ ounces white rum
1 scoop crushed ice
3 or 4 mint leaves
Juice of ½ lime
2 teaspoons sugar
2 splashes of Cointreau or triple
  sec

Combine all ingredients in a blender. Blend until smooth, letting the appliance run a few extra seconds. Pour the mixture into a large cocktail glass or champagne flute.

## Daiquiri, Peach

1¾ ounces light rum
½ ripe peach, peeled
Juice of ¼ lime
1 teaspoon sugar
1 scoop crushed ice

Mix all ingredients thoroughly in a blender. Pour the mixture into a large cocktail glass or champagne flute.

## Daiquiri, Pineapple II

1¾ ounces light rum
1 pineapple slice
Juice of ¼ lime
1 teaspoon sugar
1 scoop crushed ice

Combine all ingredients in a blender. Blend until smooth. Pour the mixture into a large cocktail glass or champagne flute.

## Daiquiri, Pineapple I

*Makes 2 servings*

4 ounces golden rum
1 ounce 151-proof rum
6 ounces pineapple, finely
    chopped
1 ounce lemon juice
1 ounce pineapple juice
1 ounce orgeat or sugar syrup to
    taste
1 egg white
Crushed ice
Club soda
Lime slices, seeded

Mix all ingredients, except the soda and lime slices, in a blender until smooth. Pour the mixture into chilled highball glasses. Top off with the soda and garnish with the lime slices.

## Daiquiri, Pink

1¾ ounces white rum
2 splashes of grenadine
1 teaspoon sugar
Juice of ½ lime
1 scoop crushed ice

Combine all ingredients in a shaker. Shake well and strain into a cocktail glass.

## Dark and Stormy

1½ ounces rum
4 ounces ginger beer
Lemon wedge
Lime wedge

Add one scoop of ice to a tall glass. Pour the rum over the ice and add the ginger beer. Squeeze the lemon and lime into the drink. Garnish with the lime wedge.

## Deep Sea Diver

2 ounces high-proof dark rum
2 ounces dark rum
¾ ounce light rum
¾ ounce triple sec
1 to 2 teaspoons sugar
¼ ounce lime syrup
Juice of 1 lime or lemon

Combine all ingredients in a shaker with crushed ice. Shake vigorously. Pour the mixture into a tall drink glass.

## Discovery Bay

3 drops of Angostura bitters
3 ounces golden or dark rum
1 teaspoon simple syrup
1 teaspoon curaçao or blue caraçao
Juice of ½ lime
Lime slices

Shake the bitters over ice in a shaker. Pour in the rum, sugar syrup, curaçao, and lime juice and shake vigorously. Strain over ice into an old-fashioned glass. Garnish with the lime slices.

## Don Juan

1 ounce dark rum
1 ounce white tequila
2 ounces pineapple juice
1 ounce grapefruit juice
1 scoop crushed ice
1 orange slice, seeded

Mix all ingredients, except the orange slice, in a shaker. Strain the mixture into a chilled cocktail glass and garnish with the orange slice.

## Fiesta Cocktail

¾ ounce light rum
¾ ounce calvados
¾ ounce dry vermouth
1 splash of grenadine
1 splash of lime juice
1 scoop crushed ice

Mix all ingredients thoroughly in a shaker or stirring glass. Pour the mixture into a chilled cocktail glass.

## Flamingo

1½ ounces light rum
Juice of ¼ lime
1 ounce pineapple juice
A few splashes of grenadine
1 scoop crushed ice
Wedge of lime with seeds
    removed (optional)

Add all ingredients, except the lime wedge, to a shaker. Mix until almost frothy. Pour the mixture into a cocktail glass and garnish with the lime wedge.

## Forbidden Jungle

1½ ounces rum
½ ounce peach schnapps
1 ounce cream of coconut
1½ ounces pineapple juice
¼ ounce freshly squeezed lime
    juice
Dash of grenadine
1 scoop crushed ice

Combine all ingredients in a blender and blend until smooth. Pour the mixture into a chilled parfait glass.

## Florida Gator

1½ ounces golden rum
¼ ounce triple sec
¾ ounce orange juice
¼ ounce maraschino liqueur
1 scoop crushed ice

Combine all ingredients in a shaker. Mix well and strain into a chilled cocktail glass.

## French Colada

1½ ounces light rum
¾ ounces cognac
Splash of cassis
1½ ounces pineapple juice
¾ ounce cream of coconut
¾ ounce sweet cream
1 scoop crushed ice

Combine all ingredients in a shaker. Mix well and pour into a chilled collins glass.

## Havana Banana Fizz

1½ ounces light rum
2 ounces pineapple juice
1 ounce lime juice (fresh or
    bottled)
⅓ ripe banana, peeled and sliced
Several dashes of bitters
1 scoop crushed ice
Bitter lemon soda

Mix all ingredients, except the soda, in a blender. Blend until smooth. Pour the mixture into a chilled highball glass and top off with the cold soda.

## Havana Special

1½ ounces light rum
2 ounces pineapple juice
2 splashes of maraschino liqueur
1 scoop crushed ice

Mix all ingredients in a shaker. Strain the mixture into a highball glass half full of crushed ice.

## Hurricane

1 ounce light rum
1 ounce golden rum
½ ounce passion fruit syrup
½ ounce lime juice
1 scoop crushed ice

Mix all ingredients thoroughly in a shaker. Strain the mixture into a chilled cocktail glass.

## Italian Colada

1½ ounces light rum
¼ ounce amaretto
2 ounces pineapple juice
¼ ounce cream of coconut
¾ ounce sweet cream
1 scoop crushed ice

Combine all ingredients in a shaker and mix well. Pour the mixture into a highball glass.

## Ixtapa

1 ounce dark rum
1 ounce gin
1 ounce dry red wine
1 ounce orange juice
1 scoop crushed ice
1 lime slice

Combine all ingredients, except the lime slice, in a shaker. Mix briefly, just to combine. Pour the mixture into a chilled old-fashioned glass and garnish with the lime slice.

## Jamaican Mule

1 ounce dark Jamaican rum
1 ounce light rum
½ ounce 151-proof rum
½ ounce triple sec or sugar syrup
½ ounce lime juice
1 scoop crushed ice
Ginger beer
1 strip fresh pineapple (optional)
1 section preserved ginger
    (optional)

Mix the first six ingredients thoroughly in a shaker. Pour the mix into a chilled collins glass. Top off with the cold ginger beer and stir gently. Garnish with the pineapple slice and ginger, if desired.

## Jamaica Rum Fix

1 teaspoon granulated sugar
1 teaspoon water
1½ ounces dark Jamaican rum
1½ ounces light rum
2 teaspoons fresh lime juice
1 scoop crushed ice
Thin slice of ripe lime or twist of
    lime peel

In an old-fashioned glass, mix together the sugar and water. Add the two rums and the lime juice. Top off the glass with the ice and stir lightly. Garnish with the lime slice or peel.

## Kamehameha Rum Punch

1 ounce light rum
2 ounces pineapple juice
½ ounce lemon juice
½ ounce sugar syrup, or to taste
1 teaspoon blackberry brandy
1 teaspoon lemon juice
1 scoop crushed ice
1 ounce dark rum
1 fresh pineapple slice

Mix all ingredients, except the dark rum and the pineapple slice, in a shaker. Pour the mix into a chilled highball glass and top with a float of dark rum. Garnish with the pineapple slice.

## Lifetimer

½ teaspoon sugar
2 ounces light rum
1 ounce apricot brandy
1 ounce brandy
1 ounce lemon juice
½ ounce triple sec
4 ounces club soda
Lemon twist

Moisten the rim of a highball glass. Coat the rim with the sugar. Shake all the remaining ingredients, except the soda and lemon twist, with a scoop of ice. Strain into a highball glass. Add more ice and the soda. Stir. Garnish with the lemon twist.

## Luau Lullaby

*Makes 2 servings*

3 ounces light rum
2 ounces passion fruit syrup
2 ounces lime juice
1 egg white
2 scoops crushed ice
2 teaspoons 151-proof Demerara
    rum

Mix all ingredients, except the 151-proof rum, in a shaker. Pour the mixture into whiskey sour glasses and top off with the high-proof rum.

## Mai Kai No

1 ounce light rum
1 ounce dark rum
½ ounce 151-proof Demerara
    rum
1 ounce lime juice
½ ounce orgeat
½ ounce passion fruit juice
1 scoop crushed ice
Club soda
Pineapple or orange slice
Mint sprig (optional)

Mix all ingredients, except the soda, fruit slice, and mint, in a shaker. Pour the mixture into a tall, chilled collins glass and top off with the soda. Garnish with the fruit slice and mint sprig.

## Mauna Kea

1½ ounces light rum
½ ounce kirsch
1½ ounces passion fruit juice
1 ounce lemon juice
½ ounce sugar syrup to taste
1 scoop crushed ice
1 coconut shell, halved
    (preparation below)
1 ounce dark rum
Red hibiscus and assorted
    tropical fruits (optional)

Mix the first six ingredients in a blender. Pour the mixture into a coconut shell and top with a float of the dark rum. Garnish with the red hibiscus and assorted fruits.

NOTE: To prepare the coconut, puncture the "eyes" and drain the coconut milk.* Saw the coconut in half across its middle and steady it, open end up, in a cup, small dish, or ashtray to keep it stable when filled with liquid. If coconuts are not available, use any large decorative glass.

*Save the milk for punches and other tropical rum drinks.

## Mauna Lani Fizz

*Makes 2 servings*

4 ounces golden rum
1 ounce 151-proof rum
6 ounces pineapple, finely
    chopped
1 ounce lemon juice
1 ounce pineapple juice
1 ounce orgeat or sugar syrup to
    taste
1 egg white
Crushed ice
Club soda
Lime slices, seeded

Mix all ingredients, except the the club soda and lime slices, in a blender until smooth. Pour the mixture into chilled highball glasses and top off with the club soda. Garnish with the lime slices.

## Monaco

1½ ounces gold rum
½ ounce brandy
½ ounce pineapple juice
1 ounce lime juice
1 teaspoon triple sec
1 scoop crushed ice
Slice of lime, seeded

Mix all ingredients, except the lime slice, in a shaker. Pour the mixture into a chilled collins glass and garnish with the lime slice.

## Outrigger

2 ounces light rum
½ ounce triple sec
½ ounce pineapple liqueur or apricot liqueur
1 ounce lime juice
1 scoop crushed ice
1 slice lime, seeded

Mix all ingredients, except the lime slice, in a shaker. Pour the mixture into a chilled old-fashioned glass and garnish with the lime slice.

## Pinky Colada

2 ounces white rum
¾ ounce pineapple juice
¾ ounce grenadine
¾ ounce cream of coconut
1½ ounces sweet cream or milk
1 scoop crushed ice

Combine all ingredients in a shaker. Mix well and strain into a chilled wine goblet.

## Polynesian Sour

1½ ounces light rum
½ ounce guava nectar
½ ounce orange juice
½ ounce lemon juice
1 scoop crushed ice

Combine all ingredients in a blender. Mix until smooth and uniform in color. Pour the mixture into a chilled deep-saucer champagne glass.

## Presidente

1½ ounces light rum
¼ ounce dry vermouth
¾ ounce sweet vermouth
1 splash of grenadine
Maraschino cherry

In a stirring glass with ice, mix together all ingredients, except the cherry. Strain the mixture into an iced cocktail glass and garnish with the cherry.

## Puffer

2 ounces light rum
1 ounce grapefruit juice
2 ounces orange juice
1 teaspoon grenadine
Orange slice

Add all ingredients, except the orange slice, to a mixing glass. Stir briefly to mix. Strain into a highball glass over crushed ice. Garnish with the orange slice.

## Robinson

1 ounce dark rum
1 ounce light rum
¾ ounce sugar syrup
Fruit of 1 papaya
Juice of ⅓ lime
1 scoop crushed ice
1 wedge lime, seeded

Combine all ingredients, except the lime wedge, in a blender. Blend until smooth. Pour the mixture into a chilled highball glass over freshly crushed ice. Garnish with the lime wedge.

## Rum Runner

1 ounce light rum
1 ounce dark rum
2¾ ounces pineapple juice
¼ ounce sugar syrup
A few splashes of bitters
Juice of ½ lime
Maraschino cherry
1 thin wedge of lime, seeded

Mix all ingredients, except the cherry and lime wedge, in a shaker. Pour the mixture into a highball glass half filled with ice. Garnish with the cherry and lime wedge.

## Sailfish Marina's Tipsy Turtle

¼ ounce dark rum
¼ ounce light rum
¼ ounce vodka
¼ ounce coconut liqueur
¼ ounce banana liqueur
Splash of grenadine
4 ounces pineapple juice
4 ounces orange juice
1 scoop crushed ice
1 fresh orange slice
1 fresh pineapple strip

Combine all ingredients, except the orange and pineapple, in a blender and mix until smooth. Pour the mixture into a chilled highball glass and garnish with the fruit.

## Strawberry Banana Colada

1½ ounces rum
2 ounces cream of coconut
2 ounces fresh or frozen
    strawberries
½ sliced banana
1 cup ice

Combine all ingredients in a blender and blend until smooth. Pour the mixture into a chilled parfait glass.

## Stress Less

1 ounce vodka
1 ounce dark rum
1 ounce pear schnapps
1 ounce orange juice
1 ounce cranberry juice
Cherry or orange slice

Add all ingredients, except the fruit, to a shaker with a scoop of ice and shake until blended. Strain into a highball glass over ice. Garnish with the cherry or the orange slice.

## Strawberry Colada

2 to 3 ounces golden rum
4 ounces piña colada mix
1 ounce fresh or frozen
    strawberries
1 scoop crushed ice
1 teaspoon strawberry schnapps
    or liqueur
1 fresh strawberry

Mix the first four ingredients in a blender until smooth. Pour the mixture into a chilled pilsner glass and top with the strawberry schnapps or liqueur. Garnish with the strawberry.

## Tipsy Turtle

¼ ounce vodka
¼ ounce white rum
¼ ounce dark rum
¼ ounce coconut liqueur
¼ ounce banana liqueur
Splash of grenadine
4 ounces pineapple juice
4 ounces orange juice
1 scoop crushed ice

Combine all ingredients in a blender. Blend well. Pour the mixture into a chilled highball glass.

## Tropical Breeze

1 ounce rum
½ ounce crème de banane
1 ounce cream of coconut
2 ounces orange juice
½ pineapple slice
1 scoop crushed ice

Combine all ingredients in a blender and blend until smooth. Pour the mixture into a chilled parfait glass.

## Zico

1 ounce light rum
1 ounce cachaca
2 ounces papaya juice
¾ ounce cream of coconut
Juice of ¼ lime

Combine all ingredients in a shaker with crushed ice. Shake well and strain into a chilled highball glass.

# Hot Drinks

## Black Marie (hot)

¾ ounce dark rum
¾ ounce brandy
¼ ounce coffee liqueur
1 to 2 teaspoons superfine sugar
1 cup hot strong coffee or
    espresso

Combine the rum, brandy, and liqueur in a nonreactive saucepan and heat until warm, but do not boil. Add the sugar to the heated mixture, stirring until it is dissolved. Pour into a heat-proof punch glass and top off with the hot coffee or espresso. Stir and serve.

## Chocolate Sin

1½ ounces dark rum
½ ounce bourbon
½ ounce dark crème de cacao
4 ounces hot chocolate
2 ounces heavy cream, whipped

Pour the first four ingredients into an Irish coffee glass. Carefully spoon the cream on top of the drink.

## Cidered Rum

2¼ ounces light rum
1 teaspoon cane or maple syrup
1 teaspoon granulated sugar
1 tablespoon fresh lime or lemon
    juice
1 slice of lemon or lime, pierced
    with two whole cloves
Hot apple cider

In a heavy mug or large cup, mix all ingredients except the fruit slice and the hot cider. Add the fruit slice with cloves and top off with cider.

## Cuban Hot Coffee

1 ounce golden rum
¼ ounce brown crème de cacao
1 teaspoon superfine sugar
1 cup hot strong coffee

Combine the rum and liqueur in a nonreactive saucepan. Heat but do not boil. Add the sugar to the heated mixture and stir until dissolved. Pour into a heat-proof punch glass and top off with the hot coffee. Stir well before serving.

## Goldie

1½ ounces dark rum
¼ ounce Galliano
¼ ounce heavy cream
1½ ounces milk
¾ ounce orange juice
1 to 2 teaspoons superfine sugar

Combine the ingredients in a non-reactive saucepan and heat until warm, stirring gently. Pour into a heat-proof punch glass and serve.

## Hot Benefactor

1 teaspoon sugar syrup, or to
    taste
2 ounces Jamaican dark rum
2 ounces dry red wine
Lemon slice
Grated nutmeg

Add the syrup to a saucepan with a little hot water and stir. Add the rum and wine. Heat the mixture until it begins to simmer. Pour into a warmed mug and garnish with the lemon slice. Sprinkle the freshly grated nutmeg on top.

## Hot Buttered Rum

1 teaspoon brown or white sugar
Boiling water
1½ ounces light or dark rum
Small piece of cinnamon stick
Pinch of ground allspice or
    nutmeg
Pat of butter

In a preheated mug or large heavy
cup, dissolve the sugar in a small
amount of the water. Stir in the
rum. Add the cinnamon stick and
the allspice or nutmeg. Top off the
mug with the boiling water and
the pat of butter.

## Hot Jamaican

2 ounces dark rum
½ ounce sugar syrup
Juice of ⅛ lime
Boiling water
½ cinnamon stick
1 wedge of lime, seeded and
    studded with cloves

Warm the rum, sugar syrup, and
lime juice in a nonreactive saucepan. Pour the mixture into a heat-
proof punch glass and top off with
boiling water. Garnish with the
cinnamon stick and the lime
wedge.

## Hot MM

1½ ounces dark rum
¾ ounce coffee liqueur
2¾ ounces heavy cream
1 to 2 teaspoons sugar

Combine the ingredients in a nonreactive saucepan and heat until
warm, stirring gently. Pour into a
heat-proof punch glass and serve.

## Hot Rum Toddy

1 teaspoon honey
Boiling water
2 ounces white or light rum
1 lemon or lime slice, pierced
    with four 4 whole cloves
1 cinnamon stick

In a heavy mug, dissolve the honey
in a small amount of hot water,
stirring constantly. Add the rum,
stirring gently, then add the lemon
or lime slice. Top off the mug with
the boiling water and drop in the
cinnamon stick.

## Hot Spiced Cider

*Makes 4 servings*

1 quart apple cider
¼ cup granulated sugar
⅛ teaspoon salt
1 cinnamon stick, broken up
12 whole cloves
8 whole allspice berries
¾ cup light rum

Combine all ingredients, except the rum, in a large saucepan, and bring to a boil. Cool and let stand for at least 4 hours, stirring occasionally. Before serving, strain and reheat, stirring in the rum at the last moment. Serve in large mugs.

## Jean Gabin

1½ ounces dark rum
¾ ounce calvados
Sugar syrup or maple syrup to
    taste
Hot milk
Freshly grated nutmeg

Warm the rum and calvados in a nonreactive saucepan. Pour the mixture into a heat-proof punch glass, stir in the syrup, and fill with the hot milk. Sprinkle the grated nutmeg on top.

## Southern Malt

1½ ounces dark rum
½ ounce Southern Comfort
4 ounces hot malted milk

Pour all ingredients into a coffee mug and stir well.

## Sweet and Hot

1½ ounces dark rum
¾ ounce coffee liqueur
¾ ounce cream
2 ounces milk
1 clove
Lemon zest

Combine all ingredients in a nonreactive saucepan and heat until warm. Pour into a heat-proof punch glass.

## Tom and Jerry II

1 egg, separated
1½ ounces light rum
1 teaspoon confectioners' sugar
¼ teaspoon ground allspice
Hot milk
Freshly grated nutmeg

In a small bowl, whisk the egg yolk for about 30 seconds. Then mix in the rum, sugar, and allspice. Continue to beat until the mixture is smooth and has thickened. In another bowl, beat the egg white for a few seconds, then blend into the rum mixture. Pour the mixture into a preheated mug or large cup, and top off with hot milk. Mix thoroughly. Dust with the nutmeg and serve immediately.

# Punches

## Blue Mountain Punch

*Makes 12 servings*

1 tablespoon powdered ginger
1 teaspoon grated nutmeg
7½ cups warmed beer
3 eggs
2 tablespoons molasses
½ cup light or dark rum

In a saucepan, mix the ginger and nutmeg with 6¾ cups of the beer. Heat until warm. Beat the eggs with the remaining beer and the molasses. Slowly add the warmed beer to this egg mixture, beating continuously. Add the rum and serve at once.

## Creamy Rum Cider

*Makes 8 servings*

1 cup dark rum
1 quart apple cider
Cider ice cubes, as needed
Vanilla ice cream to taste

In a large pitcher, combine the rum and cider and refrigerate. Just before serving, place a few of the cider ice cubes in a mug or glass. Add a scoop of the vanilla ice cream and top off with the rum cider.

# Egg Nog I

*Makes 24 servings*

12 egg yolks
½ pound granulated sugar
1 bottle light rum
1 quart whole milk
1 quart heavy cream, whipped
    until stiff but not dry
Freshly grated nutmeg

Beat egg yolks in a large bowl until they are light in color. Gradually add the sugar, beating until the mixture thickens. Stir in the rum and milk. Cover the bowl and chill for 3 to 4 hours. Pour into a chilled punch bowl. Fold in the whipped cream and dust with the nutmeg.

# Egg Nog II

*Makes 28 servings*

12 whole eggs, separated
2 cups superfine sugar
1 pint dark rum
1 pint cognac
3 pints milk
1 pint cream
Freshly grated nutmeg

Separate the eggs and beat the yolks and sugar together until the mixture becomes thick and the sugar is dissolved. Stir in the rum, cognac, milk, and cream and chill in the refrigerator until needed. Just before serving, beat the egg whites until stiff and very gently fold them into the mixture. Transfer to a chilled punch bowl and sprinkle with the nutmeg.

NOTE: Do not put ice into the punch bowl—it will dilute the drink.

# Fish House Punch I (Schumann's Variation)

*Makes 20 servings*

5 liters water
Grated peel and juice of 10
    lemons
Grated peel and juice of 10 limes
3 ⅓ cups brown sugar
3 liters dark rum
1 liter brandy
¼ flask Southern Comfort

Combine the water with the juice and grated peel of the lemons and limes in a large pot. Bring the mixture to a boil, stir in the brown sugar, and continue to boil until the liquid forms a light syrup. Add the rum, brandy, and Southern Comfort, stir well, and bring to a boil again. Serve immediately or store in sealed jars. You can also return the punch to the empty rum bottles and recap, leaving no airspace. The punch can be stored for several days.

NOTE: Fish House Punch may be served either hot or cold. When serving hot, use heat-proof punch glasses. To serve cold, serve in a highball glass filled with crushed ice and float ¼ ounce high-proof rum on top.

## Fish House Punch II

Prepare as with Fish House Punch I, substituting 2 liters of water and 3 liters of black tea for the 5 liters of water.

## Jamaican Egg Nog

*Makes 20 servings*

12 egg yolks
½ pound granulated sugar
1 bottle (750 ml.) dark Jamaican
   rum
1 quart whole milk
1 quart heavy cream
Freshly grated nutmeg

Beat egg yolks until light in color. Add the sugar, and continue to beat until the mixture is thick and pale in color. Slowly stir in the rum and milk. Chill in the refrigerator for 3 hours, stirring often. Whip the heavy cream until stiff. Pour the chilled mixture into a punch bowl, then fold in the heavy cream. Chill in the refrigerator for another hour. Pour into collins glasses and sprinkle the nutmeg on top.

## Jamaican Grand Punch

*Makes 30 servings*

Block of ice
1½ quarts dark Jamaican rum
1½ quarts unsweetened pineapple
   juice
1½ quarts mango nectar
1 cup lime juice
Club soda to taste
½ fresh peeled pineapple, sliced
   into thin strips

Place the ice block in a big punch bowl and pour in the first four ingredients. Add the club soda to taste and garnish with the pineapple strips.

## John's Mango Masterpiece

*Makes 6 servings*

1 cup light rum
1 cup mango puree (fresh or
    canned)
¼ cup freshly sqeezed lime juice,
    strained
¼ cup water, chilled
Sugar syrup to taste
1 scoop crushed ice

Chill all ingredients before starting. Mix the chilled ingredients in a blender until smooth. Pour the mixture into chilled cocktail glasses.

## The Last Resort

EAST COAST GRILL,
CAMBRIDGE, MASSACHUSETTS

*Makes 10 servings*

Last Resort Mixture: 12 ounces
    papaya juice; 12 ounces guava
    juice; 1¼ cups pineapple juice;
    1¼ cups orange juice; 1 cup
    cream of coconut; ½ cup
    grenadine
20 ounces golden rum
1 splash of dark rum per drink
1 slice of mango or papaya per
    drink

Combine all ingredients for the Last Resort Mixture in a large container and mix well. Fill a 16-ounce glass with ice and add 2 ounces of the golden rum. Fill the glass to the top of the ice level with the Last Resort Mixture. Pour the contents of the glass into a blender. Blend until completely combined, about a minute. Pour the mixture into a large wineglass and float the splash of dark rum on top. Garnish with the fruit slice. Repeat for each serving.

## Lindsay's Post College Punch

*Makes 20 servings*

1 bottle ( 750 ml.) light rum
2 to 3 pints orange juice
2 to 3 pints cranberry-raspberry
    juice
1 block of ice
1 liter ginger ale
Several sliced apples and oranges

Combine the first three ingredients in a punch bowl with the block of ice. Stir well. Add the ginger ale and fruit slices just before serving.

## Martin's Rum-Orange Punch

*Makes 1 serving*

1½ ounces dark rum
¾ ounce high-proof dark rum
¼ ounce Southern Comfort
2 teaspoons sugar
Juice of ½ lime
¾ ounce lime juice
1½ ounce orange juice
Wedges of lime and orange,
    seeded

Combine all ingredients, except for the lime and orange wedges, in a nonreactive saucepan, then heat until warm. Pour into a heat-proof punch glass and garnish with the wedges of lime and orange.

## Philadelphia Fish House Punch

*Makes 25 servings*

2 cups brown sugar
2 quarts water
1 bottle (750 ml.) dark rum or ½
    bottle dark and ½ bottle light
    rum, combined 1 (750 ml.)
    bottle brandy
½ bottle (375 ml.) peach brandy
Peel and juice of 6 ripe lemons

In a large, heavy pot, heat sugar and water together until sugar has completely dissolved, stirring often with a wooden spoon. Add the rum, brandy, peach brandy, and lemon peel and juice. Mix well, remove from heat, and allow to stand for several hours to absorb flavors. Strain over a large block of ice about an hour prior to serving in order to chill and also to dilute slightly. Serve in chilled punch cups.

## Thanksgiving Punch

*Makes 10 servings*

1 liter gold rum
½ teaspoon allspice
1 quart apple cider
3 cinnamon sticks
3 teaspoons butter

Heat all ingredients together in a saucepan. Pour into warmed mugs.

# Tonga

TRADER VIC'S, SAN FRANCISCO

*Makes 25 servings*

2 (750 ml.) bottles light rum
12 ounces brandy
12 ounces curaçao
12 ounces Passionola or passion
    fruit nectar
1 quart lemon juice
1½ pints orange juice
6 ounces grenadine

Chill all ingredients beforehand. After mixing well, pour over a block of ice in a large punch bowl.

# West Indies Punch

TRADER VIC'S, SAN FRANCISCO

*Makes 12 servings*

2 cups superfine sugar
1 pint green tea infusion
12 large limes
1 cup guava marmalade
2 cups boiling water
½ bottle (375 ml.) dark rum
½ bottle (375 ml.) light rum
1 pint cognac
1 bottle (750 ml.) Madeira wine

Dissolve the sugar in the tea. Halve the limes, squeeze, and add their juice and shells to the tea mixture. In a saucepan, dissolve the guava marmalade in the boiling water. Combine the guava mixture with the tea mixture. Add the rums, cognac, and wine and let stand overnight. The next day, remove the lime shells and pour the punch over a large piece of ice in a punch bowl. Let chill thoroughly before serving.

# BOURBON AND AMERICAN BLENDED WHISKEY

Recognized by Congress in 1964 as a "distinctive product of the United States," bourbon came of age right alongside our country. With roots sunk deep in rebellion, uprising, and plain old American gumption, this "native spirit" can track its heritage back to the early 1700s. Befitting a spirit of "the melting pot," Bourbon was the brainchild of the Scotch-Irish who emigrated from Ulster, Ireland, to western Pennsylvania. On the run from poverty, religious persecution, and famine, these settlers sought a better life in the New World. They planted easy-to-grow crops such as corn, rye, and barely and distilled the first truly American whiskey from these grains. But their journey, and the journey of bourbon, did not end there.

The onset of the Revolutionary War routed the settlers from their homes to fight against the British. Following the lengthy war, they returned to their farms and their stills to enjoy a newly won liberty. But unfortunately, the long war had left the treasury of the new country quite bare. Treasurer Alexander Hamilton proposed numerous fund-raising methods, one of which was an Excise Tax on Spiritous Liquors.

The Scotch-Irish of Pennsylvania, who used whiskey as their medium of exchange, were outraged by this incursion into their daily lives. They took drastic action to express their displeasure. Between 1791, when the law was passed, and 1794 there were countless incidents in which tax collectors were threatened, intimidated, and, in several instances, tarred and feathered.

Finally, in 1794, the western Pennsylvanians mounted an insurrection. In this first crisis faced by the new American government, the Whiskey Rebellion army of 15,000 was met by a small militia force commanded by President Washington himself. This impressive show of force put the rebels to rout and, as hoped, resulted in no bloodshed.

Many of the rebellious farmers decided to pack their families and stills into wagons and move to an area that was less accessible to the hated tax man. They left Pennsylvania and trekked over 400 miles westward to settle in the virgin lands of Bourbon County. This vast and unspoiled region eventually became the north-central part of Kentucky, as well as sections of Virginia and West Virginia. Thanks to abundant clean water and a more lenient atmosphere, distilling flourished in Bourbon County. The Excise Tax was abolished in 1802 and then reinstated in 1814 for three years. From 1817 to 1862, when the next tax was instituted, was a golden age for American whiskey.

Though bourbon was the by-product of a quest for freedom, today there are a few rules all distillers must follow. To be considered Bourbon, the whiskey must be made in the United States. It is composed of at least 51 percent corn, though many bourbons contain quite a bit more. Bourbon must be aged for a minimum of two years in new, charred American white oak barrels. As no artificial coloring may be added to the spirit, this aging is responsible for the deep, amber color of bourbon.

Bourbon takes its name from Bourbon County, Kentucky, once the major shipping point for distilled spirits heading down the Ohio and Mississippi Rivers to New Orleans. The whiskey crates were stamped "Bourbon," which led drinkers to adopt the name.

Like single-malt Scotch, bourbon is also a "single" spirit. This is to say that it is never blended with neutral spirits and the final product always comes from one distillery. Different brands of bourbon achieve their distinctive flavors through subtle changes in the components of the spirit. One such variable is the addition of wheat, barley, or rye to the standard corn mash. Another is the quality of the yeast culture. Some distillers use cultures that are more than a century old.

Though always a popular spirit, in the early 1980s bourbon began to take a backseat to premium single-malt scotches. As a result, marketing and distilling practices changed and the single-barrel and small-batch bourbons were born.

The term "small batch" was coined by bourbon giant Jim Beam to describe its line of premium bourbons, which include Booker's, Baker's, Knob Creek, and Basil Hayden's. These and other small batch bourbons are a blend of a small-batch of barrels that have been selected from a larger batch to achieve a signature taste. Other tasty small-batch bourbons include the exquisite Woodford Reserve, Elijah Craig 12 Year Old, Pappy Van Winkle Family Reserve, and a new entry from the "redheaded stranger" himself, Willie Nelson: His Old Whiskey River Bourbon is aged 6 years and made in Bardstown, Kentucky, in the serendipitously named Nelson County.

Bourbons labeled "single barrel" are, as you might imagine, bottled from a single barrel. The resulting spirit is unique and imbued with a particular mystique. Blanton's, produced by Ancient Age Distillery in Leestown, Kentucky, claims to be the first single-barrel bourbon. Introduced in 1984, this elegant drink, with its fragrant nose and a long, smooth finish, was soon joined by Benchmark, Elmer T. Lee, and Hancock's Reserve. Other fine single-barrel bourbons are Eagle Rare, which is aged ten years, and Evan Williams Single Barrel Vintage.

With high quality bourbons such as these, there's never been a better time to become a fan of this quintessentially American spirit. Though these new bourbons are bound to be a bit smoother than those original barrels that floated down the Ohio and Mississippi, I like to think when I sip that I'm still tasting a little bit of freedom.

## AMERICAN BLENDED WHISKEY

American blended whiskey is a smooth and mellow mixture of straight whiskies and grain-neutral spirits or light whiskies. It has become a fundamental part of the U.S. distilled spirits market, yet it is a relatively new product, having been introduced here only after the repeal of Prohibition in 1933.

The idea of blended American whiskey is a natural. Taking feisty American bourbons and removing some of their aggressiveness by combining them with soft, neutral-flavored spirits is a very logical concept. Such a coalition was almost a necessity just after Repeal, since most distillers had to start from scratch and had no mellow older whiskies to bottle. But I am getting ahead of the story. The government has set down guidelines for the manufacture of blended whiskey.

There must be a minimum of 20 percent straight whiskies in the blend and the rest can be grain-neutral spirits, grain spirits, or light whiskies. Grain-neutral spirits are distilled out at a very high proof and have no noticeable flavor or aroma. Grain spirits are neutral spirits that have been aged in used oak barrels to give them a subtle, soft flavor. Light whiskies are similar to grain spirits, but are distilled out at a lower proof.

Most blended whiskies are 80 proof. The finest ones are soft and balanced, mellow and smooth. The suggested way to consume blended whiskey is on the rocks or with a splash of water. People also use them extensively in cocktails and mixed drinks, most notably the "seven and seven," a mixture of Seagram's Seven Crown and 7 UP a combination that is, for many, the first alcoholic drink they ever taste.

A number of people who drink blends call them "rye." This is a complete misnomer; rye is a whiskey made from at least 51 percent rye. A true rye, such as Old Overholt, is an aggressive, strong drink that would probably horrify the people who normally drink blends.

Southern Comfort is a blend of bourbon whiskey, peach liqueur, and fresh peaches. This American product can be listed as either a liqueur or a blended whiskey. The blend is 100 proof, but is mellowed by the liqueur and fruit. It was originally created in 1875, and was first known as Cuff and Buttons. Louis Herron, a bartender in St. Louis, changed the name to Southern Comfort.

Though the interest in premium, single-barrel, and small-batch bourbons has demonstrated that the consumer is ready for a more robust and flavorful whiskey, the American blended whiskey is still a gentle and charming product.

# Bourbon • Classics

## Allegheny

1 ounce bourbon
1 ounce dry vermouth
¼ ounce blackberry-flavored
    brandy
¼ ounce lemon juice
1 Dash of bitters
Lemon twist

Stir together all ingredients, except the lemon twist, in a mixing glass with ice. Pour the mixture into a cocktail glass and garnish with the lemon twist.

## Bourbon Collins I

1½ ounces bourbon
½ ounce lime juice
1 teaspoon sugar syrup, or to
    taste
1 scoop crushed ice
Club soda
Lime peel

Mix the bourbon, lime juice, and sugar syrup in a shaker with the crushed ice. Pour the mixture into a chilled 12-ounce collins glass and top off the glass with the soda. Twist the lime peel over the glass and drop in.

## Bourbon Collins II

2 ounces 100-proof bourbon
½ ounce lemon juice
1 teaspoon sugar syrup, or to
    taste
Several dashes of bitters
Crushed ice
Club soda
Lemon slice (optional)

Mix the first five ingredients in a shaker. Pour the mixture into a chilled highball glass and top off the glass with the soda. Decorate with the lemon slice.

## Bourbon Daisy

1½ ounces bourbon
½ ounce lemon juice
1 teaspoon grenadine
1 scoop crushed ice
Club soda
1 teaspoon Southern Comfort
Orange slice
Pineapple stick

Mix the bourbon, lemon juice, and grenadine in a shaker with crushed ice. Pour the mixture into a chilled highball glass and top off with the soda and a float of the Southern Comfort. Garnish with the fruit and serve.

## Bourbon Egg Nog

2 ounces bourbon
8 ounces milk
1 teaspoon superfine sugar
1 egg
1 scoop crushed ice
Grated nutmeg

Combine all ingredients, except the nutmeg, in a shaker. Shake well and strain into a tall glass. Sprinkle the freshly grated nutmeg on top.

## Cablegram

2 ounces blended whiskey
½ ounce lemon juice
½ teaspoon superfine sugar
4 ounces ginger ale
Lemon twist

Mix the first three ingredients in a shaker with ice. Strain into a highball glass filled with crushed ice. Pour in the ginger ale and garnish with the lemon twist.

## Bourbon Sour

2 ounces bourbon
Juice of ½ lemon
½ teaspoon sugar or sugar syrup
1 scoop crushed ice
Orange slice

Mix all ingredients, except the orange slice, in a shaker. Strain the mixture into a chilled whiskey sour glass and garnish with the slice of orange.

## California Lemonade

2 ounces blended whiskey
1 ounce lemon juice
1 teaspoon superfine sugar
4 ounces club soda

Add the first three ingredients to a mixing glass along with a scoop of ice. Stir 20 times. Strain into an old-fashioned glass over ice. Add the soda.

## Classic Mint Julep

6 small mint leaves
2 ounces bourbon
1 ounce lemon juice
1 ounce sugar syrup
1 scoop crushed ice
Mint sprig

Muddle the mint leaves with the bourbon, lemon juice, and syrup in a bar glass. Add the this mixture to a blender with the finely crushed ice. Mix at high speed for about 15 seconds, or until the ice becomes mushy. Pour the mixture into a chilled double old-fashioned glass and garnish with the mint sprig.

## Commodore Cocktail

1½ ounces bourbon
¾ ounce white crème de cacao
½ ounce lemon juice
1 scoop crushed ice

In a shaker, mix together all ingredients. Strain the mixture into a chilled cocktail glass.

## Dixie Old-Fashioned

2 dashes of bitters
1 teaspoon superfine sugar
1½ ounces bourbon
1 scoop ice
1 orange slice
Twist of lemon peel
Maraschino cherry

Mix the bitters and sugar in an old-fashioned glass with ¾ ounce of water. Add the bourbon and ice,

and stir. Garnish with the orange slice, the twist of lemon peel, and the cherry.

## Manhattan, Bourbon

1½ to 2 ounces bourbon
½ ounce sweet vermouth
Dash of bitters
Ice cubes
Maraschino cherry

Combine all ingredients, except the cherry, in a large mixing glass. Stir well and strain into a chilled cocktail glass. Garnish with the cherry.

## Quick-and-Easy Mint Julep

Several mint sprigs
1 teaspoon water
1 teaspoon superfine sugar
1 scoop finely crushed ice
3 ounces bourbon

Muddle the mint sprigs in a double old-fashioned glass with the water and sugar until the sugar is dissolved. Fill the glass with the finely crushed ice and add the bourbon. Stir briskly with an iced-tea spoon. Garnish with more mint sprigs.

## *Sazerac I*

2 scoops crushed ice
1 sugar cube
1 teaspoon water
2 dashes of bitters
2 ounces rye whiskey
Dash of Pernod
Lemon peel

Fill a couple of old-fashioned glasses with the crushed ice to chill the glasses. Remove the ice from one of the glasses. Place the sugar cube and the water in the glass. Add the bitters and crush the sugar cube with a muddler until the sugar is well dissolved. Add the whiskey, along with several ice cubes, and stir well. Empty the second glass of ice. In the second glass, pour a generous dash of Pernod to thoroughly coat the inside of the glass. Pour out the excess Pernod. Add the mixture from the first glass. Twist the lemon peel over the drink but do not drop it in.

## *Sazerac II (Easy Sazerac)*

¼ teaspoon Pernod or other absinthe substitute
½ teaspoon sugar
1 tablespoon water
Dash of bitters
2 ounces bourbon, rye, or blended whiskey
Lemon peel

Coat the inside of an old-fashioned glass with the Pernod. Add the sugar, water, and bitters and muddle until the sugar is dissolved. Add the bourbon, rye, or blended whiskey, along with ice cubes, and stir well. Twist the lemon peel over the drink and drop it in.

# Bourbon • Creative Concoctions

## *Admiral Highball*

1½ ounces bourbon
1½ ounces Tokay wine
1 dash of pineapple juice
1 dash of lemon juice
Club soda

Stir together all ingredients, except the soda, in a mixing glass with ice. Pour the mixture into a highball glass with an ice cube. Top off the glass with the chilled club soda.

## Amour Paris

1½ ounces bourbon
¾ ounce apricot liqueur
½ teaspoon lemon juice
1 teaspoon grenadine
1 scoop crushed ice

Add all ingredients to a shaker. Mix well and strain into a chilled cocktail glass.

## Anchor Splash

1 ounce bourbon
2 teaspoons triple sec
2 teaspoons peach brandy
2 teaspoons maraschino liqueur
2 tablespoons heavy cream
Several drops of maraschino cherry juice
1 scoop crushed ice

Combine all ingredients in a shaker. Mix well and pour into a chilled old-fashioned glass.

## Artist's Special

1 ounce bourbon whiskey
1 ounce sherry
½ ounce lemon juice
¼ ounce grenadine

Stir together all ingredients in a mixing glass with ice. Pour the mixture into a cocktail glass.

## Banana Bird

1 ounce bourbon
2 teaspoons crème de banane
2 teaspoons triple sec
1 ounce heavy cream

In a shaker with crushed ice, mix together all ingredients. Strain the mixture into a cocktail glass.

## Bianco

1½ ounces bourbon
½ ounce dry vermouth
1 dash of Angostura bitters
Lemon twist

Stir together all ingredients, except the lemon twist, in a mixing glass with ice. Pour the mixture into a fresh cocktail glass and garnish with the lemon twist.

## Bishop

1 ounce bourbon
½ ounce sweet vermouth
1 ounce orange juice
1 dash of yellow Chartreuse

In a shaker with crushed ice, mix together all ingredients. Pour the mixture into a chilled cocktail glass.

## Blizzard

1 scoop crushed ice
1½ ounces bourbon
1½ ounces cranberry juice
½ ounce lime juice
½ ounce grenadine
1 teaspoon sugar

Place the crushed ice in a blender and add the other ingredients in the order listed. Blend on a slow speed for 15 to 30 seconds or until frozen stiff. Pour the mixture into a chilled highball glass.

## Blue Grass Cocktail

1½ ounces bourbon
1 ounce pineapple juice
1 ounce lemon juice
1 teaspoon maraschino liqueur
1 scoop crushed ice

Mix together all ingredients in a shaker. Strain the mixture into a chilled cocktail glass.

## Boomerang

¾ ounce bourbon (or rye whiskey)
¾ ounce Swedish punsch liqueur
¾ ounce dry vermouth
1 dash of Angostura bitters
1 dash of lemon juice

In a mixing glass with ice, stir together all ingredients. Pour the mixture into a chilled cocktail glass.

## Bordever

2 ounces bourbon
½ ounce ginger ale
Lemon twist

In a mixing glass with ice, stir together the bourbon and ginger ale. Pour the mixture into a chilled cocktail glass and garnish with the lemon twist.

## Bourbon Cobbler

1½ ounces bourbon
1 ounce Southern Comfort
1 teaspoon peach-flavored brandy
2 teaspoons lemon juice
1 teaspoon sugar syrup
1 scoop crushed ice
Club soda
Peach slice

Mix the first six ingredients in a shaker or blender. Pour the mixture into a chilled highball glass. Add ice cubes, top off with the soda, and decorate with the peach slice.

## Bourbon Cooler

3 ounces bourbon
½ ounce grenadine
1 teaspoon sugar syrup, or to taste
Several dashes of peppermint schnapps
Several dashes of orange bitters
1 scoop crushed ice
Club soda
Pineapple stick
Orange slice
Maraschino cherry

Mix the first six ingredients in a shaker. Pour the mixture into a

chilled, tall collins glass and top off the glass with the soda. Garnish with the fruit.

## Bourbon Flip

1½ ounces bourbon
1 egg
1 teaspoon powdered sugar
2 teaspoons sweet cream (optional)
1 scoop crushed ice
Nutmeg, grated

Mix all ingredients, except the nutmeg, in a shaker. Strain the mixture into a chilled cocktail glass. Sprinkle the nutmeg on top.

## Bourbon Milk Punch

1½ ounces bourbon
3 ounces milk or half-and-half
1 teaspoon honey or sugar syrup
Dash of vanilla extract
1 scoop crushed ice
Nutmeg, grated

Mix all ingredients, except the nutmeg, in a shaker. Pour the mixture into a chilled old-fashioned glass. Sprinkle with the nutmeg before serving.

## Bourbon Orange

1½ ounces bourbon
½ ounce triple sec
1 ounce orange juice
1 scoop crushed ice
Lemon peel

In a shaker, mix together the first four ingredients. Pour this mixture into a chilled old-fashioned glass. Twist the lemon peel over the drink and drop it in.

## Bourbon Satin

1 ounce bourbon
1 ounce white crème de cacao
1 ounce heavy cream
1 scoop crushed ice

Mix all ingredients in a shaker. Strain the mixture into a chilled cocktail glass.

## Bourbon Sidecar

1½ ounces bourbon
¾ ounce triple sec
½ ounce lemon juice
1 scoop crushed ice

Mix together all ingredients in a shaker or blender. Strain the mixture into a chilled cocktail glass.

## Bourbon Sloe Gin Fizz

1 teaspoon sugar syrup, or to taste
½ teaspoon lemon juice
1½ ounces bourbon
¾ ounce sloe gin
Club soda
Lemon slice
Maraschino cherry

Pour the first four ingredients into a 14-ounce collins glass. Add some ice and mix well. Add additional ice and top off the glass with the soda. Garnish with the lemon slice and cherry.

## Bourbonnaise

1½ ounces bourbon
½ ounce dry vermouth
½ ounce crème de cassis
1 dash of lemon juice

In a mixing glass with ice, stir together all ingredients. Pour the mixture into a chilled cocktail glass.

## Bourborita

1½ ounces bourbon
1½ ounces sweet 'n' sour mix
½ ounce triple sec
½ ounce pineapple juice
1 scoop crushed ice

In a shaker, mix together all ingredients. Strain this mixture into a sour glass or pour over ice cubes into an old-fashioned glass.

## Bull and Bear

1½ ounces bourbon
¾ ounce curaçao
1 tablespoon grenadine
Juice of ½ lime
1 scoop crushed ice
1 maraschino cherry
1 orange slice

Combine all ingredients, except the cherry and orange slice, in a shaker. Shake and strain this mixture into a chilled cocktail glass. Garnish with the cherry and orange slice.

## Campfire Sally

1½ ounces bourbon
½ ounce lime juice
½ ounce triple sec

Add all ingredients to a cocktail shaker and shake to mix. Add the ice to a highball glass and pour the cocktail into the glass.

## Dan'l Boone

1½ ounces bourbon
½ ounce orange liqueur
3 ounces chilled grapefruit juice

Pour the bourbon over ice cubes into an 8-ounce glass. Add the liqueur and juice. Stir well before serving.

## Dry Mahoney

2½ ounces bourbon
½ ounce dry vermouth
Lemon peel

In a mixing glass with ice, stir together the bourbon and vermouth. Strain the mixture into a chilled cocktail glass. Twist the lemon peel over the drink and drop it in.

## Endless Highway

1 ounce bourbon
1 ounce Baileys Irish Cream
4 ounces coffee

Combine all ingredients in a coffee mug. Stir gently.

## Flintstone

1½ ounces bourbon
½ ounce applejack
1 teaspoon lemon juice
Several dashes of grenadine
Several dashes of peppermint
　schnapps
1 scoop crushed ice

Mix together all ingredients in a shaker. Strain the mixture into a chilled cocktail glass.

## Forester

1½ ounces bourbon
¾ ounce maraschino liqueur
1 teaspoon lemon juice
1 scoop crushed ice
Maraschino cherry

Mix together all ingredients, except the cherry, in a shaker. Pour the mixture into a chilled old-fashioned glass. Garnish with the cherry.

## Golden Boy

1½ ounces bourbon
½ ounce rum
2 ounces orange juice
1 teaspoon lemon juice
Sugar syrup to taste
1 scoop crushed ice
Dash of grenadine

Mix all ingredients, except the grenadine, in a shaker. Strain the mixture into a chilled cocktail glass. Top with the grenadine.

## Green Derby

2 ounces bourbon
1 ounce green crème de menthe
Juice of ½ lime
1 teaspoon sugar syrup, or to
　taste
6 small mint leaves
Club soda
Mint sprig

Add the bourbon, crème de menthe, lime juice, syrup, and mint leaves to a mixing glass or shaker. Muddle the leaves well. Add the mixture to a blender with crushed ice and mix well. Pour this mix into a chilled collins glass, top off the glass with the soda, and garnish with the mint sprig.

## Hampton Punch

1 ounce bourbon
1 ounce cognac
¾ ounce Benedictine
Juice of ½ lemon
Juice of ½ orange
1 teaspoon sugar syrup, or to
    taste
1 scoop crushed ice
Club soda
Orange slice

Mix all ingredients, except the soda and orange slice, in a shaker. Pour the mixture into a chilled highball or collins glass. Top off the glass with the soda and stir gently. Garnish with the orange slice.

## Hawaiian Eye

1½ ounces bourbon
1 ounce vodka
1 ounce coffee liqueur
½ ounce Pernod
1 ounce cream
1 egg white
2 ounces maraschino cherry juice
1 scoop crushed ice
Pineapple chunk
Maraschino cherry

Whirl all ingredients, except the pineapple and cherry, in a blender until smooth. Pour the blend into an old-fashioned glass. Garnish with the pineapple chunk and cherry.

## Holiday Sparkle Punch

*Makes 2 (6-ounce) servings*

6 tablespoons frozen cranberry-
    raspberry juice
4 ounces bourbon
½ tablespoon frozen lemonade
2 ounces club soda

Mix all ingredients in a shaker, without ice. Pour the mixture into ice-filled cocktail glasses. This cocktail can be frozen or made into a slush by filling the shaker half full with crushed ice and adding 2 more tablespoons of juice, as well as an extra ounce of bourbon.

## Home Run

1 ounce bourbon
1 ounce light rum
1 ounce brandy
2 teaspoons lemon juice
Sugar syrup to taste

Mix together all ingredients in a shaker. Strain the mixture into a chilled cocktail glass.

## Horse's Neck

1½ ounces bourbon
Ginger ale
Lemon peel, spiral cut

Fill a highball glass with ice and add the bourbon. Fill with the ginger ale. Garnish with the spiral-cut lemon peel, having it start at the rim of the glass and continuing to the bottom.

## Imperial

1¼ ounces bourbon
1¼ ounces orange liqueur
Splash of sugar syrup
1 scoop crushed ice
Splash of club soda

In a shaker, mix together all ingredients except the soda. Strain the mixture into an old-fashioned glass over ice cubes. Top off the glass with the soda.

## Jessica's Julep Mist

1 scoop crushed ice
1½ ounces bourbon
½ ounces crème de menthe
Mint leaf

Pack a cocktail glass with crushed ice. In a mixing glass, combine the bourbon and crème de menthe. Add the this mixture to the cocktail glass and garnish with the mint leaf. Serve with short straws.

## Kentucky Breezer

2 ounces bourbon
6 ounces cranberry juice
Lime slice

Combine the bourbon and juice in a tall glass filled with ice. Stir. Garnish with the lime slice.

## Kentucky Cappuccino

1 ounce bourbon
1 ounce coffee liqueur
4 ounces heavy cream (milk or
    skim milk can be used)
1 teaspoon instant coffee
2 ounces club soda
Dark chocolate shavings
Whipped cream (optional)

Mix all ingredients, except the chocolate shavings and whipped cream, in a blender without ice. Pour the mixture into a tall glass with ice. Garnish with the chocolate shavings.

If a warm after-dinner drink is desired, omit the club soda and heat only the cream or milk. Dissolve the coffee in it. Then proceed to the blender. Add the coffee liqueur and bourbon and blend. Pour the mixture into a small stem glass with a dollop of the whipped cream if desired and chocolate shavings.

## Kentucky Cooler

1½ ounces bourbon
¾ ounce brandy
1 ounce lemon juice
2 teaspoons sugar syrup, or to
    taste
1 scoop crushed ice
Club soda
Barbados or other medium-
    weight rum

Mix together all ingredients, except the soda and rum, in a shaker. Pour the mixture into a chilled 14-ounce collins glass. Add the fresh ice and top off the glass with the soda and a float of the rum.

## Kentucky Sunrise

1½ ounces bourbon
3 ounces chilled orange juice
1 teaspoon grenadine

Pour the bourbon into an 8-ounce glass filled with ice cubes. Add the orange juice and stir. Add the grenadine, but do not stir before serving.

## Liquid Love

1 ounce bourbon
½ ounce lemon juice
Splash of grenadine

Add all ingredients to a cocktail shaker along with a scoop of ice. Shake well. Strain into a chilled cocktail glass.

## Louisville Lady

1 ounce bourbon
¾ ounce crème de cacao
¾ ounce heavy cream

In a shaker, mix together all ingredients with ice. Strain the mixture into a cocktail glass.

## Man o' War

2 ounces bourbon
1 ounce orange curaçao
½ ounce sweet vermouth
Juice of ½ lime
1 scoop crushed ice

Mix all ingredients in a shaker. Pour the mixture into a chilled cocktail glass.

## Miami Beach

1½ ounces bourbon
1 ounce orange juice
1 ounce pineapple juice
1 teaspoon lemon juice
Several dashes of bitters
Sugar syrup to taste
1 scoop crushed ice

In a shaker, mix together all ingredients. Pour the mixture into a chilled old-fashioned glass.

## Millionaire Cocktail

*Makes 2 servings*

3 ounces bourbon
1 ounce Pernod
Several dashes of curaçao
Several dashes of grenadine
1 egg white

Mix all ingredients in a shaker with crushed ice. Strain the mixture into chilled cocktail glasses.

## New Orleans Cocktail

1½ ounces bourbon
½ ounce Pernod
Dash of orange bitters
Several dashes of bitters
Dash of anisette
Sugar syrup to taste
1 scoop crushed ice
1 lemon peel twist

Mix all ingredients, except the lemon peel, in a shaker. Pour the mixture into a chilled old-fashioned glass and garnish with the lemon peel.

## Peppermint Patty

1½ ounces bourbon
½ ounce peppermint schnapps
1 tablespoon lemon juice
1 teaspoon sugar syrup, or to taste
1 scoop crushed ice
Mint sprig (optional)
Maraschino cherry

Stir together all ingredients, except the mint sprig and cherry, in a mixing glass. Pour the mixture into an old-fashioned glass. Garnish with the mint sprig if desired and the cherry.

## Painless Paul

1½ ounces bourbon
½ ounce apricot liqueur
1 ounce grapefruit juice
1 teaspoon lemon juice
Several dashes of bitters
1 scoop crushed ice

Mix together all ingredients in a shaker. Pour the mixture into an old-fashioned glass.

## Polo Dream

1½ to 2 ounces bourbon
1 ounce orange juice
¾ ounce orgeat, or to taste

Mix all ingredients in a shaker with crushed ice. Strain this mixture into a chilled cocktail glass.

## Presbyterian

2 to 3 ounces bourbon
Ginger ale
Club soda

Pour the bourbon into a chilled highball glass. Add ice cubes. Top off the glass with equal parts of the ginger ale and soda.

## Rebel Party Sour

6 ounces bourbon
6 ounces beer
1 can (6 ounces) concentrated lemon juice
1 scoop crushed ice
Maraschino cherry
Orange slice

Combine the first four ingredients in a blender. Pour the mixture into a sour glass. Garnish with the cherry and orange slice.

## Rebel Ringer

1 ounce bourbon
1 ounce gold crème de menthe
1 lemon twist
1 scoop crushed ice

In a shaker, mix together all ingredients, except the lemon twist. Strain the mixture into a chilled cocktail glass. Garnish with the lemon twist and serve.

## Reverend Craig

1½ ounces bourbon
1½ ounces concentrated frozen lemonade
6 ounces beer

Mix together all ingredients in a shaker. Shake well. Pour the mixture into a large beer glass filled with ice.

## Rhett Butler Slush

1½ ounces bourbon
1 teaspoon triple sec
Juice of ½ lime
Juice of ¼ lemon
½ teaspoon sugar
1 scoop crushed ice

Whirl together all ingredients in a blender. Pour the mixture into a chilled champagne glass.

## Royal Roost

¾ ounce bourbon or rye
¾ ounce Dubonnet rouge
Several dashes of curaçao
Several dashes of Pernod
Pineapple slice
Orange slice
Lemon peel
Generous dashes of bitters

Mix the first four ingredients in a mixing glass with crushed ice. Strain the mixture into a chilled old-fashioned glass with several ice cubes. Garnish with the fruit and top with the bitters.

## Shanty Hogan

2 ounces bourbon
1 ounce simple sugar
1 ounce lemon juice
Maraschino cherry
6 mint leaves

Combine the bourbon, sugar, lemon juice, and some ice in a blender. Blend until smooth. Pour the mixture into a hurricane glass with a straw. Garnish with the cherry and mint leaves.

## Sherry Twist

1½ ounces bourbon or blended whiskey
¾ ounce cocktail sherry
Lemon peel

Pour the bourbon or blended whiskey and sherry into a shaker with crushed ice and stir. Strain the mixture into a chilled cocktail glass. Twist the lemon peel over the drink and drop it in.

## Skyscraper

2 ounces bourbon
1 teaspoon fine sugar
1 tablespoon lime juice
Dash of bitters
1 scoop crushed ice
1 cup cranberry juice
1 cucumber rind peeling

In a shaker, mix together the first five ingredients. Strain this mixture into a highball glass with ice cubes. Top off the glass with the chilled cranberry juice and garnish with the cucumber peeling.

## Sloe 'n' Bouncy

1½ ounces bourbon
½ ounce sloe gin
½ ounce lemon juice
1 teaspoon sugar syrup
Lemon slice
Peach slice (optional)

Mix the first four ingredients in a shaker with crushed ice. Strain the mixture into a chilled cocktail glass. Garnish with the lemon and, if desired, the peach slice.

## Snowman

3 ounces bourbon
1 ounce cranberry juice
1 tablespoon lemon juice
2 tablespoons sugar syrup
1 scoop crushed ice

Mix all ingredients in a blender until the drink is frosty. Pour the blend into a chilled highball glass.

## Sonoma Fizz

1½ ounces bourbon
1 teaspoon lemon juice
1 teaspoon lime juice
1 teaspoon sugar syrup, or to
    taste
1 egg white
1 scoop crushed ice
Club soda
Maraschino cherry

In a shaker, mix together the first six ingredients. Pour the mixture into a chilled highball glass and top off with the cold soda. Garnish with the cherry.

## Southern Ginger

1½ ounces 100-proof bourbon
1 teaspoon ginger-flavored
    brandy
1 teaspoon lemon juice
1 scoop crushed ice
Ginger ale
Lemon twist

Mix the first four ingredients in a shaker. Pour the mixture into a doubled old-fashioned glass. Top off the rest of the glass with the ginger ale. Twist the lemon peel over the drink and drop it in.

## Southern Maiden

1¼ ounces bourbon
¾ ounce triple sec
2 ounces orange juice
12 ounces pineapple juice
Splash of grenadine

Combine the bourbon, triple sec, orange juice, and pineapple juice in a tall glass with ice. Top off the glass with the grenadine. Stir once and serve.

## Sunday Brunch

1½ ounces bourbon
2 ounces tomato juice
2 ounces canned beef bouillon
Dash of Worcestershire sauce
1 tablespoon lemon juice

Pour the bourbon into a tumbler filled with ice cubes. Add the remaining ingredients and stir well before serving.

## Spinner

1½ ounces bourbon
1 ounce orange juice
1 tablespoon lime juice
1 teaspoon superfine sugar
1 scoop crushed ice
½ orange slice

Combine the first four ingredients in a shaker. Shake briskly with the crushed ice. Strain the mixture into a cocktail glass or over fresh ice in an old-fashioned glass. Garnish with the half slice of orange.

## Sweet and Sour Bourbon

1½ ounces bourbon
4 ounces orange juice
1 or 2 pinches of sugar
1 pinch of salt
1 scoop crushed ice
Maraschino cherry

Mix all ingredients, except the cherry, in a shaker. Pour the mixture into a whiskey sour glass. Garnish with the cherry.

## Waldorf Cocktail

1½ ounces bourbon
¾ ounce Pernod
½ ounce sweet vermouth
Dash of bitters

In a mixing glass, stir together all ingredients with ice. Strain the mixture into a chilled cocktail glass.

## Ward Eight

1½ to 2 ounces bourbon
1 ounce lemon juice
1 ounce orange juice
Sugar syrup to taste
Dash of grenadine

Mix all ingredients in a shaker with crushed ice. Strain the mixture into a chilled cocktail glass.

## Whirlaway

2 ounces bourbon
1 ounce curaçao
Several dashes of bitters
1 scoop crushed ice
Club soda

Mix all ingredients, except the soda, in a shaker. Pour the mixture into a chilled old-fashioned glass and top off with the soda.

## Whiskey Ball

2 ounces blended whiskey
1 ounce dark rum
1 ounce añejo rum
1 teaspoon crème de cacao

Add the all ingredients to a mixing glass along with a scoop of ice. Mix well. Strain into a chilled cocktail glass.

# Bourbon • Signature Drinks

## Boilermaker

BALBOA CAFE, SAN FRANCISCO

1 shot of bourbon
½ pint beer

Pour the bourbon into a small shot glass. Drop the entire shot glass into a half-pint glass of beer.

## Café Sintra

ALFAMA, NEW YORK CITY

2 ounces Maker's Mark bourbon
1 shot of espresso
2 ounces Godiva chocolate
    liqueur
1 ounce Tia Maria

Gently stir all ingredients in a snifter. This drink is equally nice straight up and over ice.

## Cool Mint Julep

SOUTHERN CULTURE, CHARLOTTESVILLE

1½ ounces bourbon
¾ ounce peppermint schnapps
2 ounces water
2 cups ice
4 fresh mint leaves

Combine the first four ingredients in a blender. Blend until frothy. Pour the mixture into a chilled old-fashioned glass and garnish with the fresh mint.

## Geesto's Manhattan

ASTA, SAN FRANCISCO

1¼ ounces bourbon
½ ounce sweet vermouth
Splash of cherry juice
Dash of bitters
2 maraschino cherries

Combine the first four ingredients in a mixing glass with ice. Stir and strain into a chilled martini glass. Garnish with the cherries.

## Occidental "Statist" Coffee

OCCIDENTAL GRILL, WASHINGTON, D.C.

1 pint heavy cream
1½ teaspoons granulated sugar
1 teaspoon ground allspice
½ teaspoon ground cloves
Hot coffee
1½ ounces Kentucky bourbon
½ ounce coffee liqueur
Lemon twist

Whip the heavy cream at high speed, adding the granulated sugar. Whip in the ground allspice and cloves, and continue whipping until the cream holds its peaks. Fill a 10-ounce glass or snifter with the hot coffee. Add the bourbon and liqueur. Top off with the clove-scented whipped cream and garnish with the lemon twist.

## Old-Fashioned

ASTA, SAN FRANCISCO

2 maraschino cherries
2 orange slices
5 dashes of bitters
1 teaspoon sugar
1½ ounces bourbon
Splash of club soda

In a rocks glass, place 1 cherry, half an orange slice, the bitters and sugar. Muddle until the mixture is well ground. Add the bourbon and the soda while still mixing. Fill the glass with ice. Garnish with the remaining cherry and orange slices.

## Perfect Les

SX137, NEW YORK CITY

2 ounces Maker's Mark
Splash of dry vermouth
Splash of sweet vermouth
Dash of bitters
Lemon twist
Maraschino cherry

Add all ingredients to a cocktail shaker. Shake well to blend. Strain into a chilled cocktail glass. Garnish with the lemon twist and a cherry.

## Tropical Itch

MAUNA LANI BAY HOTEL,
BIG ISLAND, HAWAII

Crushed ice
½ lime
½ ounce bourbon
2 dashes of bitters
Dash of orange curaçao
½ ounce dark rum
Tropical fruit juice
1¼ ounces 151-proof rum
Maraschino cherry
Mint sprig

Fill a hurricane glass with crushed ice. Squeeze half a lime into the glass and leave the rind in the glass. Separately, blend together the bourbon, bitters, curaçao, and dark rum. Add this blend to the glass. Fill with the fruit juice just below the neck of the glass. Mix with a bar spoon and add more crushed ice. Float the 151-proof rum on top. Garnish with the cherry and mint sprig.

## Tumbleweed

"21" CLUB, NEW YORK CITY

2 ounces bourbon
Splash of Pernod
1 scoop crushed ice
Club soda
Lemon twist

Combine the bourbon, Pernod, and crushed ice in a shaker. Strain the mixture into an old-fashioned glass. Top off the glass with the soda and drop in the lemon twist.

# Bourbon • Hot Drinks

## Hot Brick Toddy

¼ teaspoon powdered cinnamon
1 teaspoon sugar syrup
1 butter pat
Boiling water
2 ounces bourbon (rye, Canadian, or blended whiskey can be used)

Rinse an old-fashioned glass in hot water. Add the cinnamon, syrup, butter, and enough of the boiling water to thoroughly mix the ingredients. Add the whiskey. Top off the glass with the rest of the boiling water.

# Canadian Whiskey •
# Creative Concoctions

## Bix Manhattan

BIX, SAN FRANCISCO

1½ ounces Canadian whiskey
½ ounce Carpano (Italian sweet
   vermouth)
Dash of bitters
Crushed ice
Maraschino cherry

Mix all ingredients, except the cherry, in a shaker. Shake vigorously. Strain the mixture into a 5-ounce chilled, stemmed martini glass. Garnish with the cherry.

## Dark Canadian Colada

FOUR SEASONS HOTEL, TORONTO

1½ ounces Canadian whiskey
1 ounce cream of coconut
2 ounces cream
½ ounce dark crème de cacao
1 cup ice

Combine all ingredients in a blender and blend until smooth. Pour the mixture into a chilled parfait glass.

## Old Pepper

1½ ounces Canadian whiskey
1 ounce lemon juice
Dash of Worcestershire sauce
Dash of chili sauce
2 dashes of Angostura bitters
Dash of Tabasco
1 scoop crushed ice

Combine all ingredients in a shaker. Mix well and strain into a sour glass.

VARIATION: Substitute ¾ ounce rye and ¾ ounce bourbon for the Canadian whiskey.

## Opening Cocktail

½ ounce Canadian whiskey
¼ ounce sweet vermouth
¼ ounce grenadine

Mix together all ingredients in a shaker with crushed ice. Strain the mixture into a chilled cocktail glass.

# Rye Whiskey •
# Creative Concoctions

### Fancy Free

Lemon juice
Powdered sugar
1½ ounces rye whiskey
2 dashes of maraschino liqueur
Dash of orange bitters
Dash of Angostura bitters

Moisten the rim of a cocktail glass with the lemon juice. Press the moistened rim into the powdered sugar. In a shaker with crushed ice, mix together the whiskey, liqueur, and bitters. Strain the mixture into the prepared glass.

# Southern Comfort •
# Creative Concoctions

### Down Comforter

1½ ounces Southern Comfort
½ ounce gin
½ ounce lemon juice
1 ounce orange juice
1 scoop crushed ice

Combine all ingredients in a shaker. Shake well and strain into a chilled cocktail glass.

### Plump Peach

2 ounces Southern Comfort
1½ ounces peach brandy
Dash of bitters
1½ ounces heavy cream
Slice of fresh peach

In a shaker, mix all ingredients, except peach slice, with ice. Strain the mixture, over ice cubes, into an old-fashioned glass. Garnish with the peach slice.

## Rhett Butler

1½ ounces Southern Comfort
1 ounce orange curaçao
¾ ounce lime juice
¾ ounce lemon juice
½ ounce orange juice
1 scoop crushed ice
Club soda
Orange slice
Mint sprig

Shake the Southern Comfort, curaçao, and juices with ice cubes. Strain the mixture into a highball glass filled with crushed ice. Top off the glass with the soda and garnish with the orange slice and mint sprig.

## Scarlett O'Hara

1½ ounces Southern Comfort
1½ ounces cranberry juice
½ ounce lime juice

In a mixing glass with ice, stir together all ingredients. Strain the mixture into a chilled cocktail glass.

## Southern Frost

1½ ounces Southern Comfort
1½ ounces amaretto
1 ounce Galliano
3 ounces orange juice
3 ounces pineapple juice
1 scoop crushed ice

Blend together all ingredients in a blender. Pour the mixture into a hurricane glass.

# SCOTCH WHISKY

From the air, Scotland is as lined and craggy as the face of an ancient mariner. Exposed to salt, wind, cold, and the constant ebb of sea water, this mass of land jutting out of the northernmost part of England is the birthplace of scotch whisky. Over 80 distilleries are scattered over a diverse countryside that includes the Highlands, the Lowlands, Speyside, which runs along the River Spey, and the island of Islay (pronounced "eye-la") off the west coast. The crevices and crags of this land influence the character of scotch whisky and reflect the rugged temperament of the Scottish natives.

While scotch whisky owes a great deal to the land where it is distilled, it owes more to the tumultuous history of the native Scots. In 1746, after the defeat of Bonnie Prince Charlie at Culloden Moor, the British crown, attempting to bring independent-minded Scotland under its thumb, banned kilts and other traditional clothes; and in 1814, distillation from any still with less than a 500-gallon capacity was outlawed in Scotland. Both these prohibitions caused anger and defiance among the Scots. The kilt and Highland dress are an integral part of the Scottish character, and so is "a wee dram" of whisky, and these meddlesome restrictions constituted a grievous insult to each and every true Scot. But, as in many other instances throughout history, this adversity only served to create a national Scottish character that was stronger and more emphatically independent than ever before. The home stills of the Highlands continued to operate, and many of them grew into flourishing businesses.

Almost 200 years later, these distilleries continue to turn out very fine "malt" whisky using very much the same process as their predecessors. To begin, top-quality barley is steeped it in water, causing it to germinate and sprout. This changes the barley's starch into sugar, which eventually is converted to alcohol during fermentation. The sprouting barley is dried in a kiln heated by a peat fire, after which it is crushed in preparation for fermentation. The peat used to heat the kiln can add a specific flavor to the whisky. This result of this process is called "malted" barley.

As this process requires substantial space and some rather heavy equipment, it can present a considerable hardship for tiny Highland distilleries. To answer this problem, malting has been concentrated— as of the early 1960s—at a relatively small number of plants that were expressly built for the intake, storage, and processing of barley malt.

The starch from the barley is infused with pure spring water and yeast and allowed to ferment. All Scots will tell you that it is the Highland water that makes their whisky special. The water, flowing in profusion out of the hills, is softened as it passes over granite and through vegetation. It also takes on a round, almost sweet flavor.

Each distillery has its own natural water supply—a spring or a stream gurgling out of the hills. The water source at each facility is tended and protected but never tampered with (despite the fact that the water does take on a slight brownish tinge as a result of its contact with peat). In fact, it was the water source that originally dictated where a given distillery would be located. The water is another factor that gives each malt its special flavor.

The type of oak barrel each distillery uses for aging also contributes to the character of the whisky. One distiller may put the clear whisky into "refill" sherry casks. These are relatively neutral and add little flavor to the spirit over time, allowing the whisky's true malty character to shine forth. At another distillery, the whisky is aged in casks that have held a couple of vintages of oloroso or cream sherry. The result, after a number of years of aging, is a dark spirit that has absorbed a great degree of complexity and richness from the inside walls of the aging barrel. Still other distilleries use American oak barrels that once held bourbon.

Though by law Scotch whisky must age a minimum of 3 years, most distillers aim for longer. Some find that their whisky hits its peak after 8 years, while others prefer to allow theirs to slumber for 10, 12, or 18 years.

While water, peat, and oak lend their flavors to the whisky, perhaps most important to the taste of the final spirit is the land on which it was made. Much as regions of France or California influence the flavor of wine, so do regions of Scotland produce scotch with recognizable regional style and flashy characteristics. The malts of Islay are a perfect example of this. This rough-hewn island is renowned for its barley, peat, and soft water. Almost constant wind and rain and the salty influence of the sea contribute strong brine and kelp flavors to the whisky produced by the distinguished distilleries Laphroaig, Bowmore, and Bruichladdich. While these malts may seem too assertive for the uninitiated scotch drinker, they provide a more than worthy target for the budding single-malt connoisseur.

Train for Islay with the softer, milder single malts from the Highlands area, the largest scotch-producing region in Scotland. The whiskies from this area can be sweet and light, with a delectable aroma of fruit and honey. Within the Highland region, Speyside is known for some of the most complex malts in the country. Speyside's distillery, the Glenlivet, may be Scotland's most famous single-malt distillery. I particularly like the Glenlivet 18-year-old with its rich, fruit flavor and long, smoky finish. Glenfiddich, another well-known single malt, is also from this region.

The Isle of Skye is home to only one single-malt distillery. Talisker, established in 1843 on the exposed west coast of the island, has been turning out spicy, smoky-flavored whisky similar in style to the sea-influenced Islay malts. The island is also home to a company making the vatted malt Poit Dubh and the blended whisky Te Bheag. Both blends are said to contain some Talisker-made whisky.

Single malts have come of age in the last decade or so. Their popularity has contributed to a new generation of so-called premium spirits, including single-barrel bourbon and aged rum. As you explore the territory of scotch whisky, you'll discover that each possesses its own unique characteristics and distinct flavors. The study of these distinctive whiskies is fascinating and can offer a lifetime of enjoyment. Each one speaks clearly of its origins and its history.

While your favorite single malt may add an exciting new dimension to the drink recipes that follow, you may prefer to save the single malt for sipping and opt for a vatted malt or blended whisky for mixing.

What is called a "vatted malt" is produced by blending a variety of single malts from more than one distillery. The whiskies going into a blend may come from vats of different ages and each may be chosen to bring a particular quality, such as a flavor or bouquet, to the final product. Just like a single-malt whisky, these vatted malts are pure malt—that is to say, they are undiluted by grain whisky or neutral spirits. The vatted malt, blended for smoothness and approachability, may be a bit less challenging than a single malt, but can still be quite delicious.

Blended whiskies are combinations of single-malt and grain whiskies. In the mid-19th century, as the British Empire became a global force, the demand for scotch whisky nearly outstripped the production capacity of the distilleries. As a result, blended Scotch was created to meet the ever-growing demand for scotch whisky. Softer and lighter than its single-malt counterpart, blended whisky was deemed more appropriate for the general public.

Today, blended scotch whiskies provide the bulk of profits for the scotch industry. Many distilleries consign the vast majority of their production to be used in blends rather than bottling it as a single malt. Though in recent years the single malt has achieved great notoriety, there are numerous blended whiskies that are arguably as delicious and complex. Companies such as Johnnie Walker, Chivas Bros., Ballantine's, Cutty Sark, and Dewar's create a number of blends that range from merely mixable to downright sippable. The only way to find your favorite is to experiment.

# Classics

## Hopscotch

1½ ounces scotch
½ ounce sweet vermouth
Several dashes of orange bitters
1 scoop crushed ice
Olive

Mix the scotch, vermouth, bitters, and ice in a shaker. Pour the mixture into a chilled cocktail glass and drop in the olive.

## Remsen Cooler

2 to 3 ounces scotch
1 teaspoon sugar syrup
Club soda
Lemon peel

Put the scotch, sugar syrup, and several ice cubes in a chilled collins glass. Top off the glass with the soda and stir. Twist the lemon peel over the drink and drop it in.

## Rob Roy

1½ to 2 ounces scotch
½ ounce sweet vermouth
Dash of orange bitters
1 maraschino cherry

In a mixing glass with ice, stir together the scotch, vermouth, and bitters. Strain the mixture into a chilled cocktail glass and garnish with the cherry.

## Rob Roy Dry

1½ to 2 ounces scotch
½ ounce dry vermouth
Dash of bitters (optional)
Lemon peel

In a mixing glass with ice cubes, stir together the scotch, vermouth, and bitters. Strain the mixture into a chilled cocktail glass. Twist the lemon peel over the drink and drop it in.

## Scotch Sour

1½ ounces scotch
½ ounce lemon juice
1 teaspoon sugar syrup
1 scoop crushed ice
Orange slice
1 maraschino cherry

Mix the together the first four ingredients in a shaker. Shake and then strain the mixture into a chilled whiskey sour glass. Garnish with the orange slice and cherry.

# Creative Concoctions

## Aberdeen Sour

2 ounces scotch
1 ounce orange juice
1 ounce lemon juice
½ ounce triple sec
1 scoop crushed ice

Combine all ingredients in a shaker or blender. Mix well and pour into a chilled old-fashioned glass.

## Affinity Cocktail

1 ounce scotch
1 ounce dry sherry
1 ounce port
Several dashes of bitters
1 scoop crushed ice
Lemon peel
Maraschino cherry

In a mixing glass with ice, stir together the scotch, sherry, port, and bitters. Strain the mixture into a chilled cocktail glass. Twist the lemon peel over the drink and drop it in. Garnish with the cherry.

## Blackwatch

1½ ounces scotch
½ ounce curaçao
½ ounce brandy
Lemon slice
Mint sprig

Pour the scotch, curaçao, and brandy over ice cubes in a chilled highball glass. Stir and then garnish with the slice of lemon and mint sprig.

## Blood and Sand

1 ounce scotch
¾ ounce sweet vermouth
¾ ounce cherry brandy
¾ ounce orange juice

Add all ingredients plus one scoop of ice to a mixing glass. Mix and strain into a chilled cocktail glass.

## Bobby Burns

1 ounce scotch
1 ounce dry vermouth
1 ounce sweet vermouth
Dash of Benedictine

Mix all ingredients with ice, then strain into a chilled cocktail glass.

## Caracas Cocktail

2 ounces scotch
½ ounce lemon juice
1 teaspoon sugar syrup
Several dashes of curaçao
Dash of amaretto
1 scoop crushed ice

In a shaker, combine all ingredients. Mix well and strain into a chilled cocktail glass.

## Farmer's Milk

2 ounces scotch
5 ounces heavy cream
1 scoop crushed ice
1 whole egg
1 teaspoon sugar syrup
Freshly grated nutmeg

Combine the scotch and cream in a shaker with the crushed ice. Beat the egg and sugar syrup together in a bowl, then add to the shaker. Shake vigorously. Pour the mixture into a chilled old-fashioned glass and sprinkle with the nutmeg.

## The Godfather

1½ ounces scotch
¾ ounce amaretto

Bill Wolkoff, bartender at the Cork Room in Los Angeles builds this sweet and smoky drink over ice in a rocks glass.

## Harry Lauder

1¼ ounces scotch
1¼ ounces sweet vermouth
½ teaspoon sugar

In a mixing glass with ice, stir together all ingredients. Strain the mixture into a chilled cocktail glass.

## Hawaiian Bull

1½ ounces scotch
Crushed ice
Fresh pineapple wedges
½ ounce orgeat

Pour the scotch into a double old-fashioned glass. Fill the glass with the crushed ice and fresh pineapple wedges. Top off with a float of the orgeat.

## Heathcliff

1 ounce scotch
1 ounce calvados
½ ounce dry gin
1 teaspoon heather honey or
   sugar syrup
1 scoop crushed ice

Mix all ingredients in a shaker. Strain the mixture into a chilled cocktail glass.

## Highland

1½ ounces scotch
3 ounces milk
1 teaspoon sugar
1 scoop crushed ice
Freshly grated nutmeg

Mix the scotch, milk, sugar, and ice in a shaker. Pour the mixture into a chilled old-fashioned glass, and sprinkle the nutmeg on top.

## Horseshoe

1 lemon, peeled in a long spiral
2 to 3 ounces scotch
½ ounce sweet vermouth
½ ounce dry vermouth
1 scoop crushed ice

Place the lemon peel in a chilled collins glass, leaving one end of the peel hanging over the rim. Pour in the scotch and vermouths. Add the crushed ice and stir well. Let the drink stand for a few minutes before serving.

## Knucklebuster

1½ ounces scotch
¾ ounce Drambuie

Fill an old-fashioned glass with ice cubes. Pour both ingredients into the glass and stir well.

## Marylou

3 ounces scotch
½ ounce lime juice
Ginger ale
Lemon slice

Pour the scotch and lime juice into a chilled collins glass filled with ice cubes. Top the glass with the ginger ale and stir. Garnish with the lemon slice.

## Miami Beach Cocktail

1 ounce scotch
1 ounce dry vermouth
1 ounce grapefruit juice
1 scoop crushed ice

Mix all ingredients in a shaker. Strain the mixture into a chilled cocktail glass.

## Prince Edward

1½ ounces scotch
½ ounce vermouth-based aperitif
    such as Lillet or St. Raphael
¼ ounce Drambuie
1 scoop crushed ice
Preserved orange slice

Mix the first four ingredients in a shaker. Pour the mixture into a chilled old-fashioned glass and garnish with the orange slice.

## Saucy Sue

2 to 3 ounces scotch
¼ ounce lime or lemon juice
1 scoop crushed ice
Cold ginger ale
Lime or lemon wedge

Mix the scotch and lime or lemon juice in a mixing glass with the crushed ice. Strain the mixture into a chilled highball glass. Top off with the ginger ale and garnish with the lime or lemon wedge.

## Scotch Orange Fix

2 ounces scotch
½ ounce lemon juice
1 teaspoon sugar syrup
1 scoop crushed ice
Orange peel, cut in a long spiral
1 teaspoon curaçao

Mix the together the first four ingredients in a shaker. Shake vigorously. Pour the mixture into a double old-fashioned glass. Add the additional ice and drop in the orange peel. Top with a float of the curaçao.

## Scotch Sangaree

1 teaspoon heather honey, or to
   taste
Club soda or water
1½ ounces scotch
Lemon twist
Freshly grated nutmeg

Mix the heather honey and a little of the soda or water in a double old-fashioned glass until the honey is dissolved. Add the scotch, lemon twist, and ice cubes. Top off the glass with the soda and sprinkle the nutmeg on top.

## Scotch Mash

1 teaspoon heather honey or
   sugar syrup
6 mint leaves
1 scoop crushed ice
2 to 3 ounces scotch
Dash of orange bitters
Mint sprig

Muddle the honey or sugar syrup with the mint in a double old-fashioned glass. Fill the glass with the crushed ice. Add the scotch and mix well. Top off with the orange bitters and the mint sprig.

## Shogun Fizz

2 ounces scotch
2 ounces dry red wine
½ ounce lemon juice
1 teaspoon sugar syrup
1 scoop crushed ice
Club soda
Pineapple spear

Mix the first five ingredients in a shaker. Pour the mixture into a chilled highball glass, top off with the cold club soda, and decorate with the pineapple spear.

## Starboard

1 ounce scotch
1 ounce grapefruit juice
1 ounce dry vermouth
1 scoop crushed ice

Mix all ingredients in a shaker.
Pour the mixture into a chilled
old-fashioned glass.

## University

2 ounces scotch
6 ounces chocolate milk
1 teaspoon curaçao
1 scoop crushed ice
Grated chocolate

Mix the scotch, milk, and curaçao
in a shaker with the crushed ice.
Pour the mixture into a chilled
double old-fashioned glass and
sprinkle the chocolate on top.

# Hot Drinks

## Oxford Grad

*Makes 2 servings*

4 ounces scotch
4 ounces boiling water
2 teaspoons sugar
2 small lemon peels

Pour the scotch and boiling water
into separate warm mugs. Ignite
the scotch. While it is blazing,
pour it back and forth between the
two mugs. Extinguish the scotch
and serve the drink in two mugs.
Add 1 teaspoon of sugar to each
mug and stir well. Garnish with the
lemon peels.

NOTE: You might want to practice
once or twice with cold water.

# IRISH WHISKEY

Irish whiskey was the first, and for a time, the only distilled spirit made in the British Isles. Today the best-known spirit from the region is, of course, scotch, but Irish whiskey has been around a good deal longer and certainly has many fans.

Some zealous constituents assure us that this heady spirit dates back to the 6th century when missionary monks brought the art of distillation to the Emerald Isle. Others insist that there was enough *uisge beatha* (Celtic for "water of life") on hand in the 12th century for Henry II's invading troops to take a supply home with them. Actually, the first recorded reference to Irish whiskey goes back to the early 1400s, which means that the spirit would still predate scotch by nearly a century. In fact, many believe that distillation was brought to Scotland from Ireland.

In the beginning of the 17th century, none other than Sir Walter Raleigh became a devotee of Ireland's mellow spirits, whiskey in particular. On his last visit to the West Indies, Raleigh stopped to visit his friend the Earl of Cork, and he happily reported in his diary that he was given "a supreme present"—a 32-gallon keg of home-distilled whiskey. Queen Elizabeth I was also fond of Irish spirits.

Soon, as a result of its burgeoning popularity in England, the spirit underwent a name change and the Celtic spelling was anglicized into "whiskey." Oddly enough, there is a spelling difference between the whiskies of the world. Irish spirits, along with those from the American continent, are named "whiskey," while the Scots drop the "e" and call theirs "whisky."

It was during the reign of Elizabeth's successor, James I, that Sir Thomas Phillips, the king's deputy in the Irish province of Ulster, was given the authority to grant distilling licenses. Those were simpler days: Ignorant of such modern ethical considerations as "conflicts of interest," Sir Thomas immediately granted himself the first license. In

1608, Phillips built his distillery on the banks of the Bush River in County Antrim, Northern Ireland. It was the world's first licensed distillery, and he christened it "Bushmills."

Whiskey distilling flourished in Ireland in the 17th century, but most stills were small cottage industries. There were many attempts—some of them violent—made to control and tax these distilling activities. But, as in Scotland and America, most of these efforts were unsuccessful.

The true beginnings of the modern Irish whiskey business came about in the late 18th century, when a group of large commercial distilleries were built. Brands that have survived include John Jameson, which opened its distillery in 1780, and John Power, which appeared in 1791. Both of these firms were established in Dublin. Later, in 1825, the Murphy brothers built a distillery in Midleton, near Cork. Here they installed the world's largest pot still—3,000 gallons in volume. It wasn't until 1975, on the still's 150th birthday, that it was taken out of service.

There are important differences between the ways scotch and Irish whiskies are made. Both methods use pot stills, but the Irish stills are much bigger. In addition, the Irish spirit is distilled 3 times, scotch just twice. As a result, Irish whiskey is purer and quite a bit more forceful coming off the still. By the addition of distilled water, both whiskies are brought down to a lower proof before bottling.

Another major difference between the two goes back to the treatment of the grain malt in the initial stages of the whiskey-making progress. In both cases, the grain is moistened, after which it begins to germinate. Scottish malt is dried in kilns over open peat fires, a process that gives the resulting spirit its distinctive smoky flavor. Irish malt is toasted over peat in enclosed kilns, which adds no noticeable character to the eventual distillate.

Scotch malt is made entirely from malted barley, while Irish whiskey is made from a blend of malted and unmalted barley, oats, rye, and wheat. Irish whiskey is aged—often for 10 to 12 years—in oak casks that previously held either bourbon, rum, or sherry. These well-seasoned barrels give the whiskey additional complexity.

Irish whiskey gained worldwide acceptance in the 19th and early 20th centuries. In America, it was the spirit of choice until the advent of Prohibition in 1919. But the bleak 13-year period that followed, plus the effects of a depression that had spread throughout the world, seriously damaged the industry. During World War II the Irish government restricted whiskey export sales in order to improve Ireland's wartime economy. As a result, American GIs returned home from Europe singing the praises of scotch.

The Irish whiskey industry remained in the doldrums until the mid-1960s, when all the distilleries in Ireland merged to form one big company, Irish Distillers Group, Limited (I.D.G.). Many of the old distilleries had become outmoded; some of them were finding it difficult to obtain a consistent supply of good water. The Dublin operations, once situated on the outskirts of the city, were slowly being engulfed by urban expansion.

After much research, it was decided to build a big new complex at Midleton. Completed in 1975, this plant now produces all Irish whiskey except Old Bushmills. The company's directors assure us that this operation is "capable of producing all the famous whiskies in exactly the way they have always been made" and that "their unique flavors and characteristics are preserved."

Old Bushmills, although part of I.D.G. since 1975, continues to make its whiskey in the ancient County Antrim distillery on the edge of St. Columb's Rill in Northern Ireland.

Like other whiskies, Irish is consumed mostly on the rocks or with water or soda. The spirit has a gentle, warm, nutlike flavor, with plenty of shadings. This complexity gives it considerable staying power and a taste that doesn't pale when sipped over the course of a long evening.

Irish whiskey can also be used with mixers or in any of the cocktails that are ordinarily made with scotch, bourbon, Canadian, or blended whiskies. Of course, the most famous of all Irish whiskey drinks is Irish Coffee. This delicious blending of coffee, sugar, and whiskey topped with whipped cream was allegedly created by Joe Sheridan, who was the chef at Ireland's Shannon Airport. Legend has it that it made its first American appearance in 1952 at the Buena Vista Cafe on San Francisco's Fisherman's Wharf, and there is a plaque outside the restaurant to commemorate the event.

But Irish can stand on its own without mixers of any sort. This historic spirit has a distinct character and a style that is unique. Different from scotch or bourbon, Irish whiskey deserves a place in every bar.

# Classics

## *Hot Irish Coffee*

1½ ounces Irish whiskey
Strong, hot coffee
Brown sugar
Whipped cream

Pour the Irish whiskey into a warm glass coffee mug. Fill the mug with the coffee and add the brown sugar to taste. Stir to combine. Top off with the dollop of freshly whipped cream.

## *Iced Irish Coffee*

4 ounces strong, hot coffee
1½ ounces Irish whiskey, warmed
1 to 2 teaspoons brown sugar
Lightly whipped heavy cream

Pour the freshly brewed coffee into a glass container. Add the Irish whiskey and sugar. Stir well until the sugar is dissolved. Chill. When you are ready to serve it, pour the cold mixture into a stemmed glass. Gently pour the cream over the back of a spoon, held just above the coffee's surface, so that the whipped cream floats on top. Do not stir before serving.

# Creative Concoctions

## *Balleylickey Belt*

½ teaspoon heather honey, or to taste
Club soda
1½ ounces Irish whiskey
Lemon peel

In a cocktail glass, mix the honey with a little club soda until it dissolves. Add the whiskey and several ice cubes, then fill the glass with the soda. Twist the lemon peel over the drink and drop it in.

## *Blackthorn*

1½ ounces Irish whiskey
1½ ounces dry vermouth
Several dashes of Pernod
Several dashes of bitters
1 scoop crushed ice

Combine all ingredients in a shaker or blender. Mix well and pour into a chilled old-fashioned glass.

## Brainstorm

2 ounces Irish whiskey
½ ounce dry vermouth
¼ ounce Benedictine
Orange peel

In a mixing glass, stir together the whiskey, vermouth, and Benedictine. Pour the mixture into a cocktail glass and garnish with the orange peel.

## Connemara Clammer

2 ounces Irish whiskey
2 ounces clam juice
3 ounces V8 juice
1 teaspoon lime juice
Several dashes of Worcestershire sauce
½ teaspoon grated horseradish
Several pinches of freshly ground black or white pepper
1 scoop crushed ice

Combine all ingredients in a shaker. Mix and strain into a chilled double old-fashioned glass.

## Dublin Sour

1½ ounces Irish whiskey
½ ounce triple sec
1 ounce lime juice
1 scoop crushed ice
¼ ounce raspberry liqueur

Mix the whiskey, triple sec, and lime juice in a shaker with crushed ice. Strain the mixture into a chilled cocktail glass. Top off with a float of the raspberry liqueur.

## Four-Leaf Clover

1½ ounces Irish whiskey
1½ ounces green crème de menthe
2 ounces heavy cream
1 scoop crushed ice
1 maraschino cherry

Mix all ingredients, except the cherry, in a shaker. Pour the mixture into a chilled old-fashioned glass and garnish with the cherry.

## Green-Eyed Monster

1¼ ounces Irish whiskey
1 ounce sweet vermouth
¼ ounce green crème de menthe
1 dash of bitters

In a mixing glass with ice, stir together all ingredients. Pour the mixture into a chilled cocktail glass.

Mix all ingredients in a shaker. Strain the mixture into a chilled cocktail glass.

## Irish Fix

2 ounces Irish whiskey
½ ounce Irish Mist
½ ounce lemon juice
½ ounce pineapple syrup or
    pineapple juice
1 scoop crushed ice
Orange slice
Lemon slice

Mix the together the first five ingredients in a blender. Pour the mixture into an old-fashioned glass. Garnish with the orange and lemon slices.

NOTE: If you use pineapple juice in place of syrup, add a little sugar syrup to taste.

## Irish Kilt

2 ounces Irish whiskey
1 ounce scotch
1 ounce lemon juice
1½ ounces sugar syrup, or to taste
Several dashes of orange bitters
1 scoop crushed ice

## Leprechaun

1½ ounces Irish whiskey
½ ounce sloe gin
½ ounce light rum
1 ounce lemon juice
1 teaspoon sugar syrup
2 peach slices, diced
1 scoop crushed ice
5 to 6 fresh raspberries
1 maraschino cherry

Mix all ingredients, except the fruit, in a blender. Pour the mixture into a chilled old-fashioned glass. Garnish with the raspberries and cherry.

## Lucky Shamrock

1½ ounces Irish whiskey
¾ ounce dry vermouth
1 teaspoon green Chartreuse
1 teaspoon green crème de
    menthe

Combine all ingredients in a mixing glass filled with ice. Stir well and strain into a chilled cocktail glass.

## Marco's Polo

1½ ounces Irish whiskey
¾ ounce triple sec
1 ounce lemon juice
1 scoop crushed ice

Combine all ingredients in a shaker or blender. Shake and strain into a chilled cocktail glass.

## Murphy Fizz

1½ ounces Irish whiskey
1 ounce medium sherry
½ ounce crème de noyaux
½ ounce lemon juice
Club soda

Pour all ingredients, except the soda, into a chilled highball glass with ice cubes. Top off the glass with the cold club soda and stir gently.

## Paddy Cocktail

1½ ounces Irish whiskey
¾ ounce sweet vermouth
Several dashes of bitters
1 scoop crushed ice

Mix all ingredients in a shaker. Pour the mixture into a chilled cocktail glass.

## Transamerica

1½ ounces Irish whiskey
1 ounce coconut syrup
3 ounces pineapple juice
1 teaspoon lemon juice
1 scoop crushed ice
Club soda

Pour the whiskey, coconut syrup, fruit juices, and crushed ice into a blender. Blend well. Pour the mixture into a chilled highball glass along with several ice cubes. Top off the glass with the cold club soda and stir gently.

## Tropical Leprechaun

1½ ounces Irish whiskey
1 tablespoon sloe gin
1 tablespoon light rum
Juice of ½ lemon
1 teaspoon powdered sugar
Raspberries, strawberries, peach
  slices, cherry

Shake all ingredients, except fruit, with ice. Strain into a highball glass. Decorate with the fresh raspberries, strawberries, peach slices, and a cherry.

# Signature Drinks

### *Perfect Irish*

MERRION HOTEL, DUBLIN, IRELAND

2 ounces Irish whiskey
Dash of Angostura bitters
1 ounce Martini & Rossi
Green cherry

Place a few pieces of ice in an old-fashioned glass. Pour ingredients, except cherry, over ice. Garnish with the green cherry.

### *Warm Creamy Bush*

FILLMORE BAR & GRILL,
SAN FRANCISCO

½ ounce warm coffee
¾ ounce Baileys Irish cream
¾ ounce Bushmill's Irish whiskey

Pour all three ingredients into a shot glass.

# Hot Drinks

### *Spirited Coffee Lopez*

½ ounce Irish whiskey
8 ounces hot coffee
½ ounce cream of coconut

In a warm mug, stir all ingredients.

# BRANDY

Brandy has been described as "fire in a glass." And, indeed, fiery warmth seems to be the definitive quality of the spirit. The word "brandy" is a derivative of the Dutch *brandewijn,* which means "burnt wine." It is made virtually everywhere wine is produced or fruit is grown. It is, put most simply, distilled fermented fruit juice. In most cases, that fermented fruit juice is wine made from grapes, though it is not uncommon to find brandies made from apples, pears, and other high-sugar fruits.

Quality wine-based brandies are produced in France, Italy, Spain, Germany, Portugal, and the United States, among other countries. Most every brandy produced in these places will be quite acceptable when used in the mixed drinks that follow. However, if you are planning to drink brandy in the more traditional manner—without ice, water, or other additives, straight up in a snifter—you should probably stick to the better (and more expensive) brandies.

When it comes to selecting a top-quality brandy, the choice narrows. There are some excellent boutique brands being made in California (Germain-Robin and Jepson come to mind), there are great Spanish brandies, and there are exquisite brandies made in southwestern France called Armagnac. But all of these must be held up to the standard set by cognac.

What is it that sets cognac apart from these others? What's so special about cognac anyway? Actually there are several things that make this brandy unique. Each of these elements is important on its own, but in combination they can make magic.

Let's start with location. The cognac-producing region is directly north and east of the best vineyards of Bordeaux. But even more important is the fact that cognac's growing area extends to the banks of the Gironde River, which enters from the Atlantic Ocean and opens out into a wide and well-protected waterway. This unusually serene and inviting marine thoroughfare became, early on, a popular trading stop for ships from Holland, Scandinavia, and Britain. The secure Atlantic port of La Rochelle also attracted many vessels. It is because of the Dutch trade that there was any brandy even made in the region at all. In the 16th century Charentais wine merchants, looking for a way to reduce taxes and shipping costs to Holland, decided to distill their tart and rather ordinary white wine, thereby reducing its weight. Since the distillation essentially dehydrated the wine, they theorized that all they would have to do was add water at the other end of the voyage to reconstitute it. Of course, this didn't work; what resulted instead was the first cognac brandy.

Interest in this distilled wine was immediate, especially from the British Isles. Mr. Hine arrived from Dorset, Mr. Martell came from the Channel Islands, and Mr. Hennessy appeared, having traveled from his home in Ireland. The cognac business had begun. This strong British presence in Cognac has been an extremely important influence on the development of the unique style of the region's brandy. Indeed, the English obsession with elegance and finesse dictated right from the beginning what cognac was to become.

Next, let's talk about soil. Although the grapes used to make the rather pedestrian wine that eventually becomes cognac are considered incidental to the final product, the soil in which they are grown is crucial. (For the record, the grapes are mostly Ugni Blanc, with some Folle Blanche and Colombard mixed in.)

The stony, chalky, lime-rich earth around the town of Cognac and along the southern banks of the Charente River produces brandy with the greatest finesse and the finest bouquet. This small subregion, with its 32,100 acres of white wine vineyards, is called Grande Champagne, and its brandies are Cognac's most highly prized. Petite Champagne (39,500 acres), the next-best area, forms a collar around Grande Champagne. Borderies (9,900 acres), to the north of the river and to the west of Cognac, is next.

These three prime areas are surrounded by three lesser subdivisions, Fins Bois, Bons Bois, and Bois Ordinaires (154,400 acres total), which produce coarser, earthier, less complex spirits from soils that are heavier and contain less limestone. (By contrast, in Bas-Armagnac—

the best section of the only other region that is ever mentioned in the same breath as Cognac—the soil is mostly sandy.)

Another unique aspect of Cognac's soil is the special yeast that grows there, which provides a complete and natural fermentation as well as adding a singular note to the brandy's bouquet.

Technique is another important element in the cognac story. Nearly all distilled spirits and most brandies (including Armagnac) are made in a continuous or column still, a fast, efficient, and relatively inexpensive process. Cognac, on the other hand, is made in distinctive, onion-shaped copper pot stills.

The distillation procedure, known as *double chauffe,* requires that the wine be distilled twice. This method allows for greater control and also, because the alembic pot stills are small, permits individual growers to distill their own brandy.

There are some 50,000 winegrowers in the Cognac region, which was delimited by the French government in 1909. Most of these take their grapes to one of 250 small distilleries or cooperatives in the region. There are 6,000 growers, however, who actually distill their own brandy.

It is a lonely task for those who choose to be their own distillers. The wood fire that keeps the still operating must never be allowed to go out, and it must be tended, day and night, during the many cold weeks of the wintertime distillation period. The resulting cognac, made in a way that has been handed down from father to son for generations, is produced drop by drop.

Wood is another significant element in the production of cognac. After distillation the clear, white eau-de-vie is put into small barrels made from oak that comes from the forests of Limousin or Troncais, not far to the northeast of the Cognac district. This oak is highly porous and quite low in the harsh wood tannins which can add an unwelcome bitterness to a young brandy.

There are some 300 cooperages in the Cognac district. Most important distillers operate and strictly oversee their own barrel-making operation. Cognac barrels are made entirely by hand from staves that have been air-dried for at least 4 years. The staves are carefully bent with the use of heat and fitted together. No nails may be used in making barrels because, if any metal were to come in contact with the brandy, its effect on flavor could be disastrous.

Now we come to one of the most important of all ingredients in fine cognac: age. The early brandies of the region were sold fresh from the still—harsh, fiery white liquors which were rather difficult to stomach. But the Wars of the Spanish Succession changed the course of cognac history. This 12-year conflict effectively stopped the brandy trade with England. When it ended in 1713 with the Treaty of Utrecht, merchants discovered that the eau-de-vie they had barreled back in 1701 had turned a lovely golden color and had lost much of its harshness.

Since then, aging has become a standard part of cognac production. The raw young brandy is put into new oak barrels and stored in a well-ventilated warehouse called a *chai*. Then a subtle but remarkable natural procedure begins. The brandy extracts tannins, color, and taste from the wood while at the same time the alcohol gradually evaporates through the porous oak. The annual amount of evaporation, called by some "the angel's share," is equivalent to a quarter of the annual world consumption of cognac. As a result of this, the air around the city of Cognac, where many of these *chais* are located, has a persistent, delightful perfume.

The youngest cognac which may be sold must have aged for a minimum of 2½ years. The least expensive cognac, 3-star, is a blend that actually averages closer to 5 years of age. Some houses call their 3-star brandies "V.S." (Very Superior).

The next step on the age scale is V.S.O.P. (Very Superior Old Pale), which by law must be at least 4½ years old, but is usually closer to 7 to 10.

Next comes X.O. (Extra Old) or Napoleon. The law says these must contain no brandies that are less than 5½ years old, but most of them average between 15 and 25.

Finally there are the Grande Réserves. These are not defined by law, but most of them average around 50 years of age. Some of the best known of this group are Hennessy Paradis, Martell Extra, Rémy Martin Louis VIII, and Delamain Réserve de la Famille.

Incidentally, cognac ages only when it is in oak. Unlike wine, once brandy is bottled it doesn't change; it neither deteriorates nor improves. Also unlike wine, brandy should be stored upright to avoid cork deterioration. Once opened, a properly stored bottle of brandy will keep for many months.

The last and ultimately most important aspect of cognac production is people. The Cognacais take their local brandy seriously and are willing to expend the extra effort required to make it special. There is the vast network of growers, the hardworking distillers, and, most remarkable of all, the tasters.

Each of the 320 cognac houses has a head taster on staff. His taste buds are responsible for the success (or failure) of the house product. His job is to taste and judge the thousands of samples brought to him each year by local growers and distillers. From these he selects and buys sound brandies which eventually will find their way into one of the house cognacs.

Each house, not unlike key champagne producers, has its own distinctive style. A consumer who enjoys a glass of a particular cognac in Paris should be able to buy the same brandy in Chicago and have the identical sensory experience. This distinctive characteristic of a good cognac is the result of the head taster's talents.

When the master taster decides to make a superpremium cognac he goes to the *paradis,* the cellar where the oldest brandies are stored. From the barrels there he selects a blend—the oldest cognacs for complexity and oaky richness, some others for smoothness and finesse, perhaps younger ones for fruit and liveliness. The result is superb, a true artistic expression.

Cognac has been called "the distilled quintessence of wine." In fact, there is no more perfect finale to a succession of good wines than a toasty, rich, softly fruity, intensely perfumed few ounces of this unique liquid. Swirling shimmering amber up the walls of a graceful glass, one can appreciate all the things that make this elegant brandy so special: the location of its vineyards, the Charente soil, the time-honored techniques, the wood, the aging, and the people who have devoted their lives to making cognac the world's finest brandy.

It used to be that the only brandy made in the United States was the mass-produced kind, brewed in tall column stills. These brandies, which still represent the lion's share of the domestic brandy market, are usually simple and a little sweet, pleasant in mixed drinks and for cooking.

Over the past 20 years, however, a few hardy souls have attempted to reproduce the handmade, oak-aged, pot still brandies that have made cognac so renowned, and some have also set about to make serious "pomace" brandies—distillates produced from the grape solids that remain after the wine-making process—such as grappa or marc.

Notable California producers such as Germain-Robin, Jepson, and RMS, along with Oregon's Clear Creek Distillery, are producing amazing spirits that can easily hold their own in the company of some of the best distilled products of Europe.

French-born Hubert Germain-Robin and his American partner, Ansley Coale, produce a superb brandy using premium varietal wines such as pinot noir. Both the Anno Domini and Select Barrel XO compare to the finest cognacs. These brandies are made using a traditional alambic still. This type of pot still works only one batch at a time, setting these fine brandies apart from other mass-produced American brandies which are made in a continuously processing column still.

Clear Creek Distillery in Oregon not only makes a wonderful wine-based brandy, but also distills from fruit. Its Eau de Vie Pomme is an American take on apple brandy. Calvados, the world's best-known apple brandy, is made in Normandy, where there are many more apple trees than grapevines. Whether American bred or foreign-born, this fiery spirit makes a lovely after-dinner *digestif*.

Finally, I would be remiss if I did not mention pomace brandies. These are the less-polished stepsisters of the brandies mentioned above. They are made by distilling the remnants of the wine-making process, and they can be strong and fiery.

Grappa is an unaged brandy made from the residue left after wine-making. When grapes are pressed in the beginning stages of the wine-making process, the juice is put into a fermenting tank, where it continues the dramatic progression of transformation from grape juice to wine. Left behind, after the pressing, is a dense mass of grape skins, pulp, and seeds, plus stems and leaves. This residue is called "pomace," or, in Italian, *vinaccie*.

Since the grapes are not pressed so hard that all the juice is extracted, the remains still contain liquid. This pomace can be fermented and then distilled. The result, in Italy, is called grappa, in France it is called marc (pronounced "marr").

This harsh distillate was directly descended from the medicines and digestive tonics of the Middle Ages. Grappa was a rough, completely unrefined country brandy, almost like moonshine. As recently as

1933, it was decreed that this traditional spirit must be bottled instead of sold directly from the barrel.

Today's grappa can be very different. Yes, there is still plenty of fiery grappa around that tastes like a fermented compost heap, but it is the carefully made, premium grappas that have captured the attention of connoisseurs.

The gentle process of making modern grappa begins the moment the grapes are first crushed. The pomace is only lightly pressed, kept fresh, and quickly distilled—preferably within 6 hours—to minimize oxidation and to preserve fresh perfumes and flavors.

In the old days, very little attention was paid to the variety of grapes used to make grappa. Whatever pomace was left after wine-making was combined and eventually processed; the residues of various crushings were customarily distilled together. The result was a distillate that was high in alcohol but missing specific flavor and complexity.

Today, a sizable number of the best grappas are made from an individual grape variety, and frequently they derive from a particular vineyard. A few of them are even vintaged. Many of the finest versions carry some very well-known wine names. Lungarotti, Ceretto, Gaja, Marchesi de Gresy, and many other notable Italian wineries now release their own branded grappas.

There are grappas made from Nebbiolo (the red grape from Barolo and Barbaresco), Sangiovese (the red grape from Chianti), Chardonnay, Barbera, Moscato, and Prosecco (the sweet white grape that is made into sparkling wine in the Veneto). Some grappas are made from pomace that comes from specific cuvées for certain wines such as Chianti Classico (a blend of Sangiovese, Canaiolo, Malvasia, and Trebbiano) or Rubesco Torgiano (Sangiovese, Canaiolo, Trebbiano, and Ciliegiolo), while others are vineyard-designated, such as Ceretto's grappa from Brunate, a Barolo vineyard.

Until 1970, wine-makers had stills on their own property and made their own grappas. That year, however, a law was passed forbidding distillation on a winery estate. Most wineries either arranged to have their pomace turned into grappa by a reliable local distiller or built their own distillery, off the property but nearby.

The growth of independent distillers and the increased popularity of grappa in the United States has belatedly introduced consumers to an extremely important name—Nonino. This remarkable family has been distilling grappa in Friuli since 1897.

Nonino has been a leader in the metamorphosis of the grappa industry. In the 1960s, when grappa first became widely known among consumers and sales began to increase, most distillers switched from the slow, discontinuous stills—similar in style to the pot stills used in the production of cognac—to speedy continuous column stills. They managed to produce the quantity of spirits the market demanded, but quality slipped significantly. The Noninos, on the other hand, added more costly *bagna-Maria* (double boiler) stills and decided to focus on quality.

In 1974 Nonino introduced the first varietal grappa, made from Picolit, Friuli's rarest grape. It was packaged in a graceful, hand blown clear glass cruet designed by one of Italy's best architects. This bottle, topped with a plated stopper, has become the Nonino trademark.

The Noninos have been fastidious in encouraging the cultivation of varieties that are in danger of becoming extinct. They now produce a whole line of grappas from these obscure varieties: Fragolino, Ribolla, Tacelenghe, Verduzzo di Ramandolo, Pignola, and Schiopettino. The company has also invented a completely new drink called *ue* (the Italian word for "grape") which is made by distilling whole, uncrushed grapes.

Jacopo Poli of Distilleria Poli in Schiavon enjoys one of the highest reputations not only in Italy but around the world. The brandies of Poli are superb and well presented in delicate crystal bottles. These grappas are produced using fresh pomace, and distilling is done only during the month and a half of grape harvest. In addition to their standard-quality grappa, Sarpa di Poli, the Polis distill single-variety grappas called Amarosa using cabernet, merlot, pinot, and tocolato. The distillery also produces a number of fine fruit brandies and the brandy L'Arzente.

There are a number of special grappas on the market that contain various kinds of fruit or herbs. After several months of steeping, the brandy will begin to pick up the flavors of whatever it contains. Many Northern Italians like to make their own flavored grappas. They buy a good clean grappa and pour it into a wide-mouthed jar, add fresh fruit, seal it, and allow it to stand for a year or two. Several American restaurants have amassed fine collections of this type of grappa.

In the past, grappas were never aged; they were sold almost right out of the still. The new trend is to age the top-of-the-line grappa for a year or two in oak or some other type of wood. This mellows and softens the brandy's harshness.

As seems to be the case with many premium spirits, packaging is part of the allure. Many of these grappas are available in beautiful handblown glass bottles. These bottles range from the beautiful to the whimsical. In some bottles, blown-glass fruit or flowers may provide colorful accents to the clear liquor, while in others the purity of the spirit is highlighted by the simplicity of the bottle's form.

In addition to the lovely Poli and Nonino grappas, there are a number of other fine, high-quality versions that I have tried. Here are my favorites:

- *Lungarotti Rubesco* is distilled from the pomace of the famous Umbrian wine, Rubesco. It is rich and clean, with complex, refined licorice flavors.

- *Andrea da Ponte* makes a lovely Prosecco grappa that is aged 3 years in wood.

- *Ceretto* grappa is made entirely from Nebbiolo grapes grown in Piedmont for the production of Barolo and Barbaresco. This spirit is spicy and dry and has an appealing herbal quality.

- *Ceretto Grappa delle Brunate* is also produced from Nebbiolo. The difference is that this earthy, rich, and herbal spirit is made from the fruit of one single vineyard. The Ceretto firm makes grappa in its own distillery.

- *Gaja Costa Rusi* is a crisp and austere Nebbiolo grappa made from a single Barbaresco vineyard.

Other excellent grappas include L'Aquavite de Castello, Castello di Querceto (Tuscany); Grappa di Capezzana (Tuscany); Monte Vertine (Tuscany); Conte di Cavour (Piedmont); Zeni (Friuli); Jermann (Friuli); and Castello di Gabbiano (Tuscany).

The popularity of imported grappa has inspired some American producers to make grappas of their own. The results have been quite good. Bonny Doon, Creekside, Germain-Robin, and St. George Spirits have made very attractive versions.

The simple distilling process that in Italy creates grappa has been used in Peru and Chile to create pisco. The extracted pulp and juice from grapes, primarily the varietal muscatel, is fermented in large containers before being distilled and cooled. Pisco originates in Peru, where it has been made for over 400 years. It is believed that the name *pisco* is the Incan word for a clay vessel used by the tribe to distill a kind of crude beer from corn mash.

Pisco from Peru is generally of a much higher quality than its Chilean cousin. Unlike Chilean pisco, the production of Peruvian pisco is regulated. Pisco from Peru is not blended with water or other neutral spirits. While pisco from Chile gets some of its flavor from being aged in oak casks, Peruvian pisco is aged in casks lined with paraffin, which keeps the liquor clear and the flavor pure.

There are three types of Peruvian pisco. Acholado is distilled from a variety of grapes, while Aromatico uses only muscatel. Puro, the highest-quality pisco and the only one exported in any quantity, is distilled form Quebranta grapes. While Puro is lovely in the traditional Pisco Sour or other mixed drinks, its distinctive dry flavor and aromatic nose make it ideal for sipping alone or on the rocks. It is difficult to find a good pisco in the United States, but the search is definitely worth your while.

# Classics

## Betsy Ross

1½ ounces brandy
1½ ounces port
1 egg yolk
1 teaspoon sugar syrup, or to
    taste
Several dashes of curaçao
Several dashes of bitters
1 scoop crushed ice
Freshly ground nutmeg

Mix all ingredients, except the nutmeg, in a shaker. Strain the mixture into a chilled cocktail glass. Top with a sprinkle of the nutmeg.

## Bob Danby

1 ounce brandy
2 to 3 ounces Dubonnet rouge

Put both ingredients in a mixing glass filled with ice cubes. Stir well and strain into a chilled cocktail glass.

## Brandy Alexander

1½ ounces brandy
1 ounce crème de cacao

1 ounce heavy cream
1 scoop crushed ice

Mix all ingredients in a shaker. Strain the mixture into a chilled cocktail glass.

## Brandy Daisy I

2 ounces brandy
1¼ ounces lemon juice
½ teaspoon sugar
¼ ounce grenadine
Crushed ice

Mix all ingredients in a shaker. Shake well and pour into a large cocktail glass.

## Brandy Daisy II

2 to 3 ounces brandy
Juice of ½ lemon
½ ounce raspberry syrup or
    grenadine
1 teaspoon sugar syrup
1 scoop crushed ice
Club soda
Dash of Pernod
Peach or orange slice
Pineapple stick
Maraschino cherry

Mix the first five ingredients in a shaker. Pour the mixture into a chilled wineglass and add additional ice. Stir briskly until the glass is frosted. Top off with the cold club soda and the Pernod. Garnish with the fruit.

## Brandy Eggnog

2 to 3 ounces brandy
½ ounce sugar syrup, or to taste
1 cup milk
1 egg
1 scoop crushed ice
Freshly ground nutmeg

Mix all ingredients, except the nutmeg, in a shaker. Strain the mixture into a chilled highball glass. Sprinkle the nutmeg on top.

## Brandy Manhattan

2 ounces brandy
½ ounce sweet or dry vermouth
Dash of bitters
1 maraschino cherry

In a mixing glass, stir the brandy, vermouth, and bitters. Strain the mixture into a chilled cocktail glass and garnish with the cherry.

## Brandy Old-Fashioned

1 sugar cube
Several dashes of bitters
3 ounces brandy
Lemon peel

Place the sugar cube in a chilled old-fashioned glass. Add the bitters and a dash of cold water and stir until the sugar cube is dissolved. Add ice cubes and the brandy. Twist the lemon peel over the drink and drop it in.

## Brandy Sour

2 ounces brandy
1 ounce lemon juice
½ ounce orange juice (optional)
1 teaspoon sugar syrup, or to taste
1 scoop crushed ice
1 maraschino cherry

Combine all ingredients, except the cherry, in a shaker. Mix well and strain into a chilled whiskey sour glass. Garnish with the cherry.

## Pisco Sour

3 parts chilled pisco
1 part fresh lemon or lime juice
Powdered sugar to taste
1 egg white

Add all ingredients to a cocktail shaker. Shake hard to blend. Strain into a champagne glass.

# Creative Concoctions

## Alabama

1 ounce brandy
1 ounce curaçao
½ ounce lime juice
½ teaspoon sugar syrup, or to taste
1 scoop crushed ice
Orange peel

Combine all ingredients, except the orange peel, in a shaker. Mix well and strain into a chilled cocktail glass. Twist the orange peel over the drink and drop it in.

## American Rose

1½ ounces brandy
1 teaspoon grenadine
½ fresh peach, peeled and mashed
Several dashes of Pernod
1 scoop crushed ice
Champagne or sparkling wine

Mix all ingredients, except the champagne or wine, in a shaker. Pour the mixture into a chilled wineglass. Top off with the champagne or wine and stir gently.

## Apple Blossom

1½ ounces brandy
1 ounce apple juice
1 teaspoon lemon juice
1 scoop crushed ice
Lemon slice

Mix all ingredients, except the lemon slice, in a shaker. Strain the mixture into a chilled cocktail glass and garnish with the lemon slice.

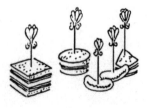

## Apple Brandy Cooler

2 ounces brandy
1 ounce light rum
4 ounces apple juice
½ ounce lime juice
1 teaspoon sugar syrup to taste
1 scoop crushed ice
1 teaspoon dark rum
Lime slice

Mix all ingredients, except the dark rum and lime slice, in a shaker. Pour the mixture into a chilled collins glass. Top off with a float of the dark rum and garnish with the lime slice.

## Banana Peel

1½ ounces brandy
¾ ounce crème de banane
½ ounce lemon juice
1 scoop crushed ice
Club soda
Lemon wedge
Banana slice

Mix the first four ingredients in a shaker. Pour the mixture into a chilled collins glass. Top off with the cold club soda and stir gently. Decorate with the lemon wedge and banana slice.

## Beach Street Cooler

1½ ounces brandy
½ ounce curaçao
½ ounce lemon juice
1 scoop crushed ice
Cola

Mix all ingredients, except the cola, in a shaker. Pour the mixture into a chilled collins glass. Top off with the cold cola.

## Beau's Sister

1½ ounces brandy
1 ounce white crème de menthe
1 ounce heavy cream
1 scoop crushed ice

Combine all ingredients in a shaker. Mix well and pour into a chilled cocktail glass.

## Blackberry Slammer

1 ounce cognac or other brandy
½ ounce blackberry brandy
1 ounce coffee brandy
½ ounce dry vermouth
½ ounce amaretto
1 ounce lemon juice
1 scoop crushed ice

Mix all ingredients in a shaker. Pour the mixture into a chilled brandy snifter.

## Bombay

1 ounce brandy
1 ounce dry vermouth
½ ounce sweet vermouth
½ teaspoon curaçao
Dash of Pernod
1 scoop crushed ice
Orange slice

Mix all ingredients, except the orange slice, in a shaker. Pour the mixture into a chilled old-fashioned glass. Garnish with the orange slice.

## Bosom Caresser

1½ ounces brandy
½ ounce triple sec or curaçao
1 teaspoon grenadine
1 scoop crushed ice

Mix all ingredients in a shaker. Strain the mixture into a chilled cocktail glass.

## Bowdoin Appleball

2 ounces apple brandy
Ginger ale or club soda
Lemon peel

Pour the apple brandy into a chilled highball glass with several ice cubes. Top off the glass with the ginger ale or club soda. Stir gently. Twist the lemon peel over the drink and drop it in.

## Bracer Highball

1½ ounces brandy
¼ ounce anisette
1 dash of Angostura bitters
½ teaspoon sugar
½ ounce lemon juice
1 egg
Club soda

In a shaker with crushed ice, mix all ingredients except the soda. Strain the mixture into a highball glass. Top off with the cold club soda and add ice if necessary.

## Brandied Apricot

Granulated sugar
1½ ounces brandy
½ ounce apricot-flavored brandy
1 ounce lemon juice
Orange peel

Press the moistened rim of a cocktail glass into the sugar. In a shaker with crushed ice, mix the brandies and lemon juice. Pour the mixture into the sugar-rimmed glass and garnish with the orange peel.

## Brandied Banana Collins

1½ ounces brandy
1 ounce crème de banane
1 ounce lemon juice
Cold club soda
Lemon wedge
Banana slice

Pour the brandy, crème de banane, and lemon juice into a shaker. Mix well and strain into a tall glass. Top off the glass with ice cubes and the soda. Garnish with the lemon wedge and banana slice.

## Brandied Apricot Flip

1½ ounces brandy
½ ounce apricot-flavored brandy
1 egg
1 teaspoon sugar
1 scoop crushed ice
Freshly grated nutmeg

Mix all ingredients, except the nutmeg, in a shaker. Pour the mixture into a cocktail glass and sprinkle the nutmeg on top.

## Brandied Cordial Médoc

1½ ounces brandy
½ ounce Cordial Médoc
½ ounce lemon juice
Crushed ice
Orange peel

Mix all ingredients, except the orange peel, in a shaker. Pour the mixture into a cocktail glass and garnish with the orange peel.

## Brandied Ginger

1½ ounces brandy
½ ounce ginger-flavored brandy
¼ ounce lime juice
¼ ounce orange juice

Combine all ingredients in a shaker with crushed ice. Shake well and strain into a cocktail glass.

## Brandied Madeira

1 ounce brandy
1 ounce Madeira
½ ounce dry vermouth
Lemon twist

In a mixing glass, stir the brandy, Madeira, and vermouth. Pour the mixture into a cocktail glass and garnish with the lemon twist.

## Brandied Peach Fizz

1½ ounces brandy
½ ounce peach-flavored brandy
½ ounce lemon juice
½ teaspoon sugar
¼ ounce banana liqueur
Club soda
Peach slice

Combine all ingredients, except the soda and peach slice, in a shaker with crushed ice. Mix well and strain into a tall glass. Top off with the cold club soda and several ice cubes. Garnish with the peach slice.

## Brandied Peach Sling

1½ ounces brandy
½ ounce peach-flavored brandy
1 ounce lemon juice
1 teaspoon sugar
Club soda
Lemon twist
Peach slice

In a shaker with crushed ice, mix the first four ingredients. Strain the mixture into a tall glass with fresh ice cubes. Top off with the cold club soda. Garnish with the lemon twist and peach slice.

## Brandied Port

¾ ounce brandy
¾ ounce tawny port
¼ ounce maraschino liqueur
¾ ounce lemon juice
Crushed ice
Orange slice

Mix all ingredients, except the orange slice, in a shaker. Strain the mixture into a cocktail glass and garnish with the orange slice.

## Brandt

2 ounces brandy
½ ounce white crème de menthe
2 dashes of bitters
Lemon twist

In a mixing glass with ice, stir the brandy, crème de menthe, and bitters. Pour the mixture into a cocktail glass and garnish with the lemon twist.

## Brandy Apricot Frappe

Finely crushed ice
¾ ounce brandy
¼ ounce crème de noyaux
½ ounce apricot-flavored brandy

Pack a cocktail glass with crushed ice, building the ice into a snow cone. Stir the ingredients in a mixing glass and pour over the crushed ice.

## Brandy Berry Fix

1 teaspoon superfine sugar
Splash of water
2 ounces brandy
¼ ounce strawberry liqueur
¾ ounce lemon juice
1 scoop crushed ice
Lemon wedge
Several fresh strawberries

In a highball glass, dissolve the sugar in the splash of water. Pour in the brandy, liqueur, and lemon juice. Fill the glass with the crushed ice and stir well. Garnish with the lemon wedge and fresh strawberries.

## Brandy Blizzard

1½ ounces brandy
¼ ounce white crème de menthe
½ ounce lemon juice
1 scoop crushed ice
Ginger ale
Several seedless grapes

Mix the first four ingredients in a shaker. Pour the mixture into a chilled highball glass. Top off the glass with the ginger ale and stir gently. Garnish with the seedless grapes.

## Brandy Champerelle

½ ounce brandy
½ ounce curaçao
½ ounce yellow Chartreuse
½ ounce anisette

Prechill all the ingredients, and carefully pour each ingredient, in the order listed, into a chilled sherry glass. Each layer should float on the one beneath it. To properly layer, slowly pour the liqueurs over the back of a spoon.

## Brandy Cooler

2½ ounces brandy
Ginger ale
Lemon peel, cut in a spiral

Pour the brandy into a glass filled with ice cubes. Top off with the ginger ale and garnish with the lemon spiral.

## Brandy Crusta

Lemon wedge
Sugar
1½ ounces brandy
¼ ounce maraschino liqueur
1 dash of bitters
¼ ounce lemon juice
½ ounce orange curaçao

Moisten the rim of a glass with a lemon wedge. Press the rim into the sugar, then drop the lemon wedge into the glass. In a shaker with crushed ice, mix the rest of the ingredients. Strain the mixture into the prepared glass.

## Brandy Fancy

2 ounces brandy
¼ ounce maraschino liqueur
1 dash of orange bitters
1 dash of bitters

In a mixing glass with ice, stir all ingredients. Pour the mixture into a fresh cocktail glass.

## Brandy Fix

2 to 3 ounces brandy
1 teaspoon sugar syrup
1 teaspoon water
Juice of ½ lemon

Pour all ingredients into a chilled old-fashioned glass. Fill the glass with ice and stir until frosty.

## Brandy Float

Club soda
1½ ounces brandy

Place several ice cubes in an old-fashioned glass. Fill the glass three quarters full with the cold club soda. Top off with a float of the brandy.

## Brandy Fizz

1½ ounces brandy
1¼ ounces lemon juice
1 teaspoon superfine sugar
Club soda
2 dashes of yellow Chartreuse
  (optional)

In a shaker with crushed ice, mix the brandy, lemon juice, and sugar. Strain the mixture into a tall collins glass. Top off with the cold club soda and fresh ice. If desired, float the Chartreuse on top.

## Brandy Frappe

1½ ounces brandy
1 ounce dark rum
½ ounce lemon or lime juice
1 teaspoon orgeat
1 egg yolk
1 scoop crushed ice

In a blender, mix all ingredients until slushy. Spoon the blend into a chilled wineglass.

## Brandy Gump Cocktail

1½ ounces brandy
1¼ ounces lemon juice
¼ ounce grenadine
1 scoop crushed ice

In a shaker, mix all ingredients. Strain the mixture into a cocktail glass.

## Brandy Julep

6 mint leaves
1 teaspoon sugar syrup
1 scoop finely crushed ice
Brandy
Mint sprig
Confectioners' sugar

Place the mint leaves in a chilled double old-fashioned glass. Add the syrup and a small amount of cold water. Muddle the leaves until bruised, then fill the glass with the crushed ice. Top off with the brandy and stir until the glass is frosted. Add the more ice if necessary. Garnish with the mint sprig and dust with the sugar.

## Brandy Melba

1½ ounces brandy
½ ounce peach schnapps
¼ ounce raspberry liqueur
½ ounce lemon juice
Several dashes of orange bitters
1 scoop crushed ice
Peach slice

Mix all ingredients, except the peach slice, in a shaker. Strain the mixture into a chilled cocktail glass and garnish with the peach slice.

## Brandy Mint Fizz

1½ ounces brandy
¼ ounce white crème de menthe
¼ ounce light crème de cacao
¾ ounce lemon juice
½ teaspoon sugar
1 scoop crushed ice
Club soda
Mint sprigs

Mix all ingredients, except the soda and mint sprigs, in a shaker. Strain the mixture into a tall glass. Top off with the cold club soda and ice. Garnish with the mint sprigs.

## Brandy Puff

1½ ounces brandy
3 ounces milk
Club soda

Pour the brandy into a chilled highball glass with several ice cubes. Add the milk and top off with the chilled club soda.

## Brandy Punch

2 ounces brandy
¼ ounce orange curaçao
¼ ounce rum
½ teaspoon superfine sugar
Squirt of club soda

Add all ingredients, except the soda, to a highball glass. Fill the glass with ice and top off with the soda.

## Brandy Sangaree

½ teaspoon superfine sugar
Dash of water
2 to 3 ounces brandy
Freshly ground nutmeg

Dissolve the sugar with a little water in a double old-fashioned glass. Add the ice cubes and the brandy. Stir well and top with a sprinkle of the nutmeg.

## Brandy Swizzle

1½ ounces lime juice
1 teaspoon sugar
Club soda
1 scoop crushed ice
2 ounces brandy
2 dashes of bitters
Lime peel

In a tall glass, mix the lime juice, the sugar, and 2 ounces of the club soda. Fill the glass with the crushed ice and stir well. Add the brandy and the bitters. Top off with the rest of the club soda and stir vigorously. Garnish with the lime peel.

## Brandy Zoom

1 teaspoon honey
Hot water
2 ounces brandy
¼ ounce heavy cream

In a mixing glass, dissolve the honey in a splash of the hot water. Pour the honey into a shaker with the brandy, cream, and crushed ice. Shake well and pour into a cocktail glass.

## Chicago

Lemon wedge
Superfine sugar
1½ ounces brandy
Dash of curaçao
Dash of bitters
Sparkling wine or champagne

Using a lemon wedge, moisten the rim of a chilled wineglass. Roll the rim in the sugar until it is evenly coated. Mix the brandy, curaçao, and bitters with crushed ice in a mixing glass. Strain the mixture into the glass. Top off with the wine or cold champagne.

## Coffee Cocktail

1½ ounces brandy
¾ ounce port
Several dashes of curaçao
Several dashes of sugar syrup
1 egg yolk
1 scoop crushed ice
Freshly ground nutmeg

Mix all ingredients, except the nutmeg, in a shaker. Strain the mixture into a chilled cocktail glass. Sprinkle the nutmeg on top.

## Columbia

1½ ounces brandy
½ ounce sweet vermouth
¼ ounce lemon juice
1 teaspoon grenadine
Dash of bitters
1 scoop crushed ice

Combine all ingredients in a shaker. Mix well and strain into a chilled cocktail glass.

## Continental

1½ ounces brandy
1 ounce gin
1 teaspoon dry vermouth
Lemon peel or green olive

Combine the first three ingredients in a mixing glass with ice cubes. Stir well and strain into a chilled cocktail glass. Twist the lemon peel over the drink and drop in, or garnish with the cocktail olive.

## Cool Java

1 ounce brandy
1 ounce triple sec
1 ounce cold black coffee
1 scoop crushed ice

Mix all ingredients in a shaker. Pour the mixture into a chilled parfait glass.

## Creamsicle

*Makes 4 servings*

½ cup brandy
Orange juice
Heavy cream

Fill a blender with ice. Add the brandy. Fill blender to the three-quarter mark with the orange juice. Add the cream to top. Blend well. Pour into rocks glasses.

## Deauville

1 ounce brandy
¾ ounce apple brandy
½ ounce triple sec
½ ounce lemon juice
1 scoop crushed ice

Mix all ingredients in a shaker. Strain the mixture into a chilled cocktail glass.

## Fantasio

1 ounce brandy
¾ ounces dry vermouth
1 teaspoon white crème de cacao
1 teaspoon maraschino liqueur
1 scoop crushed ice

Mix all ingredients in a shaker. Pour the mixture into a chilled cocktail glass.

## Feather Boa

2 ounces brandy
1 ounce dry vermouth
½ ounce Cointreau
Dash of bitters
Lemon twist

Stir the first four ingredients with cracked ice. Strain into a chilled cocktail glass. Garnish with the lemon twist.

## Foghorn

*Makes 2 servings*

4 ounces brandy
2 ounces curaçao
1 egg white
2 scoops crushed ice
Freshly ground nutmeg

In a shaker, mix the first four ingredients. Pour the mixture into chilled cocktail glasses. Sprinkle the nutmeg on top.

## Foxhound

1½ ounces brandy
½ ounce cranberry juice
1 teaspoon kümmel
1 teaspoon lemon juice
1 scoop crushed ice
Lemon slice

Mix all ingredients, except the lemon slice, in a shaker. Pour the mixture into a chilled old-fashioned glass. Garnish with the lemon slice.

## French Green Dragon

1½ ounces brandy
1½ ounces green Chartreuse

In a shaker with crushed ice, mix the brandy and Chartreuse. Strain the mixture into a chilled cocktail glass.

## Frozen Frenzy

1½ ounces brandy
½ ounce peach schnapps
4 ounces orange juice
1 scoop crushed ice

Mix all ingredients in a shaker. Pour the mixture into a chilled double old-fashioned glass.

## Gazette

1½ ounces brandy
1 ounce sweet vermouth
1 teaspoon lemon juice
1 teaspoon sugar syrup
1 scoop crushed ice

Mix all ingredients in a shaker or blender. Pour the mixture into a chilled cocktail glass.

## Georgia Peach Fizz

1½ ounces brandy
½ ounce peach brandy
½ ounce lemon juice
1 teaspoon crème de banane
1 teaspoon sugar syrup
1 scoop crushed ice
Club soda
Fresh or brandied peach slice

Mix the first six ingredients in a shaker or blender. Pour the mixture into a chilled collins glass. Top off with the cold club soda and stir gently. Garnish with the peach slice.

## Gold Dragon

1½ ounces brandy
1½ ounces yellow Chartreuse
1 scoop crushed ice
Lemon peel

In a mixer, shake the brandy, Chartreuse, and ice. Strain the mixture into a chilled cocktail glass. Garnish with the lemon peel.

## Goodbye

*Makes 2 servings*

2 ounces brandy
2 ounces sloe gin
½ ounce lemon juice
1 egg white
2 scoops crushed ice

In a shaker, mix all ingredients. Strain the mixture into chilled cocktail glasses.

## Island Milk

2 ounces brandy
½ ounce dark rum
6 ounces milk
1 teaspoon sugar syrup, or to taste
1 scoop crushed ice
Powdered cinnamon or freshly ground nutmeg

Mix all ingredients, except the cinnamon or nutmeg, in a shaker. Pour the mixture into a chilled highball glass. Sprinkle with the cinnamon or nutmeg.

## Japan Town

2 ounces brandy
¼ ounce orgeat
¼ ounce lime juice
Dash of bitters
1 scoop crushed ice
Lime peel

Mix all ingredients, except the lime peel, in a shaker. Strain the mixture into a chilled cocktail glass. Twist the lime peel over the drink and drop it in.

## Kiss from Heaven

1 ounce brandy
¾ ounce Drambuie
¾ ounce dry vermouth

Stir all ingredients in a mixing glass with ice. Pour the mixture into a chilled cocktail glass.

## La Jolla

1½ ounces brandy
½ ounce crème de banane
¼ ounce lemon juice
1 teaspoon orange juice
1 scoop crushed ice

Combine all ingredients in a shaker. Mix well and strain into a chilled cocktail glass.

## Lifesaver

1½ ounces brandy
¾ ounce cherry brandy or cherry liqueur
½ ounce curaçao
½ lemon juice
¼ ounce grenadine
1 teaspoon sugar syrup
1 scoop crushed ice

Mix all ingredients in a shaker. Strain the mixture into a chilled cocktail glass.

## Loudspeaker

1 ounce brandy
1 ounce gin
¼ ounce triple sec
½ ounce lemon juice
1 scoop crushed ice

Combine all ingredients in a shaker. Mix well and strain into a cocktail glass.

## Montecito

1½ ounces brandy
½ ounce triple sec
Cola
Lemon slice

Pour the brandy and triple sec over ice in a chilled collins glass. Top off with the cold cola and garnish with the lemon slice.

## Olympic Lady

1½ ounces brandy
1 ounce apricot brandy
½ ounce amaretto
1 scoop crushed ice

In a shaker, mix all ingredients. Strain the mixture into a chilled cocktail glass.

## Santa Barbara Bracer

*Makes 2 servings*

2 ounces brandy
2 ounces anisette
1 egg white
Crushed ice

Mix all ingredients in a shaker. Pour the mixture into 2 chilled cocktail glasses.

## Southern Belle

1½ ounces brandy
¾ ounce Southern Comfort
½ ounce lemon juice
Several dashes of orange bitters
1 scoop crushed ice

Combine all ingredients in a shaker. Mix well and strain into a chilled cocktail glass.

# Signature Drinks

## Anatole Coffee

LOEWS ANATOLE HOTEL, DALLAS

½ ounce brandy
½ ounce coffee liqueur
½ ounce hazelnut liqueur
Cold black coffee
Whipped cream
Chocolate shavings

Mix the first four ingredients in a blender with ice. Pour the mixture into a chilled wineglass. Top off with the whipped cream and chocolate shavings.

## Boss McClure Cocktail

VISTA INTERNATIONAL HOTEL, WASHINGTON, D.C.

1 ounce brandy
1 ounce gin
½ ounce orange curaçao
½ ounce apricot liqueur
1 scoop crushed ice
Lemon twist

Mix all ingredients, except the lemon twist, in a shaker. Strain the mixture into a chilled cocktail glass and garnish with the lemon twist.

## Piscorita

CIUDAD, LOS ANGELES

1 lime, cut into 5 slices
Margarita or kosher salt
2 ounces pisco
1 ounce triple sec
1 tablespoon freshly squeezed
    lemon juice
½ cup ice cubes

Arrange 3 lime slices on a small plate and cover another plate with salt to a depth of a quarter-inch. Place a martini glass upside down on the limes and turn to dampen, then dip in salt to coat the rim. Combine the pisco, triple sec, lemon juice, and ice in a blender. Blend at high speed until smooth. Pour into the prepared glass. Garnish with the remaining lime slices and serve.

## The Raphael Kiss

RAPHAEL HOTEL, CHICAGO

½ ounce brandy
4 ounces vanilla ice cream
2 ounces chocolate ice cream
½ ounce coffee liqueur
½ ounce Sambuca
½ ounce heavy cream
Lime wedge
Cinnamon and sugar mixture

In a blender, mix the brandy, ice cream, coffee liqueur, and cream. Prepare a wineglass by moistening it with the lime wedge and then coating it with the cinnamon-sugar mixture. Pour the blended ingredients into the wineglass. Float the Sambuca on top.

# Tropical Drinks

## Sunshine Colada

¾ ounce brandy
1 ounce cream of coconut
1½ ounces orange juice
½ ounce heavy cream
½ ounce orange liqueur
1 cup ice

Combine all ingredients in a blender and blend until smooth. Pour the mixture into a chilled parfait glass.

# Hot Drinks

## *Alahambra Royale*

1 cup hot chocolate
1 orange peel
1½ ounces brandy
1 tablespoon whipped cream

Fill a mug nearly to the brim with the hot chocolate. Add the orange peel. Warm the brandy in a ladle over hot water. Ignite the brandy and, as it blazes, pour it into the hot chocolate. Stir well and top with a dollop of the whipped cream.

## *Café Diablo*

*Makes 4 servings*

2 cinnamon sticks
8 whole cloves
6 whole coffee beans
2 ounces brandy or cognac
1 ounce Cointreau or triple sec
1 ounce hot curaçao
1 pint hot, strong black coffee

Place all ingredients, except the coffee, in a chafing dish. Warm the contents over a low, direct heat. Ignite and allow to blaze for a few seconds. Add the coffee and mix well. Pour into mugs.

## *Hot Brandy Flip*

2 ounces brandy (rum, gin, or whiskey may also be used)
1 whole egg
1 teaspoon sugar syrup, or to taste
Freshly ground nutmeg

Mix the brandy, egg, and sugar syrup in a saucepan. Heat and pour into a warm mug or glass. Sprinkle with the nutmeg.

# Applejack

## Apple Blow Fizz

*Makes 2 servings*

5½ ounces applejack
½ teaspoon lemon juice
2 teaspoons sugar syrup, or to
   taste
1 egg white
1 scoop crushed ice
Club soda

Mix all ingredients, except the soda, in a shaker. Pour the mixture into 2 chilled highball glasses with ice cubes. Top off the glasses with the cold club soda and stir gently.

## Apple Buck

1½ ounces applejack
½ ounce lemon juice
1 teaspoon ginger-flavored
   brandy
1 scoop crushed ice
Cold ginger ale
Preserved ginger

Mix the first four ingredients in a shaker. Pour the mixture into a chilled highball glass. Top off with the ginger ale. Stir gently and garnish with the ginger.

## Apple Fizz

2 ounces applejack
4 ounces apple juice
Dash of lime juice
Club soda
Lime slice

Add all ingredients, except the lime slice, to a chilled collins glass filled with ice cubes. Stir well and garnish with the lime slice.

## Apple Sidecar

1½ ounces applejack
½ ounce triple sec
½ ounce lime juice
1 scoop crushed ice

In a shaker, mix all the ingredients. Pour the mixture into a chilled cocktail glass.

## Applejack Collins

2 ounces applejack
1 ounce lemon juice
1 teaspoon sugar syrup
Several dashes of orange bitters
1 scoop crushed ice
Club soda
Lemon slice

Mix all ingredients, except the soda and lemon slice, in a shaker or blender. Pour the mixture into a chilled collins glass. Top off with the cold club soda and stir gently. Garnish with the lemon slice.

## Applejack Manhattan

1¾ ounces applejack
¾ ounce sweet vermouth
Dash of orange bitters
1 maraschino cherry

Mix the applejack, vermouth, and bitters in a glass with ice cubes. Stir well and strain into a chilled cocktail glass. Garnish with the cherry.

## Big Apple

2 ounces applejack
½ ounce amaretto
3 ounces apple juice
1 tablespoon applesauce
Ground cinnamon

Mix all ingredients, except the cinnamon, in a blender with ice. Blend until smooth. Pour the mixture into a chilled parfait glass and sprinkle with the cinnamon before serving.

## Central Park

1 ounce applejack
1 ounce apricot brandy
½ ounce gin
½ ounce orange juice
1 scoop crushed ice
Several dashes of grenadine

Mix all ingredients, except the grenadine, in a shaker. Strain the mixture into a chilled cocktail glass. Top off with a float of the grenadine.

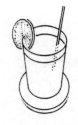

## Corpse Reviver

1½ ounces applejack
¾ ounce brandy
½ ounce sweet vermouth
1 scoop crushed ice

In a shaker, mix all ingredients. Strain the mixture into a chilled cocktail glass.

## Jack-in-the-Box

1½ ounces applejack
1 ounce pineapple juice
1 ounce lemon juice
Several dashes of bitters
1 scoop crushed ice

In a shaker, mix all ingredients. Strain the mixture into a chilled cocktail glass.

## Jackrose

2 ounces applejack
½ ounce lime or lemon juice
1 teaspoon grenadine
1 scoop crushed ice

In a shaker, mix all ingredients. Strain the mixture into a chilled cocktail glass.

## Java Flip

1 ounce brandy
½ ounce port
4 ounces coffee
½ teaspoon sugar syrup
1 scoop crushed ice
Freshly ground nutmeg

Mix all ingredients, except the nutmeg, in a shaker. Pour the mixture into a chilled wineglass and sprinkle with the nutmeg.

## Marconi Wireless

1½ ounces apple brandy
½ ounce sweet vermouth
Several dashes of orange bitters
1 scoop crushed ice

Combine all ingredients in a shaker. Mix well and pour into a chilled cocktail glass.

## Midnight Oasis

1 ounce apricot brandy
½ ounce triple sec
1 tablespoon lemon juice

Shake all ingredients along with a scoop of ice in a cocktail shaker. Strain into a chilled cocktail glass.

## Mount Fuji

1½ ounces applejack
1½ ounces light rum
1 ounce Southern Comfort
1 ounce sugar
Juice of ½ lime
1 scoop crushed ice
1 ounce 151-proof rum
Scooped-out ½ lime shell

Mix all ingredients, except the 151-proof rum and the lime shell, in a blender. Pour the mixture into a sour glass. Place the lime shell on top so that it forms a small bowl. Fill the lime shell with the 151-proof rum and ignite it. The heat will melt the icy drink so you can sip it through a straw.

## Red Apple

1½ ounces applejack
1½ ounces grapefruit juice
Several dashes of grenadine
1 scoop crushed ice

Mix all ingredients in a shaker. Pour the mixture into a chilled cocktail glass.

## Snap Apple

3 ounces applejack
½ ounce sweet vermouth
4 ounces orange juice
½ ounce sugar syrup, or to taste
1 teaspoon lemon juice
1 scoop crushed ice

Mix all ingredients in a shaker. Pour the mixture into a chilled collins glass with additional ice.

## Sour Apple

2 ounces applejack
1 ounce lemon juice
1 teaspoon sugar syrup, or to taste
1 scoop crushed ice

Mix all ingredients in a shaker. Strain the mixture into a chilled cocktail glass.

## Sweet Apple

1½ ounces applejack
½ ounce lime juice
1 teaspoon raspberry syrup
1 scoop crushed ice
Club soda
1 teaspoon ginger brandy
Lime slice

Mix the first four ingredients in a shaker. Pour the mixture into a chilled highball glass and top off with the cold club soda. Stir gently.

Carefully pour the ginger brandy over the back of a spoon so that it floats on top. Garnish with the lime slice.

# Apricot Brandy

## Apricot

2 ounces apricot brandy
1 ounce orange juice
1 ounce lemon juice
Several dashes of gin
1 scoop crushed ice

In a shaker, mix all ingredients. Pour the mixture into a chilled cocktail glass.

## Big Dipper

1 ounce apricot brandy
¾ ounce crème de cacao
¾ teaspoon cream
1 teaspoon grenadine
1 scoop crushed ice

Combine all ingredients in a shaker. Mix well and pour into a chilled cocktail glass.

## Apricot Brandy Fizz

2 ounces apricot brandy
Several dashes of grenadine
Lemon peel
Orange slice
Club soda

Pour the brandy and grenadine into a chilled old-fashioned glass. Add several ice cubes, the lemon peel, and the orange slice. Top off the glass with the soda and stir gently.

## Bronx Cheer

2 ounces apricot brandy
6 ounces raspberry soda
Orange peel

In a chilled collins glass, mix the brandy, soda, and several ice cubes. Twist the orange peel over the drink and drop it in.

## Golden Gate

1½ ounces apricot brandy
2 ounces orange juice
1 ounce lemon juice
½ ounce orgeat, or to taste
1 scoop crushed ice

Mix all ingredients in a shaker. Pour the mixture into a chilled cocktail glass.

## Nob Hill Cricket

2 ounces apricot brandy
½ ounce sloe gin
½ ounce lime juice
1 scoop crushed ice

In a shaker, mix all ingredients. Pour the mixture into a chilled cocktail glass.

## Hotel California

2 ounces apricot brandy
4 ounces orange soda
1 scoop orange sherbet
1 cup ice cubes

Combine all ingredients in a blender. For a foamier drink, add additional ice cubes. Blend until smooth. Pour the mixture into a parfait glass.

## Tempter Cocktail

2 ounces apricot brandy
2 ounces port

In a mixing glass with ice, stir the brandy and port. Strain the mixture into a chilled cocktail glass.

## Midnight Oasis

1 ounce apricot brandy
½ ounce triple sec
1 tablespoon lemon juice

Shake all ingredients along with a scoop of ice in a cocktail shaker. Strain into a chilled cocktail glass.

## Why Not

1 ounce apricot brandy
1 ounce gin
½ ounce dry vermouth
Dash of lemon juice

Place all ingredients along with a scoop of ice in a cocktail shaker. Shake vigorously to mix. Strain into a chilled cocktail glass.

# Blackberry Brandy

## Black Sheep

2 ounces blackberry brandy
1 ounce blackberry liqueur
½ ounce lime juice
1 scoop crushed ice

Mix all ingredients in a shaker. Strain the mixture into a chilled cocktail glass.

## Yellowfingers

BULL AND BEAR BAR,
WALDORF-ASTORIA, NEW YORK CITY

1 ounce blackberry brandy
1 ounce crème de banane
½ ounce gin
½ ounce heavy cream
1 scoop crushed ice

Combine all ingredients in a shaker. Mix well and strain into a chilled old-fashioned glass.

# Cherry Brandy (Kirsch)

## Cherry Cola

1 ounce cherry brandy
½ ounce maraschino liqueur
4 ounces cola
1 maraschino cherry

Pour the brandy, liqueur, and cold cola into a highball glass over ice cubes. Stir well and garnish with the cherry.

## Ostend Fizz

1 ounce cherry brandy
1 ounce crème de cassis
Club soda
Lemon peel

In a highball glass, stir the brandy, crème de cassis, and ice. Top off with the cold club soda. Twist the lemon peel over the drink and drop it in.

## Spinster

1½ ounces cherry brandy
1 ounce maraschino liqueur
1 scoop crushed ice
1 maraschino cherry

Mix all ingredients, except the cherry, in a shaker. Strain the mixture into a chilled cocktail glass and garnish with the cherry.

## Villa Bella Fizz

1½ ounces cherry brandy
1 ounce light rum
1 egg white
½ teaspoon granulated sugar
1 tablespoon fresh lime juice
1 scoop crushed ice
Club soda
1 maraschino cherry

Combine all ingredients, except the soda and cherry, in a shaker. Mix well and strain into a highball glass. Top off the glass with the cold soda and garnish with the cherry.

# Grappa

## Caffe Corretto

One shot of espresso
1 ounce grappa
Sugar to taste

Brew the espresso. Add the grappa. Stir. Add sugar as needed.

## Caffe Corretto on Ice

One shot espresso
Sugar to taste
4 teaspoons grappa
Ground cloves and cinnamon

Brew the espresso. Stir in the sugar and let it dissolve. Allow the espresso to cool. Stir in the grappa. Sprinkle with ground cloves and cinnamon.

## Grappa Highball

1 ounce grappa
Dash of orange bitters
Splash of club soda
Lemon twist

In a rocks glass over ice, combine the grappa and bitters. Add the splash of soda and stir. Garnish with the twist of lemon.

## Grappa Sour

3 tablespoons grappa
4 to 6 teaspoons lemon juice
2 to 4 teaspoons sugar syrup

Combine all ingredients in a mixing glass with ice. Stir well. Strain over ice into a highball glass.

## Venetian Sunset

FELIDIA, NEW YORK CITY

1 ounce grappa
¼ ounce Campari
2 ounces orange juice
1 teaspoon sugar
½ orange slice
1 mint leaf

In an ice-filled shaker, mix the first four ingredients. Strain the mixture into a large chilled cocktail glass. Garnish with the orange slice and mint leaf.

# Pear Brandy

## Pear Sour

FOUR SEASONS HOTEL, NEW YORK CITY

2 ounces pear brandy or pear schnapps
1 ounce lemon juice
½ ounce sugar syrup
Brandied pear slice

Combine all ingredients, except the pear slice, in a shaker with crushed ice. Mix well and strain into a chilled cocktail glass. Garnish with the pear slice.

# LIQUEURS AND BITTERS

Like that last bit of chocolate licked from the lips, liqueurs are lusciously sweet drinks meant to be savored. Capturing the essence of some of the world's most unique and beautiful flavors, these potions provide an ideal endnote to a wonderful meal. Explore the world of liqueurs and you'll taste oranges from the Orient, herbs from western France, coffee beans from Mexico, and cream from Ireland.

The word "liqueur" comes from the Latin *liquefacere,* which means "to melt" or "to dissolve." Liqueurs get their character from nuts, beans, seeds, spirits, herbs, fruits, and cream. These elements give their essence to the liqueur in one of two basic ways, maceration or distillation.

Maceration is usually used for the production of liqueurs flavored with fruits and grains. This very simple technique consists of soaking the fruits and/or grains in the base alcohol. The flavor of the liqueur is determined by the length of the soaking process and the condition of the fruit.

Distillation is used to concentrate aromatic elements, not to produce alcohol, since the base liquid is alcohol. The object is to marry the aromatic essences of plants and herbs as they rise with the ascending alcoholic vapors. After a double distillation, the distillate is aged.

Distillates are often blended with the products of maceration in the production of a liqueur, as the flavors of liqueurs are frequently very complex. After blending, the mixtures are often aged in oak casks. The blends can be altered by the addition of sugar, honey, water, alcohol, or an aged brandy for more complexity. Color can also be added through the infusion of different plants or fruits such as saffron or berry. After blending and aging, the liqueur is filtered, then bottled.

Liqueurs, like other spirituous beverages, should always be stored in an upright position so that the cork will not deteriorate as a result of prolonged exposure to alcohol. Liqueurs that have been opened will not deteriorate provided they are kept tightly corked.

There is also a group of odd potions called bitters which, for want of a more appropriate placement, are also listed here. These are some of the most popular concoctions in this category:

# Nut, Bean, and Seed Liqueurs

## ALMOND

*Amaretto di Saronno (Italy, 56 proof)*

The most popular nut liqueur is not really made from nuts at all. It is flavored with the almondlike pits of apricots grown in orchards northwest of Milan. These pits have a nutty but slightly bitter flavor, which explains why the liqueur is called amaretto—"a little bitter" in Italian. The reason many people think this lush liqueur is made from almonds is that the very popular almond cookies made in the region are called amaretti.

There is a lovely story associated with the invention of the Amaretto di Saronno liqueur. It may be just a legend, but it is widely accepted as truth. The year 1525 was a horrendous one for Lombardy, the province in which Milan is located. Famine and war had ravaged the land and the people were destitute. An obscure young artist, Bernardino Luini, a disciple of Leonardo da Vinci, was painting a fresco in the sanctuary of Santa Maria della Grazie in Saronno, a small village north of Milan near Lake Como.

He chose as the model for the Madonna in his painting the proprietress of the small inn in which he was staying. The poor young innkeeper was a beautiful widow raising two small children. She wanted to express her gratitude to the talented artist, but she had no money to spend on a gift. Instead she invented a special drink made from the apricot pits that her daughter gathered in nearby orchards. She combined the pits with herbs and alcohol, and the rest is history. The drink, a true love potion, was the beginning of an ardent romance, and Luini went on to become quite a celebrated artist. The painting of his charming blond lover hangs to this day in the church in Saronno.

The formula for the drink was passed down from innkeeper to innkeeper until 1800, when Carlo Domenico Riena obtained the recipe and began selling it in his apothecary shop. His signature encircles the neck of the product to this day. Since 1939, Amaretto di Saronno has been produced commercially by Illva in Saronno. It is sold in a distinctive square antique bottle with a gold label.

Amaretto di Saronno is deep amber in color and has a unique almond and herb flavor with hints of mint, cinnamon, and vanilla. The liqueur is fairly thick in texture. Its intense sweetness is nicely balanced by the gentle bitterness of the apricot pits.

Successfully marketed in the United States, Amaretto di Saronno is consumed by itself after dinner, on the rocks, or as part of several mixed drinks. It has joined a precious few other liqueurs—Cointreau, Grand Marnier, Chartreuse—as a frequently used ingredient in pastries and other desserts.

The success of the original amaretto has, of course, brought forth a stream of imitators, some made in Italy and some domestically. Other Italian amarettos include Lazzaroni (48 proof), Galliano (56 proof), Patrician (48 proof), Trave (54 proof), Stock (56 proof), and Amaretto di Torani (56 proof). Domestic versions include Amaretto di Amore (42 proof), DeKuyper Amaretto di Cupera (56 proof), Gaetano (56 proof), Boston (34 proof), Bols (56 proof), Arrow (56 proof), Hiram Walker (50 proof), and Dubouchett (56 proof). These versions are quite pleasant, if not as complex as the original. Most of them, particularly those made in this country, are considerably less expensive.

### Crème de noyaux

Domestic and foreign producers make a cordial flavored with bitter almonds, mace, nutmeg, and other spices. This product is not as strongly almond-flavored as amaretto. It is consumed straight, on the rocks, mixed with vodka, or combined with crème de cacao. Some call this liqueur "crème de noyaux," some "crème de noya."

Some American liqueur producers make crème de almond, a clear red cordial based on almond oil or, occasionally, apricot pits. Typically it has a snappy cinnamon flavor and is a colorful addition to mixed drinks.

## COCOA

*Crème de cacao*

Crème de cacao is a liqueur made from cacao and vanilla beans. It is produced in either a white or brown version and there is generally no discernible flavor difference between the two.

## COFFEE

The coffee bean has had a long voyage from obscurity to its present position on most of the world's breakfast tables and desks. It was first discovered growing in Abyssinia, which is now Ethiopia. Four thousand years ago warriors from northern Africa went off to battle with apple-sized balls of ground coffee beans mixed with fat as rations.

By the beginning of the 5th century, coffee had made its way to Arabia, and not too long afterwards it arrived in Turkey. Yemeni Arabs actually made wine from coffee beans.

As the trade routes to the mysterious East opened, coffee was gradually introduced into Europe. One story, perhaps apocryphal, tells about how in 1683, after their defeat near Vienna, the Turks fled, leaving behind sacks of coffee in their deserted tents. The curious Viennese found immediate use for the booty. This and other less dramatic incidents kindled a European passion for coffee that endures to this day.

In the 18th century, coffee houses in Vienna, London, and other places became centers of social, political, and literary activities. At about the same time, coffee was introduced into the Americas, where it gained immediate acceptance. Coffee plants were cultivated in the Caribbean and on the mountains of Mexico, where the climate and soil were ideal for the proliferation of this tropical crop.

At some point during this process of world proliferation—probably toward the end of the last century—someone got the bright idea to blend coffee with distilled spirits to make a drink that combined the unique, toasty flavor of coffee with the smoothness and sweetness of a liqueur. The results of this alchemy included the big two coffee liqueurs, Kahlúa and Tia Maria.

*Kahlúa (Mexico, 53 proof)*

This mahogany-colored, smooth, and syrupy liqueur in the distinctive high-neck bottle with the yellow label was being made in Mexico before World War II. Since its introduction into the United States in 1962, it has dominated the liqueur market.

Kahlúa, the industry standard among coffee liqueurs, has a smoky, toasty coffee flavor with a background of vanilla. It is bright and clean-flavored, with a snappy finish and an attractive coffee candy sweetness.

*Tia Maria (Jamaica, 53 proof)*

Although still fairly sweet, Tia Maria is drier and lighter than Kahlúa. It is a product of the Caribbean island of Jamaica and claims to derive from a formula that has been continually handed down since 1655. In that year, the English stormed this then-Spanish island, causing the family that had developed the recipe for the liqueur to flee their plantation. The family's youngest daughter and the recipe were saved by a courageous housekeeper, Tia Maria.

The daughter kept the formula and passed it on to her eldest daughter on her wedding day. In this way, the family tradition continued for nearly 300 years.

In the late 1940s, Dr. Kenneth Lee Evans, a Jamaican physician, was served the liqueur at a friend's home. He immediately got permission to produce the liqueur commercially.

Tia Maria is made from the Blue Mountain coffee grown north of Kingston, at 6,000 feet above sea level. The amber-colored liqueur has a smoky, roasted aroma and a crisp, tangy coffee and herb flavor, with a silky café au lait smoothness.

The success of these two coffee liqueurs has spawned a bunch of wanna-bes, some of which can compete only on the basis of their price. But there are actually some good ones, too. The best of the lot is Sabra, a delicious Israeli-made 60-proof version.

Most of the large quantity of coffee liqueur sold in America is not consumed straight up or even on the rocks. The bulk of it goes into mixed drinks, the most popular of which is the Black Russian.

## HAZELNUT

*Frangelico (Italy, 56 proof)*

Frangelico is a relative newcomer from northern Italy that has had a significant recent sales success in the United States. Its main flavoring ingredient is the wild hazelnut. A light amber liqueur, Frangelico is crisp and fairly dry, with a lush texture and the taste of toasty hazelnuts. There are hints of vanilla and white chocolate in the complex herbal flavors.

The Frangelico legend concerns a 17th-century hermit-monk who created this liqueur out of woodland nuts and herbs. It is made commercially by Barbero in Piedmont, not far from Torino. The bottle is made in the shape of a pious, robed cleric.

Frangelico is a lovely after-dinner drink, served straight in a snifter. It is also quite good on the rocks. For a refreshing cocktail, blend it half and half with vodka.

There are a few domestic cordials that use a hazelnut base. As with the Amaretto reproductions, these are less complex and less expensive but usually quite pleasant. Gaetano and DeKuyper make widely distributed versions.

*Pisa Nut Liqueur (Italy, 48 proof)*

A recent addition to the roster of nut-flavored liqueurs, Pisa offers a complex blend of several nut essences, with a definite slant toward almond and hazelnut. It has a smooth, sweet taste and a pleasing bitter-almond finish. The ingenious slanted bottle is modeled after the Leaning Tower of Pisa. The liqueur is delicious on its own and also makes a nice addition to coffee or cappuccino and in mixed drinks.

## MAPLE SYRUP

*Sortilege (Canada, 43 proof)*

An unusual recent entry, this Canadian distilled spirit is a blend of premium Canadian whiskey and maple syrup. Delicate and not too sweet, it is delightful when served on its own and is actually quite sinful when drizzled over ice cream or baked apples. If you let your imagination wander, you might even find it on the weekend breakfast table next to a tall stack of buttermilk pancakes.

# Fruit Liqueurs

Americans love fruit, and fruit liqueurs provide an accessible and luscious orchard of captivating natural flavors. Although many of the world's most aromatic fruit liqueurs are made abroad, several domestic companies also offer complete lines. Arrow, Bols, J.W. Dant, DeKuyper, Dubouchett, Garnier, Jacquin, Leroux, Mohawk, Old Mr. Boston, Regnier, and Hiram Walker all provide excellent products.

Here are some of the fruit liqueurs you might encounter at your favorite spirits merchant.

## BANANA

*Crème de banane (Foreign and United States, 50 to 60 proof)*

Many producers make this white or gold liqueur. It is generally very sweet and syrupy. Banana liqueurs are used in desserts and a few mixed drinks.

## BLACK CURRANT

*Crème de cassis (France and United States, 32 to 40 proof)*

A deep red, low-alcohol, syrupy, sweet concoction, this liqueur was of little use until someone mixed it with Aligote, the extremely tart white Burgundy. The resulting aperitif, called kir after the wartime mayor of Dijon, showcases the good qualities of both ingredients, and became a fixture at parties in the 1980s. It can be made with any crisp, dry white wine. The combination of crème de cassis and champagne, called a Kir Royale, is another nice showcase for this liqueur. I particularly like the Double Crème de Cassis de Dijon liqueur from Lejay-Lagoute.

## BLACK RASPBERRY

*Chambord (France, 33 proof)*

This thick, sweet, low-alcohol liqueur is flavored mainly by French black raspberries, but other fruits and herbs are used as well, and the mixture is sweetened with honey. It is a deep amber color tinged with ruby, and its appealing flavor suggests candy fruit. Chambord is made by La Maison Delan et Cie in France and packaged in the United States. The bottle is squat and round, with a gold crown. Chambord is particularly delicious poured over vanilla ice cream, and a tablespoon or so in a glass of champagne makes a charming aperitif.

Several domestic producers sell blackberry liqueurs. These are mostly 60 proof and purplish red. They are quite sweet and dense, and are attractive when poured over fruit or ice cream.

## CHERRY

*Cherry Marnier (France, 48 proof)*

Like Grand Marnier, this spirit uses brandy as a base. It is medium sweet and slighty thick.

*Maraschino (Italy and United States, 50 to 60 proof)*

This clear, relatively dry liqueur is made from the spicy Marasca cherries of Italy and Dalmatia (in Yugoslavia). The cherry pits are distilled separately and contribute to a charming bitter-almond nuance. Maraschino is used frequently in mixed drinks.

## LEMON

*Villa Massa (Italy, 60 proof)*

Limoncello is a sweet liquor made up of lemons, sugar, and alcohol. Created by the farmers along the Gulf of Naples, it is one of Italy's most popular drinks. I particularly enjoy Villa Massa (Italy, 60 proof). Made exclusively from the peels of Sorrento lemons, this fresh-tasting liqueur is a little like sunshine in a bottle. It's lovely chilled or over ice and makes a nice addition to mixed drinks and desserts.

## MELON

*Midori (Japan, 46 proof)*

This bright green liqueur, a recent addition to the bar, is made by the giant Japanese distiller Suntory. Midori is fairly sweet but its muskmelon flavor is delicious and quite charming.

## ORANGE

*Cointreau (France, 80 proof)*

One of the most popular of all fruit liqueurs, Cointreau sells nearly 2 million cases in 217 different countries annually. It was formulated in 1879 by Edouard Cointreau Sr., the head of a successful confectionery and distillery located in the Loire Valley. Three generations and 142 years later, the same secret formula is still closely guarded by the family at their plant in Angers.

Cointreau is bittersweet, with a delicate orange flavor derived from the peels of oranges from Europe, the Caribbean, North Africa, and the Middle East. It has a silky texture, and, although sweet, it leaves a decidedly dry impression on the palate.

Since its American introduction at the 1893 International Exhibition in Chicago, Cointreau has had a devoted following here. To handle the demand, a marketing subsidiary was established in New York City.

Cointreau can be used in any mixed drinks that call for triple sec, but this elegant liqueur is best served on the rocks or on its own.

*Grand Marnier (France, 80 proof)*

Marnier-Lapostelle was founded by Jean-Baptiste Lapostelle in 1827. At first, the company bottled a number of liqueurs, but by the turn of the century its orange version had taken center stage. Grand Marnier is based on cognac and the peels of bitter oranges from Haiti. It is amber in color and its dry citrus component combines congenially with the rich toastiness it receives from the cognac. Grand Marnier has become indispensable in dessert making. It is used in many pastries and soufflés. It is also delicious over ice or served neat in a cordial glass or snifter.

## Curaçao (United States, 60 proof)

Curaçao is a generic name referring to the island that produces some of the Caribbean's best bitter oranges. In the 17th century the peel was brought to Holland, where the Dutch created the first orange liqueur.

Today, there are many curaçaos on the market. Most are produced in the United States but are made with imported peels. These liqueurs are usually amber and sweet, with a charming taste of bitterness. Curaçaos are about 60 proof; some use a brandy base. A number of distillers make one that has been tinted blue. There is no significant difference in flavor or proof between this product and the regular variety, or between the amber and the few clear curaçaos available.

## Triple Sec (United States, 48 to 60 proof)

Triple sec is an orange liqueur made from both sweet and bitter orange peels. The name means "triple dry," but triple secs are not all dry. The best of them are smooth, sweet, and nicely balanced with fresh fruit flavors and considerable finesse.

Triple sec can be poured over ice or enjoyed on it is own, but it is most frequently used for margaritas.

## SLOE

## Sloe Gin (England and United States, 40 to 60 proof)

The sloe is a small wild plum. The liqueur made from it is misnamed, because it is not a gin, although early versions were made by macerating the fruit in gin.

Bright red and medium sweet, it has an intriguing flavor of wild cherry and bitter almond. Sloe gin is almost never consumed on its own; it is used in mixed drinks such as sloe gin fizzes.

# Herbal Liqueurs

*Absente (France, 110 proof)*

Not to be confused with absinthe, the now-illegal drink of decadent Parisian poets, Absente packs all the licorice flavor of its predecessor and none of the possibly deadly wormwood extract. But even without the wormwood, all that alcohol may have you recklessly reciting Baudelaire, so it's a good idea to dilute Absente with four parts water. With absinthe, this was done by pouring the water through a slotted spoon containing a sugar cube. The drink will turn milky like pastis and lose a bit of its kick.

*Benedictine (France, 40 proof)*

The closely guarded formula for the liqueur Benedictine was first produced in 1510 in the Benedictine Abbey de Fecamp in France. Today, it is still made in the same location. D.O.M. Benedictine is an herbal liqueur made on a cognac brandy base. After several separate distillations, Benedictine is aged for 4 years before it is bottled. D.O.M., which appears on every label, stands for the latin *Dio Optimo Maximo*— "To God, Most Good, Most Great." Hundreds of imitations have arisen, but the original formula still stands alone.

*Chartreuse (France, 84 to 110 proof)*

Chartreuse dates from the beginning of the 17th century, when the recipe for an *Elixir de Longue Vie* (Elixir of Long Life) was given to a Carthusian monastery outside of Paris by one of Henry IV's captains.

For more than 150 years the monks tinkered with the formula, and in 1764, at the Carthusian monastery in the Massif de la Chartreuse in southeastern France, they settled on a blend made from 130 different plants and herbs.

Two Chartreuse liqueurs were produced, *Elixir de Sante* and *Elixir de Table*. The latter version was the green drink that is still popular today—the liquid that actually gave a color its name. Green Chartreuse has a minty, spicy flavor. It is crisp, peppery, and very high in alcohol—55 percent, to be exact.

In 1838, a yellow version of Chartreuse was created. It is sweeter and mellower than the green. Honey was added to the mix and the alcoholic content was dropped to 43 percent.

In addition, small lots of both green and yellow Chartreuse are specially aged in oak for 12 years and labeled V.E.P. (*Vieillissement Exceptionnellement Prolongé*, which stands for "exceptionally prolonged aging"). These aged liqueurs develop a softer, more complex flavor. The green V.E.P. is 54 percent alcohol and the yellow 42 percent.

In the early 1920s the production and marketing of Chartreuse was sold into nonchurch hands. The formula and the direction of production, however, remain under the control of Carthusian monks, who work every day at the Chartreuse distillery in Voiron, a small city in the foothills of the Alps not far from Grenoble.

### Elisir du Dr. Roux (France, 94 proof)

A gorgeous green liqueur concocted by Michel Roux, this elixir is filled with 14 different herbs and aromatics. Many of the ingredients are derived from energy-enhancing plants common to the landscape of Provence. Straight, it's an acquired taste, but it adds a wonderful flavor to mixed drinks like the Green Envy cocktail.

### Liquore Galliano (Italy, 70 proof)

The most popular of Italian herbal liqueurs, Galliano is lush and moderately syrupy in texture, and has a smooth herbal-vanilla flavor that finishes with a pleasant twinge of bitterness. This liqueur is less complex than its French cousins, but, for many consumers its flavors may be easier to like.

Liquore Galliano was first made around the turn of the 20th century in Livorno, on the Tuscan coast; it is now produced in a modern plant near Milan. Unlike its French counterparts, this Italian liqueur is given very little age. After several separate distillations, the various lots are blended before being held for three months while their flavors marry. Then, after being adjusted to 40 percent alcohol, Galliano is bottled. In the United States it had a tremendous upsurge in popularity when the Harvey Wallbanger became a fashionable cocktail.

In Trieste, near the Austrian border, Stock, one of Italy's biggest distillers, makes an attractive Galliano clone called Roiano.

*Barenjager (German, 70 proof)*

One of the classic German liqueurs, Barenjager was developed in the late 15th century. It is made from highland honey and fine vodka. The name means "bear hunter."

*Jagermeister (Germany, 70 proof)*

Jagermeister is an herbal concoction made in Wulfenbuttel, Germany, that tastes at first like a liqueur but finishes like bitters with spicy, peppery, and decidedly bittersweet flavors. It is classed here as an herb liqueur, such as Benedictine or Chartreuse, but its flavors would also make it welcome in the bitters category.

Made from 56 different herbs, Jagermeister has its share of medicinal herbs, such as rhubarb roots from the Himalayas, gentian roots from the Alps, valerian roots from Japan, and chamomile blossoms from Egypt. In addition, there are plenty of barks, seeds, and resins.

Jagermeister, which is quite popular in the New Orleans area, has been made since 1878 by the Mast family, which has passed its formula down from generation to generation. It is reddish brown in color. The producers recommend that Jagermeister be served chilled and some like to follow it with a beer.

*Pernod (France, 80 proof)*

Pernod is a commercial name that, through the years, has become synonymous with absinthe. Absinthe is prepared with aromatic plants, balm-mint, hyssop, fennel, star anise, and a high-proof spirit. In fact, absinthe is so powerful, 136 proof, that its sale is prohibited in Switzerland, France, the United States, and other countries. Because of this, the Pernod firm produces an anise-flavored spirit that is 80 proof. It is a light yellow-green color with a strong licorice aroma.

*Pimm's No. 1 (England, 67 proof)*

More than one hundred years ago, a bartender in Pimm's restaurant in London invented the gin sling. This drink became very popular and customers would ask to bring it home for private parties and weekends away. Eventually, this drink was prepared commercially as

Pimm's No. 1. It is produced in England, and sweetened with spices, fruits, and herbs.

### Tuaca (Italy, 70 proof)

This handsomely packaged Italian liqueur is a relative newcomer to the marketplace. It is light amber in color and has an attractive, moderately sweet herbal-vanilla flavor.

# Cream Liqueurs

Cream liqueurs are the hottest thing to hit the liquor business in years. It all started in 1979 when a company called International Distillers and Vintners (I.D.V.) brought a totally new product to market. This "cream liqueur" was the result of a technological breakthrough that allowed fresh cream and alcohol to be combined in such a way that they were completely homogenized—and remained so indefinitely. Made in Ireland, this smooth blend was mixed with sweeteners and flavorings to make something unique. The total effect was reminiscent of the classic Brandy Alexander; the big difference was that this drink would never separate.

### Baileys Original Irish Cream (Ireland, 34 proof)

The I.D.V. liqueur sold a scant 17,000 cases that first year. The next year, more than 10 times as much was consumed. In 1983, over 1 million cases were purchased. It was the most dramatic product introduction in the history of the wine and spirits industry. Today sales are even greater, and are still growing. It appears that cream liqueurs have a bit more staying power than coolers did.

As might be expected, this impressive success prompted a number of companies to come up with their own variations. Some were flavored with rum or coffee, while others were very much like Baileys, only less expensive. So far, none of them has been able to slow the phenomenal surge in sales of the leader. There was room for other cream liqueurs, however, and a number of them have made modest inroads.

Cream liqueurs are very nice at the end of a meal, served either chilled or at room temperature, neat or on the rocks. They are also delicious poured over ice cream or mixed with brandy to create a less sweet, more potent drink.

Baileys Irish Cream has a grayish brown color and contains fresh dairy cream, Irish whiskey, and natural flavorings such as vanilla and chocolate. The mixture is then homogenized to ensure uniformity in every bottle, pasteurized to preserve freshness, and then cooled and bottled. Baileys has medium viscosity and is smooth and creamy without being cloying. It has a fresh and appealing milk chocolate flavor.

## *Vermeer Dutch Chocolate Cream (Netherlands, 34 proof)*

Real Dutch chocolate combined with vodka and dairy cream make for a delectably smooth and chocolaty experience. This grown-up version of chocolate milk is quite nice on the rocks, but mixes easily into Chocolate Martinis, White Russians, and other coffee drinks.

# Bitters

Bitters are the essences of bark, roots, fruits, plants, stems, seeds, and other botanicals incorporated into an alcohol base. This type of distillate is a relatively modern development—dating from the 19th century—but it is really descended directly from the original medicinal elixirs that were the forerunners of today's liqueurs. Actually, the line of demarcation between bitters and liqueurs is a bit fuzzy. A number of bitters fit the definition of liqueur, and vice versa.

The characteristic that sets bitters apart, besides their obvious bitterness, is their original use as a medicine, usually as a stomachic or digestive aid. Within the definition, however, there are two distinct categories of bitters as defined by the Internal Revenue Service: those fit for use as beverages and those not fit for use as beverages. The first group pays a sizable tax, while the second pays practically nothing.

## *Amer Picon (France, 78 proof)*

Amer Picon is a reddish-brown bitter liqueur that has been made in France since 1837. It contains gentian and cinchona bark, which yields quinine, but the most prominent flavor is bitter orange. Aficionados like to drink Amer Picon on the rocks with soda.

### Angostura (Trinidad, 90 proof)

The formula for Angostura was developed in 1824 by Dr. Johann Siegert, who was the surgeon-general in the army of the South American hero Simón Bolívar. The introduction of the tonic came after Dr. Siegert spent four years trying to find a potion that would improve the health and appetites of troops. The name derives from the fact that the good doctor was headquartered in the port of Angostura, Venezuela, which is now known as Ciudad Bolívar.

The Angostura formula contains herbs and spices in a combination that is still kept secret by the Siegert family. The only herb actually named on the label is gentian. Angostura is currently manufactured in Trinidad in the West Indies.

Angostura is a powerful 90 proof, which explains why it is dispensed only in drops and dashes. It has a unique ability to enhance and intensify the flavors of other ingredients in both drinks and foods.

### Cynar (Italy, 33 proof)

Artichokes? That's right—this Italian bitter *aperitivo* is made from a maceration of several herbs, but the main flavor comes from artichoke leaves. Cynar (pronounced "chee-nahr") is sipped before dinner in Italy, often on the rocks with a slice of orange. It is also frequently used in mixed drinks.

### Campari (Italy, 48 proof)

The world's most popular bitters was created by Gaspare Campari in 1860, the year Italy was united into a single nation. His idea was to offer a new drink to the patrons of his elegant Milan café, and it became an immediate success. By the turn of the century, thanks to the marketing savvy of his son Davide, Campari had become a national fixture, and soon after that it grew into an international triumph. Today, this bright red, spirit-based *aperitivo* is available in 169 countries, and over 5 million cases are sold worldwide.

The Campari company still uses Gaspare's original formula, which utilizes herbs and fruits from four continents. These ingredients are blended and then aged in oak. Campari's flavor is soft, sweet, and pleasantly bitter. In Italy Campari is so popular mixed with soda that premixed "Campari-Soda" sells more than 400 million bottles each year. In addition, there are two world-famous cocktails made from Campari: the Americano and the Negroni. The Americano is equal parts of Campari and sweet vermouth, and the Negroni is equal parts of Campari, sweet vermouth, and gin.

## Fernet Branca *(Italy, 80 proof)*

I first tasted this strange brown liquid in Gascony when it was proffered as a sure cure for extreme gastric distress. It worked. This elixir was originally introduced in 1845 by a young Milanese woman named Maria Scala who subsequently married into the Branca family. The mysterious "bitters liqueur" is made from a secret formula that contains some 40 herbs and spices—things like rhubarb, chamomile, anise, cardamom, clove, gentian, and myrrh. Many of these ingredients come from the Alpine foothills not far from Milan, but others are imported from various parts of the world. Each component is carefully tested for quality before being used in production.

The word "fernet" translates as "hot iron," which refers to a poker-like tool that was used to stir the mixture in the early days of Fernet Branca's production. Since the beginning, this popular brand of bitters has been made exclusively in Milan by the Branca family. The secret formula has been carefully passed down from generation to generation, and today the ingredients are put through a computerized measuring program to ensure consistency in the product.

Europe's most popular digestif, Fernet Branca sells more than a million cases a year in Italy alone. Most Italians drink this elixir straight or on the rocks. In Argentina it is often taken as an aperitif, while in Germany it is sometimes followed by beer. Some people like to add it to their coffee after a meal.

## Gammel Dansk *(Denmark, 76 proof)*

Forty thousand cases of Gammel Dansk are sold in tiny Denmark every year. This bitters is made from an "age-old" recipe that includes

20 different herbs and fruits. The dark amber drink is peppery, assertively herbal, and completely dry. Its flavor is one of the liveliest and bitterest among bitters.

*Peychaud's (United States, 70 proof)*

Antoine Amedie Peychaud was a New Orleans apothecary who in 1793 concocted a tonic that was supposed to cure virtually every disease known to man. Although its curative powers may have been somewhat overstated, Peychaud's tonic became a local favorite as a flavoring for mixed drinks.

Peychaud's is usually dispensed a few drops at a time. It is also used in a number of Creole recipes.

# Liqueurs • Classics

## Angel's Tip

1 ounce white crème de cacao
Dash of heavy cream
1 maraschino cherry

Pour the crème de cacao into a liqueur glass. Float the heavy cream on top and garnish with the cherry.

## Cape Cod Cooler

2 ounces sloe gin
1 ounce gin
5 ounces cranberry juice
½ ounce lemon juice
½ ounce orgeat
Crushed ice
Lime slice

Combine all ingredients, except the lime slice, in a shaker or blender. Pour the mixture into a chilled collins glass and garnish with the lime slice.

## Grasshopper

1 ounce crème de menthe
1 ounce crème de cacao
1 ounce light cream

Combine all ingredients in a shaker. Shake vigorously. Strain the mixture into a chilled cocktail glass.

## *Pousse Café*

Use equal amounts (usually ½ ounce) of each of the following ingredients:
Raspberry syrup (or grenadine)
Crème de cacao
Maraschino liqueur
Curaçao
Crème de menthe (green)
Parfait Amour
Cognac

Layer ingredients one on top of the other in the order given in a pousse-café glass or parfait glass. This is best accomplished by pouring them slowly over the back of a spoon.

## *Sloe Gin Fizz*

2 to 3 ounces sloe gin
½ ounce lemon juice
1 teaspoon sugar syrup
1 scoop crushed ice
Club soda
Lemon slice

In a shaker, mix the first four ingredients. Pour the mixture into a chilled collins glass. Top off with the cold club soda and stir gently. Garnish with the lemon slice.

# Almond Liqueur

## *Coco Amandine*

1 ounce almond liqueur
1 ounce cream of coconut

Pour both ingredients into a snifter filled with ice. Stir gently.

## *Toasty Almond Colada*

1 ounce almond liqueur
1 ounce coffee liqueur
1 ounce cream of coconut
2 ounces heavy cream
1 cup ice

Combine all ingredients in a blender and blend until smooth. Pour the mixture into a chilled parfait glass.

# Amaretto

## Amaretto Sour

2 to 3 ounces amaretto
¾ ounce lemon juice
1 scoop crushed ice
1 orange slice

In a shaker, mix the amaretto, lemon juice, and crushed ice. Strain over ice cubes in an old-fashioned glass and garnish with the orange slice.

## Amaretto Stinger

2 ounces amaretto
1 ounce white crème de menthe

In a shaker, combine both ingredients with ice. Shake well and strain over fresh ice cubes in an old-fashioned glass.

## Café Amaretto

1 ounce amaretto
1 ounce coffee liqueur
1 cup hot coffee
Whipped cream

Pour the liqueurs into the cup of hot coffee. Top generously with the whipped cream.

## Café Prego

1½ ounces amaretto
4 ounces hot coffee
½ ounce brandy
2 ounces heavy cream

Pour the first three ingredients into an Irish coffee glass. Stir well. Hold a spoon just above the surface of the coffee and carefully pour the cream over the back of the spoon. The cream should float on top of the coffee.

## Dynasty

1½ ounces amaretto
1½ ounces Southern Comfort

In a shaker or blender, mix both ingredients with ice. Strain the mixture into an old-fashioned glass over fresh ice cubes.

## Fairmont Freeze

PYRAMID LOUNGE,
FAIRMONT HOTEL, DALLAS

1½ ounces amaretto
1 scoop vanilla ice cream
Sliced toasted almonds

Blend the amaretto with the ice cream until thoroughly mixed and creamy in texture. Pour the blend into a chilled cocktail glass and sprinkle the almonds on top.

## Little Italy

2 ounces amaretto
5 ounces orange juice

Pour both ingredients into a highball glass filled with ice cubes. Stir well before serving.

## Radisson Snowball

RADISSON HOTEL, OASIS LOUNGE, SCOTTSDALE, ARIZONA

1 ounce amaretto
½ ounce white crème de cacao
1 teaspoon cream of coconut
1 scoop vanilla ice cream
2 ounces heavy cream
1 scoop crushed ice
½ fresh pineapple slice

Blend all ingredients, except the pineapple slice, until the mixture reaches a slushy consistency. Pour into a tulip glass and garnish with the pineapple slice.

## Secret Love

QUEEN ELIZABETH HOTEL, MONTREAL

1 ounce coconut amaretto liqueur
½ ounce white rum
½ ounce lemon juice
1 ounce orange juice
½ ounce cranberry juice
Maraschino cherry

Combine the first five ingredients in a shaker with ice. Shake well. Strain into a cocktail glass and garnish with the cherry.

## Southern Slammer

1½ ounces amaretto
1 ounce Southern Comfort
½ ounce sloe gin
½ ounce lemon juice

In a shaker or blender, shake all ingredients with ice. Strain the mixture into an old-fashioned glass filled with fresh ice cubes.

# Benedictine

## Annabelle Special

ANNABELLE'S, LONDON

1½ ounces Benedictine
⅓ ounce dry vermouth
⅛ ounce lime juice
1 scoop crushed ice

Mix all ingredients in a shaker. Strain the mixture into a chilled cocktail glass.

## Friar's Coffee

4 ounces hot coffee
½ teaspoon superfine sugar
2 ounces Benedictine
2 ounces heavy cream

Add the coffee and sugar to an Irish coffee glass. Stir until the sugar dissolves. Add the Benedictine and stir again. To layer the cream on top, hold a spoon just above the surface of the coffee and carefully pour the cream over the back of the spoon.

## Quiet Nun

1 ounce Benedictine
½ ounce triple sec
1 ounce light cream
1 scoop crushed ice

Combine all ingredients in a shaker. Shake well and strain into a chilled cocktail glass.

# Black Raspberry Liqueur

## Cádiz

¾ ounce black raspberry liqueur
¾ ounce amontillado sherry
½ ounce triple sec
½ ounce heavy cream
1 scoop crushed ice

In a shaker, mix all ingredients. Pour the mixture into a chilled old-fashioned glass.

## Di Nuovo

YELLOWFINGER'S, NEW YORK CITY

1 ounce black raspberry liqueur
¾ ounce hazelnut liqueur
¼ cup pureed rasberries
½ cup heavy cream
Whipped cream
Chopped nuts
Fresh berries

In a blender, combine the first four ingredients with approximately half a cup of ice. Blend well. The blend should have a smooth, light pink consistency. Pour the mixture into an 8-ounce tulip glass. Add a dollop of the whipped cream and a light sprinkling of the chopped nuts. Garnish with a large strawberry or a few fresh raspberries.

## Latin Love

1 ounce Chambord
1 ounce Frangelico
Cream

Fill a rocks glass with ice. Carefully add the Chambord and Frangelico and float the cream for a lovely layered effect.

## Nuts and Berries

BISTRO TOUJOURS, PARK CITY, UTAH

Espresso
Lemon wedge
⅛ ounce finely chopped hazelnuts
1 ounce Chambord
1 ounce Frangelico
½ cup steamed milk
Dollop of whipped cream

Heat a latte glass with hot water. Grind and make 1 serving of espresso. Pour the hot water out of the latte glass and coat the rim with the lemon wedge. Dip the rim in the hazelnuts. Add the liqueurs and espresso. Steam the milk and add to the mixture. Garnish with the freshly whipped cream.

# Chocolate Liqueur

## Café Diana

OLD LYME INN,
OLD LYME, CONNECTICUT

1¼ ounces chocolate liqueur
1¼ ounces Chambord
Hot coffee
Whipped cream
Fresh raspberry (optional)

Pour the first two ingredients into a warm coffee mug. Top off with the hot coffee and a dollop of the whipped cream. In season, garnish with the fresh raspberry.

## Treasure Chest

1 ounce chocolate almond
    liqueur
¼ ounce golden rum
½ ounce amaretto
1 ounce heavy cream
1 scoop crushed ice

Mix all ingredients thoroughly in a blender. Pour the mixture into a chilled cocktail glass.

# Coffee Liqueur

## Coco Java

1 ounce coffee liqueur
1 ounce cream of coconut

Pour both ingredients into a snifter filled with ice. Gently stir.

## Cool Irish Coffee Colada

1 ounce coffee liqueur
1 ounce Irish whiskey
1½ ounces cream of coconut
1 ounce heavy cream
1 cup ice

Combine all ingredients in a blender and blend until smooth. Pour the mixture into a chilled parfait glass.

## Keoke Coffee

REDWOOD ROOM,
CLIFT HOTEL, SAN FRANCISCO

¾ ounce coffee liqueur
½ ounce brandy
Hot coffee
Freshly whipped cream

Pour the liqueur and brandy into an Irish coffee glass. Add fresh hot coffee to within an inch of the rim. Spoon three quarters of an inch of the whipped cream on top of the coffee.

## Kona Gold

1½ ounces crème de cacao
1 ounce peach brandy
Large scoop vanilla ice cream
½ ripe banana, peeled and sliced
Pinch of ground nutmeg
1 maraschino cherry

In a blender, combine the first four ingredients. Blend until smooth. Pour the mixture into a wineglass. Top with a sprinkle of the nutmeg and the cherry.

## Margi's Mocha Mint

¾ ounce coffee liqueur
¾ ounce crème de menthe
¾ ounce crème de cacao
1 scoop crushed ice

Combine all ingredients in a shaker. Mix well and strain into a chilled cocktail glass.

## Root Beer

1 ounce coffee liqueur
1 ounce Galliano
1 ounce lemon juice
½ teaspoon superfine sugar
3 ounces cola

Combine all ingredients, except the cola, in a shaker with ice cubes. Shake vigorously. Strain the mixture into a highball glass over fresh ice cubes. Top off with the cola. Stir well.

## Sombrero

1½ ounces coffee liqueur
1 ounce heavy cream

Pour the liqueur over ice cubes in a chilled old-fashioned glass. Float the cream on top of the liqueur by slowly pouring it over the back of a spoon.

## Toasted Almond

WINDOWS ON THE WORLD,
NEW YORK CITY

1½ ounces coffee liqueur
1 ounce amaretto
1½ ounces heavy cream
Pinch of ground nutmeg or
    cinnamon

Mix the first three ingredients in a shaker with ice. Strain into a chilled cocktail glass and sprinkle a little of the nutmeg or cinnamon on top.

## Velvet Dress

1 ounce coffee liqueur
¾ ounce brandy
¾ ounce triple sec
1½ ounces heavy cream

In a shaker, mix all ingredients with ice. Strain the mixture into a cocktail glass.

# Crème de Cacao

## Angel's Tit

¼ ounce crème de cacao
¼ ounce maraschino liqueur
¼ ounce heavy cream
1 maraschino cherry

Layer the ingredients, except the cherry, in a pony glass. Chill for a half hour before serving. Garnish with the cherry.

## Angel's Wings

1 ounce white crème de cacao
Dash of heavy cream
½ ounce brandy
1 maraschino cherry

Pour the crème de cacao into a cocktail glass. Float the cream on top. Gently pour the brandy over the cream. Garnish with the cherry.

## Beetlejuice

1 ounce white crème de cacao
1 ounce dark crème de cacao
½ ounce coffee liqueur
2 teaspoons peppermint schnapps
1 ounce light cream

Combine all ingredients in a shaker with ice cubes. Shake and strain into a cocktail glass.

## Caribbean Grasshopper

1 ounce white crème de cacao
½ ounce green crème de menthe
1½ ounces cream of coconut
Mint sprig

Pour all ingredients into a large snifter filled with ice cubes. Stir gently and garnish with the sprig of mint.

## Morton's Coffee

MORTON'S OF CHICAGO, BOSTON

Ground cinnamon
Granulated sugar
1 ounce dark crème de cacao
1 ounce amaretto
1 ounce Irish cream
Hot coffee
Unsweetened whipped cream

Press the moistened rim of a coffee mug into a mixture of equal parts cinnamon and sugar. Pour the crème de cacao, amaretto, and Irish cream into the mug. Top off with the hot coffee and a generous dollop of the freshly whipped cream.

## Pink Squirrel

1 ounce crème de cacao
1 ounce crème de noyaux
1 ounce heavy cream
1 scoop of crushed ice

Combine all ingredients in a shaker. Mix well and strain into a chilled cocktail glass.

## Sea Cow

FOUR SEASONS HOTEL, TORONTO

¾ ounce dark crème de cacao
½ ounce rye whiskey
½ ounce anisette
1½ ounces heavy cream
Green crème de menthe
Sugar
Grated nutmeg

Shake the first four ingredients with ice. Strain the mixture into a wineglass rimmed with the crème de menthe and sugar. Sprinkle the nutmeg on top.

### Snow Cap Colada

1 ounce white crème de cacao
1 ounce almond liqueur
½ ounce brandy
2 ounces cream of coconut
1 ounce cream
1 cup ice

Combine all ingredients in a blender and blend until smooth. Pour the mixture into a chilled parfait glass.

# Crème de Menthe

### Diana

2 ounces white crème de menthe
½ ounce brandy

Pour the crème de menthe into a pony glass. Float the brandy on top.

NOTE: This drink can also be served with crushed ice, using an extra ounce of crème de menthe and 3 teaspoons of brandy.

### Green Orchid

¾ ounce green crème de menthe
½ ounce Pernod
1 egg white
Club soda

Mix all ingredients, except the soda, in a shaker with crushed ice. Strain the mixture into a highball glass. Top off with the cold club soda and ice.

### London Fog

½ ounce white crème de menthe
1 ounce anisette
1 scoop vanilla ice cream
1 scoop crushed ice

Put all ingredients in a blender. Blend briefly. Pour the mixture into a chilled parfait glass.

## Mint Twist

1 teaspoon white crème de
  menthe or peppermint
  schnapps
1 teaspoon green crème de
  menthe
1 scoop vanilla ice cream

Combine all ingredients in a blender and blend until smooth. Pour the mixture into a chilled parfait glass.

## Mocha Mint

*Makes 4 servings*

1 cup cold coffee
1 pint chocolate ice cream
¼ cup crème de menthe
4 very thin chocolate mint wafer
  candies

In a blender, combine the coffee, ice cream, and crème de menthe. Spoon the blend into sherbet glasses or wineglasses. Garnish each serving with one of the chocolate mint wafers.

## Pacifier

1 scoop crushed ice
1½ ounces white crème de
  menthe
Several dashes of Fernet Branca

Pack a sherry glass with the crushed ice. Pour in the crème de menthe and top off with a float of the Fernet Branca.

## Shirley McLake

1½ ounces crème de banane
1½ ounces white crème de
  menthe

Pour both ingredients into a chilled old-fashioned glass. Add several ice cubes and stir well.

# Curaçao

## Fog City Blues

1½ ounces blue curaçao
½ ounce white crème de cacao
½ ounce light cream
1 scoop crushed ice

Mix all ingredients in a shaker. Pour the mixture into a chilled cocktail glass.

## Gloom Chaser

1 ounce curaçao
1 ounce orange liqueur
½ ounce lemon juice
¼ ounce grenadine
1 scoop crushed ice

Mix all ingredients in a shaker. Pour the mixture into a chilled cocktail glass.

## Ice Cream Flip

1 ounce orange curaçao
1 ounce maraschino liqueur
1 egg
1 scoop vanilla ice cream
Freshly grated nutmeg

Combine all ingredients, except the nutmeg, in a blender. Blend and pour into a cocktail glass. Sprinkle the nutmeg on top.

## Paradise

1 ounce curaçao
1 ounce hazelnut liqueur
1 ounce heavy cream

In a shaker, mix the liqueurs, the cream, and a few ice cubes. Strain the mixture into a chilled cocktail glass over crushed ice.

# Galliano

## Golden Dream

1½ ounces Galliano
1 ounce triple sec
1 ounce orange juice
1 teaspoon cream

In a shaker with ice cubes, mix all ingredients. Strain the mixture into a chilled cocktail glass.

## Jaguar

2 ounces Galliano
1 ounce white crème de cacao
1 ounce heavy cream
1 scoop crushed ice

Combine all ingredients in a blender. Blend for about 10 seconds. Strain the mixture into a chilled cocktail glass.

## Tyrol

1 ounce Galliano
½ ounce brandy
½ ounce green Chartreuse
½ ounce heavy cream
Freshly grated nutmeg

Mix all ingredients, except the nutmeg, in a shaker filled with crushed ice. Pour the mixture into a cocktail glass and sprinkle the nutmeg on top.

# Grand Marnier

## The Palace Café Royale

THE PALACE CAFE, SANTA BARBARA

*Makes 4 servings*

2 teaspoons Grand Marnier
1 teaspoon cognac
¼ cup sugar
½ cup heavy cream
½ teaspoon vanilla extract
2 teaspoons sour cream
Granulated sugar
Hot coffee
Grated chocolate

Combine the first six ingredients in a mixer or blender. Mix well, until the cream holds a stiff peak. Coat the rim of a clear mug or champagne glass with the sugar. Pour the hot coffee into a prepared glass. Dollop the whipped cream mixture on top of the coffee. Sprinkle the chocolate on top.

# Hazelnut Liqueur

### Nutcracker

1½ ounces hazelnut liqueur
1½ ounces coconut amaretto
1½ ounces heavy cream
Crushed ice

Combine all ingredients in a shaker or blender. Shake well and strain into a chilled cocktail glass.

### Robin Hood

1½ ounces hazelnut liqueur
2 teaspoons brandy
1 ounce lemon juice
1 teaspoon grenadine
1 maraschino cherry

Combine all ingredients, except the cherry, in a shaker with ice.

Shake well. Strain into a cocktail glass and garnish with the cherry.

### Snickers Bar

FOUR SEASONS HOTEL, BOSTON

1½ ounces hazelnut liqueur
1 ounce coffee liqueur
Handful of cocktail peanuts
Large scoop vanilla ice cream
Milk
Whipped cream

Combine the first four ingredients in a blender. Add the cold milk while blending on low speed until a medium thickness is reached. Pour the mixture into a cocktail glass and top off with a dollop of the whipped cream.

# Herbal Liqueur

### Green Envy

1 ounce Elisir du Dr. Roux
1 ounce lime juice
1 ounce dry vermouth

Shake all ingredients with ice and strain into a chilled cocktail glass.

# Irish Cream Liqueur

## Chip Shot

BALBOA CAFE, SAN FRANCISCO

¾ ounce Irish cream
¾ ounce Tuaca
1½ ounces hot coffee

Pour all ingredients directly into a shot glass.

## Irish Berry

1 ounce Irish cream
½ ounce vodka
1 ounce cream of coconut
1½ ounces strawberries
Dash of grenadine
½ cup ice

Combine all ingredients in a blender. Blend until smooth and pour the mixture into a saucer-shaped champagne glass.

## Slippery Nipple

BALBOA CACFE, SAN FRANCISCO

¾ ounce Irish cream
¾ ounce Sambuca

Combine the both ingredients in a shaker with ice. Mix and strain into a shot glass.

# Jagermeister

## Bee Sting

BALBOA CAFE, SAN FRANCISCO

¾ ounce Jagermeister
¾ ounce Barenjager

Chill both ingredients and pour them into a shot glass.

## Dead Nazi

BALBOA CAFE, SAN FRANCISCO

¾ ounce Jagermeister
¾ ounce Rumplemintz

Chill both ingredients and pour them into a shot glass.

## Poison Milk

CREATED BY AARON RAMSEY,
PARAGON, SAN FRANCISCO

¾ ounce Jagermeister
¾ ounce Irish cream

Chill the Jagermeister. Pour both ingredients into a shot glass.

# Lemon Liqueur

## Lem 'n' Tonic

1 ounce gin
½ ounce lemon liqueur
Tonic water
Lemon wedge

Fill a tall glass with ice. Add the first two ingredients. Fill with the tonic water. Garnish with the wedge of lemon.

## Lemon Sunset

1 ounce lemon liqueur
Sugar
1 ounce rum
1 teaspoon grenadine
¼ ounce lemon juice
Maraschino cherry

Dip rim of rocks glass into the lemon liqueur and then into the sugar. Shake all ingredients, including the remaining lemon liqueur, with ice and pour into the glass. Garnish with the cherry.

## Sorrento Sunrise

1 ounce lemon liqueur
1½ ounces tequila
2 ounces orange juice
½ ounce grenadine

Add the ice to a collins glass. Stir together the lemon liqueur, tequila, and orange juice. Slowly pour in grenadine and allow it to settle. Before drinking, stir.

# Melon Liqueur

## Midori Sour

2 ounces melon liqueur
1 ounce light rum
1 ounce heavy cream

Mix all ingredients in a shaker with ice. Strain the mixture into a chilled whiskey sour glass.

## Sniapin Verde

FELIDIA, NEW YORK CITY

2 ounces melon liqueur
1 ounce grappa
1 scoop crushed ice
1 orange slice

Combine all ingredients, except the orange slice, in a shaker. Mix well. Pour the mixture into an old-fashioned glass and garnish with the orange slice.

## St. Patrick's Irish Breeze

GRISWOLD INN, ESSEX, CONNECTICUT

1½ ounces melon liqueur
Grapefruit juice
Cranberry juice

Pour the liqueur into a large glass filled with ice. Top off the glass with equal parts of grapefruit and cranberry juice.

# Pernod

### Pernod Cocktail

½ ounce water
Several dashes of sugar syrup
Several dashes of bitters
1 scoop crushed ice
2 ounces Pernod

In an old-fashioned glass, combine the first four ingredients and stir well. Add the Pernod and stir again before serving.

### Suissesse

*Makes 2 servings*

3 ounces Pernod
1 ounce anisette
1 egg white
Several dashes of cream
 (optional)
1 scoop crushed ice

Combine all ingredients in a shaker. Mix well and strain into chilled cocktail glasses.

# Pimm's No. 1

### Pimm's Cup

1 ounce Pimm's No. 1
Lemon-lime soda
1 cucumber slice or spear

Pour the Pimm's into a highball or double old-fashioned glass. Add ice and fill the glass with lemon-lime soda. Garnish with the cucumber. (This is a traditional accompaniment to Indian food.)

# Raspberry Liqueur

### Raspberry Rickey

AUREOLE, NEW YORK CITY

1 to 2 tablespoons raspberry
   liqueur
Club soda
2 lime wedges
4 to 6 raspberries (red, yellow, or
   black)

Pour the liqueur into a large wine-glass. Fill the glass with ice and top it off with the cold club soda. Squeeze 1 lime wedge into the drink. Garnish with the raspberries and the second lime wedge. Serve with a straw.

# Rum Cream Liqueur

### Aloha

KAHALA HILTON HOTEL, HONOLULU

1½ ounces rum cream liqueur
1 ounce dark rum
½ ounce lime juice
2 ounces pineapple juice
2 ounces orange juice
1 ounce coconut syrup, or to
   taste

Small scoop vanilla ice cream
1 scoop crushed ice
1 fresh pineapple strip

Mix all ingredients, except the pineapple strip, in a blender until smooth. Do not overmix. Pour the blend into a chilled hurricane or collins glass. Garnish with the pineapple strip.

# Sambuca

### Fox Tail

1 ounce Sambuca
½ ounce heavy cream
Pinch of instant coffee powder

Pour the Sambuca into a pony glass. Using the back of a spoon, slowly pour the cream in so that it floats on top. Finally, dust the drink with the coffee powder.

## Hot Shot

BALBOA CAFE, SAN FRANCISCO

½ ounce Sambuca
½ ounce hot coffee
Whipped cream

Pour the Sambuca and coffee into a pony glass. Layer the freshly whipped cream on top.

## Roman Snowball

1 scoop crushed ice
2 to 3 ounces Sambuca
5 coffee beans

First fill a tulip glass with the ice, then pour in the Sambuca. Drop the coffee beans into the glass and serve this drink with a straw. You can chew the coffee beans after they have soaked in the Sambuca.

# Sloe Gin

## Love

*Makes 2 (4-ounce) servings*

4 ounces sloe gin
1 egg white
1 ounce lemon juice
Several dashes of grenadine
2 scoops crushed ice

Combine all ingredients in a shaker. Mix well and pour into chilled cocktail glasses.

## Moulin Rouge

1½ ounces sloe gin
½ ounce sweet vermouth
Several dashes of bitters
1 scoop crushed ice

In a shaker, mix all ingredients. Strain the mixture into a chilled cocktail glass.

## Sloe Gin Cocktail

1½ ounces sloe gin
½ ounce dry vermouth

Combine both ingredients in a shaker with ice. Shake well. Strain the mixture into a chilled cocktail glass.

## Sloe Screw

1½ ounces sloe gin
Orange juice

Pour the sloe gin over ice cubes in an old-fashioned glass. Top off the glass with the orange juice and stir.

## Stoplight

2 ounces sloe gin
1 ounce gin
1 ounce lemon juice
1 scoop crushed ice
1 maraschino cherry

Mix the sloe gin, gin, and lemon juice in a shaker with crushed ice. Strain the mixture into a chilled cocktail glass. Garnish with the cherry.

# Triple Sec

## Alfonso Special

1½ ounces triple sec
¾ ounce gin
1 teaspoon dry vermouth
1 teaspoon sweet vermouth
Several dashes of bitters
Crushed ice

Combine all ingredients in a shaker. Mix well and strain into a chilled cocktail glass.

## Beverly's Hills

1½ ounces triple sec
½ ounce cognac
¼ ounce coffee liqueur
Crushed ice

Mix all ingredients in a shaker. Strain the mixture into a chilled cocktail glass.

## Café du Franc

GORDON RESTAURANT, CHICAGO

Burnt sugar
Cinnamon
½ ounce triple sec
½ ounce hazelnut liqueur
½ ounce Irish cream
Hot coffee
Whipped cream

Coat the rim of a coffee mug with the sugar and cinnamon. Pour all three liqueurs into the coffee mug. Top off with the hot coffee and a dollop of the whipped cream.

## *Lollipop*

1 ounce triple sec
1 ounce green Chartreuse
1 ounce kirsch
Dash of maraschino liqueur

In a shaker, mix all ingredients with ice. Strain the mixture into a cocktail glass without ice.

## *Stewart Plaid*

1 ounce triple sec
¾ ounce coffee liqueur
½ ounce Irish cream

Combine all ingredients in a shaker with ice. Shake well and strain into a cocktail glass.

## *Two-Wheeler*

2 ounces triple sec
3 ounces orange juice
2 ounces heavy cream

Mix all ingredients in a shaker with ice. Strain the mixture into a chilled cocktail glass or a wineglass.

## *Velvet Hammer*

1 ounce triple sec
1 ounce white crème de cacao
1 ounce heavy cream
1 scoop crushed ice

Combine all ingredients in a shaker. Mix well. Strain the mixture into a chilled cocktail glass.

# Tuaca

## *Griswold Inn Hot Apple Cider*

GRISWOLD INN, ESSEX, CONNECTICUT

1½ ounces Tuaca
Hot apple cider
Whipped cream

Pour the Tuaca into a glass coffee mug. Top off the mug with the hot cider and a dollop of the whipped cream.

## *Hot Apple Pie*

BALBOA CAFE, SAN FRANCISCO

1½ ounces Tuaca
Hot apple juice or cider
Whipped cream
Freshly grated nutmeg
Cinnamon stick

Add the Tuaca to a mug of the hot apple juice or cider. Layer fresh whipped cream on top and sprinkle on the nutmeg. Garnish with the cinnamon stick.

# WINE DRINKS

Wine drinks are not trendy. A dalliance with dreadfully sweet, bottled wine coolers has left discerning drinkers with a bad taste in their mouths regarding this category. In this age of single-malt scotches, small-batch bourbons, and vodka martinis as big as your head, the idea of a wine-based drink seems a bit like . . . well, Kool-Aid. Erase the memory of that last bubbly berry sipper by sampling a well-made wine drink and you'll realize that a great cocktail doesn't necessarily have to include spirits. Certain wines and fortified wines add as much style and complexity to mixed drinks as the latest whiskey or well-packaged vodka, and their lighter touch makes these drinks ideal for summer barbecues and afternoon gatherings.

Drinks using champagne or sparkling wines make splendid aperitifs before formal dinners and lend an air of elegance and sophistication to any special meal or occasion. In addition, still wine is wonderful in punches and some mixed drinks.

A whole other group of drinks use fortified wines—sherry, port, and Madeira. These rich, intense wines have had brandy blended into them to stabilize their flavors and increase their alcohol content.

## MADEIRA

Madeira is a fortified wine made in a group of islands located 350 miles off the coast of Morocco. Through a series of shipping mishaps, it was discovered that Madeira aged best under rough treatment. The extra time it spent in the warm hull of ships added a desirable "cooked effect" to the wine. For a time, Madeira was aged while being used as ballast on ships sailing back and forth to the New World. For this reason, Madeira was known as *vinho da roda*, or "wine of the round voyage." Today, this aging process is duplicated using a heating process in which cement tanks or casks of wine are heated using hot water pipes and steam. Very fine Madeiras known as *vinhos do cantiero* are aged for at least 20 years and are warmed only by natural sunlight. During colonial times, Madeira was extremely popular in America. Legend has it that the signing of the Declaration of Independence was celebrated with a toast of Madeira. The wine was reputedly George Washington's favorite.

Madeira's popularity hit its peak in the mid-19th century, but then the vineyards suffered a double tragedy. First they fell victim to oidium, a damaging mildew, and then a few years later phylloxera, the vine louse that destroyed most of the vineyards of Europe. By the time the Madeira vineyards had recovered enough to produce adequate commercial quantities, Madeira's popularity had evaporated.

In 1925 several of the largest Madeira producers founded the Madeira Wine Company, a trade organization determined to increase worldwide awareness of the wine. The original members of the company—Blandy's, Leacock; and Lomelina, Miles and Cossarts—continue to produce wonderful Madeira today.

Madeira uses varietal grape names to label its wines. Although some of the great varieties have been replaced with others since the phylloxera blight, the wines are labeled "Sercial," the driest type; "Verdelho," off-dry to medium; "Boal" (also called "Bual"), sweet; and "Malmsey," sweetest of all. Bottles are also labeled according to age. "Reserve" signifies 5 years, "special reserve" 10 years, and "extra reserve" 15 years or longer.

Madeira can be a wonderful surprise for fans of port and sherry, and because it does not share the popularity of these fortified wines, very fine vintages can often be found at bargain prices.

## PORT

Port is a wine that was designed for export by the exporters. The wine as we know it today was created to please wine drinkers in England, not Portugal. English wine merchants were looking for a wine to replace popular French varieties, the supply of which was frequently being cut off because of hostilities between Britain and France. In the late 1600s, these merchants discovered the wines of the Douro in Portugal.

The Douro River winds through the green hills of northern Portugal and empties into the Atlantic at Oporto, a handsome city whose name translates as "the port." The wine that was being grown on the slopes along the river was harsh, strong, and lacking in finesse.

English merchants, recognizing the basic soundness of the wines, suggested wine-making improvements to the peasant farmers who produced them. They even brought coopers from England to teach the Portuguese how to make barrels. Eventually, they were able to reconstruct the wine in the style that they knew would sell back home.

The wine did get better and did become popular in England. But it changed again, this time dramatically. In the mid-18th century, many growers began adding brandy to the wine in the fermenting tank. The effect of this was to stop the fermentation process while there was still some natural grape sweetness in the wine.

Forty-eight different grape varieties are grown in the delimited region of the Douro Valley, with vineyards ranging over steep slopes and narrow terraces. There are 20 white grapes and 28 red. Fifteen of the varieties are considered particularly desirable, while the others are acceptable or merely tolerated. Among the best reds is Pinot Noir, known in Portugal as Tinta Francisca. White port is often made from Malvasia grapes, a variety that is also grown in Madeira, South Africa, and California.

There are two basic types of port: wood and bottle. Wood port is aged in wood until it is ready to drink. After bottling, wood ports do not need further aging, although some of them will improve when kept for a year or two.

Wood ports come in three types: ruby, tawny, and white. Ruby, the most popular of all ports, is deep and full-bodied. A blend of wines from three or four vintages, ruby port is usually sweet and fruity in flavor.

Tawny ports can be made by blending red and white ports, or by using older ruby ports that have developed an amber hue. Tawny differs from ruby in that it is subtler, deeper, less sweet, with a nutlike flavor which is known as *rancio*.

White ports are made the same way red ports are; the only difference is that white grapes are used. The wine is usually drier than either red or tawny, but it has the same rich, nutty flavor.

Bottle ports are wines that are meant to age and improve in the bottle rather than in the barrel. The finest bottle port is vintage port. These wines come from the best vineyards in the best years and are vinified in the painstaking traditional manner, which includes crushing by treading.

A classic vintage will approach its peak between 15 and 25 years after the harvest. It maintains its character for another 15 years or more then slowly loses depth and color. However, a good vintage almost never becomes undrinkable, because its high alcohol content and sugar act as preservatives. Wines more than 100 years old can be very attractive. The most important vintages declared since 1960 were: 1960, 1962, 1963, 1966, 1967, 1970, 1972, 1975, 1977, 1979, 1980, 1983, 1985, 1991, 1992, 1994, 1997, and 1999.

While vintage ports are blended from the grapes of numerous fine vineyards grown in a particularly successful year, there has been a recent trend toward producing wines from a single estate. Called "Colheita," or "single vineyard," these ports are made in good years that are not declared for vintage port. Like vintage port, Colheita port is bottle-aged and so should be allowed to age in the cellar for a number of years.

Late-bottled vintage, or LBV, port is made from grapes grown in numerous vineyards over the same year. What sets it apart from vintage port is that like ruby, tawny, and Colheita, it is aged in wood for a period of 4 to 6 years, which makes it ready to drink now.

As you search the stores for this luscious, velvety wine, a few shippers to consider are Dow's, Taylor Fladgate, Calem, Cockburn, Croft, Delaforce, Ferreira, Fonseca, Graham, Sandeman, and Warre.

Port should be sipped from a small, stemmed glass and is a lovely accompaniment to cheese (Stilton is the preferred type), fruit, or nuts.

## SHERRY

Sherry is produced in and around the town of Jerez de la Frontera in Spain's sunny southern province of Andalusia; the name "sherry" is an anglicization of Jerez. This region, north of Cadiz and Gibraltar on the Atlantic coast, has an ideal climate for growing wine grapes. The vineyards surround the town and the two neighboring villages of Sanlucar de Barrameda and Puerto de Santa Maria.

The Palomino grape is the major varietal used in sherry and is grown on vines with a life span of 20 to 30 years. At that age, when the vines begin to decline in productivity, they are pulled out and the soil is allowed to rest for five years or more. Every year land is rotated, some being retired, some coming into service anew.

Palomino vines are planted only in albariza soil, which due to its high chalk content is almost white. This earth, though troublesome to cultivate and low in yield, is valued because of its ability to soak up water in the rainy season.

This unusual soil requires approximately two dozen distinct operations to assure a successful vintage. Besides such time-consuming jobs as fertilizing, pruning, staking, and tying, vineyard workers must make bowl-shaped hollows around each vine to collect water during the rainy season. The procedure is begun only when there are sure signs of approaching rain, lest the delicate exposed roots be scorched by the sun. At the end of the rainy period, the water holes have to be filled and the soil leveled.

This leveling goes on all during the spring, and the earth is also tamped to minimize the evaporation of moisture. Eventually, this difficult work leads to the harvest in September, when the tight bunches of plump, tough-skinned greenish grapes are picked. The harvest lasts until all the vines have been picked over several times.

It took several centuries for the sherry we now drink to evolve. The wine that Falstaff refers to as "sack" was a product of Jerez, but it was very different from the wine produced there today. In the early 1700s, large aboveground warehouses (called *bodegas*) were erected in and around Jerez, and after almost a century of experimentation, the *solera* system, the method that sets sherry apart from all other wines, was perfected.

Sherry lives its first seven or eight years in 132-gallon butts (casks) made of fine-grained American oak. After the crush, which in some locations is still accomplished by treading, the new wine is left to ferment slowly for two to three months in these casks until all its sugar content has been converted to alcohol. By New Year's Day, the young wine "falls bright," meaning that all the impurities drop to the bottom of the cask, clarifying the wine.

At this point, the wine is given its first tentative classification. Like the men who make it, sherry is ruggedly individualistic, and actually decides for itself whether to be a pale fino or a heavier, more darkly colored oloroso. The process by which the wine does this is still a mystery. Two butts harvested and crushed at the same time from grapes grown side by side in one vineyard often develop differently. And how very different they are. Fino is completely dry and very light in color. It has a light to medium body and a flavor that is elegant and crisp. Oloroso, on the other hand, is a deeply golden-amber wine with a nutty aroma and a flavor that is somewhat sweet.

It is possible to distinguish between a fino and an oloroso at this early stage because a fino develops a thick coating of yeast on its surface, while an oloroso does not. This yeast cap is called the *flor.*

Some fino becomes amontillado, a wine that acquires the burnished character of an oloroso, with a full body, a crisp nutty taste, and, depending on the shipper, a dry to slightly sweet taste.

After this period of declaration and maturation, called the *anadas* stage, fino and amontillado wines are fortified with grape brandy to 15.5 percent alcohol, while olorosos are raised to 18 percent. Then the sherry is introduced to the solera, where young wines are blended with older ones to produce a wine of consistent taste and quality. The solera system consists of row upon row of identical butts, each row containing wine a year older than that in the row above it. Soleras are often ten rows high.

Wine for shipment is always drawn from the oldest (bottom) row of casks, but never is more than half the wine in this tier withdrawn in a single year. The bottom butts are replenished by wine drawn from the row above it, which is in turn refilled from the row above it, and so on. This complex method of fractional blending eliminates the effect of any differences in vintages and creates a wine of extraordinary depth and complexity.

Prior to shipping, the wines are fined (clarified) with beaten egg whites, which settle slowly through the wines, removing impurities as they go. Then the alcoholic content is adjusted by the addition of neutrally flavored grape brandy. Finally, dryness and paleness are regulated through the addition of sweet solera wine made from the Pedro Ximenez (or PX) grape. All of these options give each individual shipper a personal and distinctive style.

Several of the big Jerez shippers maintain bodegas in the town of Sanlucar de Barrameda, where the salt air from the Atlantic Ocean adds a definite fragrance and lightness, tinged with a slight bitterness. The fino made there, called manzanilla, is a marvelously delicate wine that ranges from pale green to gold in color. Unfortunately, manzanilla is the ultimate example of a wine that doesn't travel well, and if moved from Sanlucar it loses some of its special characteristics. Cream sherries are dark olorosos that have been sweetened. They are rich, luscious, and very creamy in texture.

A few names to keep in mind when searching for a good sherry are Lustau, Sandeman, Osborne, Domecq, Harvey, and Gonzalez Byas.

## VERMOUTH

There are two basic types of vermouth—dry and sweet. Dry vermouth is the pale French style that is herbal and soft and that has a nutty, sherry-like finish. This is the type of vermouth that is used in the martini. Noilly Prat (a French firm), Martini & Rossi, and Cinzano (two Italian firms) are the primary producers. There are also domestic versions.

Sweet vermouth—the Italian style—is ruby to dark amber in color. It has a sweet, lush, smooth, and spicy flavor. It is the type of vermouth used in such mixed drinks as Manhattans and Negronis. Punt e Mas is the richest and most flavorful version, but there are also excellent sweet vermouths made in northern Italy by Cinzano and Martini & Rossi, and there are domestic versions as well.

There are a few interesting vermouths on the market that are intended to be consumed on their own, as aperitifs. Martini & Rossi offers the sweet, lush white vermouth "Bianco," plus "Rosso," a red vermouth with a slightly bitter taste. Vya Extra-Dry, an American vermouth, is produced by Andrew Quady, a northern California winemaker who specializes in dessert wines.

The base wine for Vya Extra-Dry is made from Colombard (for its herbaceous qualities) and Orange Muscat (for its lovely aromatic character). This is a very dry, crisp, and nicely balanced vermouth with a touch of astringency. Another delightful new vermouth comes to us from Duckhorn Vineyards. The King Eider is made using a base of sauvignon blanc. It is then mixed with brandy and a blend of botanical extracts such as chamomile flower, star anise, bitter orange rind, cinnamon, and Moroccan rosebuds. A portion of the vermouth is aged for 5 to 6 weeks in French oak barrels. Served over ice with a twist of orange or lemon, it's a delightful aperitif. All vermouths range from 16 to 19 percent alcohol. In addition, many aperitif wines are made with a mostly vermouth base. These wines are usually spiced, slightly, sweet, and can be either red or white.

*Punt e Mes (Italy, 33 proof)*

The Carpano company has been producing vermouth in the Piemonte region of northern Italy since 1786. At the café on Turin's Piazza Castello, the bartender's specialty was mixing various flavorings into vermouth. The addition of bitter quinine was particularly fashionable. It was so popular, in fact, that the Carpano company decided to bottle this particular combination so that it could reach a wider audience. The result was Amaro vermouth.

Punt e Mes was named inadvertently by a member of the Turin Stock Exchange, who was so preoccupied by his work that he mistakenly asked for a "point and a half" instead of a bitter vermouth. Punt e Mes is always served very cold, straight up in a chilled shot glass or over ice with a splash of club soda water and an orange slice.

# Madeira

### Boston Eggnog

1 egg yolk
¾ teaspoon sugar
4 ounces Madeira
½ ounce brandy
¼ ounce rum
Cold milk
Freshly grated nutmeg

In a shaker, beat the egg and sugar. Add crushed ice and the Madeira, brandy, and rum to the shaker. Shake well and strain into a tall glass. Top off with the cold milk and fresh ice. Sprinkle the nutmeg on top.

### Champagne Santa

3 ounces Sercial Madeira
½ ounce raspberry brandy
Dash of orange bitters
Champagne

In a shaker, combine the Madeira, brandy, and bitters. Shake vigorously and pour into a champagne flute. Fill the glass with the chilled champagne and stir to blend.

# Port

## Broken Spur

1½ ounces white port
1 ounce gin
1 ounce sweet vermouth
1 teaspoon anisette
1 egg yolk
1 scoop crushed ice

Combine all ingredients in a shaker. Mix well and pour into a chilled old-fashioned glass.

## Chocolate Cocktail

3 ounces ruby port
1 ounce yellow Chartreuse
1 egg yolk
1 teaspoon grated chocolate

Mix the port, Chartreuse, and egg yolk in a shaker with ice. Strain the mixture into a chilled cocktail glass and sprinkle with a bit of the grated chocolate.

# Port • Signature Drinks

## Amalia

ALFAMA, NEW YORK CITY

2 ounces Offley white port
1½ ounces Stoli Ohranj
Splash of tonic
2 drops Angostura bitters
1 white grape

In a shaker filled with ice, pour all ingredients, except grape, and stir for about 20 seconds. Strain into a cocktail glass and garnish with the white grape.

## Chiado

ALFAMA, NEW YORK CITY

2 ounces Royal Oporto extra-dry white port
1½ ounces Midori
Splash of gin
Splash of club soda
Lemon wedge

In a shaker filled with ice, pour all ingredients, except lemon, and stir gently for about 20 seconds. Strain into a cocktail glass. Squeeze the lemon wedge and drop it into the cocktail.

# Red Wine

## *Appetizer*

2 to 3 ounces red aperitif wine
Juice of 1 orange
1 scoop crushed ice

Combine all ingredients in a blender. Mix well and strain into a cocktail glass.

## *The Locomotive*

6 ounces dry red wine
½ ounce curaçao
½ ounce maraschino liqueur
½ ounce honey
1 egg
Lemon slice
Ground cinnamon

In a flaming saucepan, mix the red wine, curaçao, maraschino liqueur, and honey. Stir well until the honey is dissolved. Gradually warm the mixture over direct heat, but do not boil. Beat the egg lightly and stir it into the wine mixture. Bring the mixture to a simmer. Pour into a warmed mug. Top with the lemon slice and a bit of the ground cinnamon.

## *Portland Cocktail*

1½ ounces red aperitif wine
1½ ounces light rum
4 dashes of orange bitters
Twist of ripe lime peel

Stir the wine, rum, and bitters with ice until well chilled. Strain the mixture into a chilled cocktail glass and garnish with the lime peel.

## *SX Sangria Red*

SX137, New York City

⅔ pitcher red wine
4 ounces triple sec
Orange juice
Lemon-lime soda
Orange wedges, apple slices, and Asian pear wedges

Add the wine and triple sec to a pitcher. Fill with ice. Add equal parts of the orange juice and lemon-lime soda to fill. Garnish with the orange wedges, apple slices, and Asian pear wedges.

## T Street Punch

*Makes 48 (4-ounce) servings*

2 pounds confectioners' sugar
Juice of 24 lemons
1 pint strong tea
3 (750 ml.) bottles dry red wine
1 (750 ml.) bottle brandy
1 (750 ml.) bottle chilled
    champagne (or sparkling wine)
Lemon slices

In a large punch bowl, dissolve the sugar in the lemon juice. Add the tea and large chunks of ice. Pour in the wine and brandy and chill for 2 hours. Before serving, pour in the champagne. Serve the punch in wine goblets and decorate with the lemon slices.

## Trump's Sangria

TRUMPS, WEST HOLLYWOOD

Orange slice
Lemon slice
8 ounces red wine
Dash of anisette
1½ ounces triple sec
1 ounce orange juice
Club soda

Squeeze the orange and lemon slices into a 16-ounce balloon glass. Add ice and wine, anisette, triple sec, and juice. Top off with the cold club soda.

# Sherry

## Adonis Cocktail

3 ounces fino sherry
1 ounce sweet vermouth
Dash of orange bitters
Twist of orange peel

Mix all ingredients, except the orange peel, in a small pitcher with ice. Strain the mixture into a cocktail glass. Drop the orange peel into the glass.

## Brandy Bonanza

1½ ounces sherry
1 ounce brandy
Chilled Riesling or other crisp
    white wine

Pour the sherry and brandy into a highball glass. Top off with the wine.

## Sherry Cobbler

1 scoop crushed ice
Several dashes of curaçao
Several dashes of pineapple syrup
4 ounces amontillado sherry
Twist of lemon
Mint sprig
Pineapple stick

Fill a large wine goblet with the crushed ice. Add the curaçao and syrup. Add the sherry and churn until the outside of the glass appears frosty. Drop the lemon peel into the drink. Garnish with the mint and pineapple.

## Straight Law Cocktail

2 ounces fino sherry
1 ounce gin
Twist of lemon

Mix the sherry and gin with ice. Strain the mixture into a chilled cocktail glass. Twist the lemon peel over the drink and drop it in.

# Sparkling Wine and Champagne

## American Flyer

1 scoop crushed ice
1½ ounces light rum
¼ ounce lime juice
½ teaspoon sugar syrup, or to taste
Champagne (or sparkling wine)

Combine all ingredients, except champagne or wine, in a shaker and mix thoroughly. Strain the mixture into a chilled wineglass. Top off with the chilled champagne.

## Black Velvet

½ pint champagne (or sparkling wine)
½ pint Guinness stout or other dark porter

Chill both ingredients and pour them into a chilled highball glass. Stir minimally in order to preserve the fizz.

## Breakers's French 75

1 ounce gin
½ ounce lemon juice
Champagne (or sparkling wine)

In a highball glass, mix the gin and lemon juice. Add the ice cubes and top off with the champagne.

## Caribbean Champagne

4 ounces dry champagne
½ teaspoon white rum
½ teaspoon banana liqueur
2 dashes of orange bitters
½ scoop crushed ice
1 banana slice

In a saucer-shaped champagne glass, stir the first five ingredients. Garnish with the banana slice.

## Champagne Cooler

1 ounce brandy
1 ounce triple sec
Champagne (or sparkling wine)
Mint sprigs

Pour the brandy and triple sec into a chilled wine goblet. Top off with the champagne and stir gently. Garnish with the mint sprigs.

## Champagne Julep

6 mint leaves
1 teaspoon sugar syrup
1 scoop crushed ice
3 ounces bourbon
Brut champagne or dry sparkling
   wine
Mint sprig

Muddle the mint leaves in a tall collins glass with the syrup. Fill the glass two-thirds full with the crushed ice. Pour in the bourbon and stir briskly. Add additional ice if necessary. Top off with the cold champagne or sparkling wine. Stir gently and garnish with the large mint sprig.

## Earthquake Cooler

1 ounce vodka
1 ounce orange liqueur
Dash of lime juice
Dash of orange bitters
Champagne (or dry sparkling
   wine)

Mix all ingredients, except the champagne, in a shaker with crushed ice. Strain the mixture into a large chilled wineglass. Top off with the chilled champagne and stir gently.

## French 75

1 ounce lemon juice
½ ounce sugar syrup, or to taste
1½ ounces cognac (or other good
   brandy)
Brut champagne (or sparkling
   wine)

In a collins glass, mix the lemon
juice and sugar syrup with several
ice cubes. Stir until the sugar is dissolved. Add the cognac and top off
with the cold champagne.

## Luscious Lisa

1 ounce brandy
½ ounce raspberry liqueur
Brut champagne (or sparkling
   wine)
½ teaspoon framboise (raspberry
   dessert wine)

Stir the brandy and raspberry
liqueur in a mixing glass with ice
cubes. Strain the mixture into a
chilled tulip glass. Top off the glass
with the cold champagne and a
float of the framboise.

## Imperial Kir

2 ounces crème de cassis
1 ounce kirsch
Crushed ice
Champagne, sparkling wine, or
   white wine

Mix the cassis and kirsch in a
shaker with the crushed ice. Pour
the mixture into a large wineglass.
Top off with the cold champagne
or wine and stir gently.

## Mimosa

6 ounces brut champagne (or
   sparkling wine)
3 ounces orange juice, preferably
   freshly squeezed

Chill both ingredients. Mix in a
chilled wine goblet.

## Poinsettia

¼ ounce triple sec
Splash of cranberry juice
Champagne
Lemon twist

Combine the first two ingredients
in a champagne glass. Add the
champagne to fill. Garnish with
the lemon twist.

## Soyer au Champagne

2 tablespoons vanilla ice cream
Several dashes of curaçao
Several dashes of maraschino
    liqueur
Several dashes of brandy
Champagne (or sparkling wine)
Orange slice
1 maraschino cherry

Put the ice cream into a large champagne flute. Add the curaçao, liqueur, and brandy. Mix well. Top off the glass with the cold champagne and stir. Garnish with the orange slice and the maraschino cherry.

# Sparkling Wine and Champagne • Signature Drinks

## Aureole Cocktail

AUREOLE, NEW YORK CITY

½ teaspoon raspberry wine
Champagne (or sparkling wine)

Pour the raspberry wine into a champagne flute. Top off the flute with the chilled champagne.

## Ballroom Derby

THE BALLROOM, NEW YORK CITY

Champagne (or sparkling wine)
Dash of dry sherry
Twist of lemon

Combine all ingredients in a fluted champagne glass and serve.

## Beau Nash Splash

HOTEL CRESCENT COURT, DALLAS

1 tablespoon Mandarin Napoleon
    liqueur
4½ ounces brut champagne (or
    sparkling wine)
Twist of orange peel

Pour the liqueur into a champagne flute. Add the champagne to the flute. Garnish with the orange twist.

## Bellini

BELLINI BY CIPRIANI, NEW YORK CITY

3 ounces champagne (or
  sparkling wine)
1 ounce fresh white peach juice

Mix the ingredients in a mixing
glass or bowl. Pour the blend into
a champagne flute.

## Champagne Cocktail

SIGN OF THE DOVE, NEW YORK CITY

1 small sugar cube
2 to 3 drops of Angostura bitters
Splash of brandy
Splash of Grand Marnier
Champagne (or sparkling wine)

Place the sugar cube in a glass. Add
the bitters, then a touch each of
the brandy and Grand Marnier.
Top off with the champagne or
sparkling wine. (This drink has an
attractive amber color and only a
hint of bitterness, and the sugar
cube causes bubbles to rise furi-
ously and steadily.)

## Champagne Royal

PUMP ROOM, CHICAGO

½ ounce black raspberry liqueur
½ ounce pear brandy
1 fresh strawberry
Champagne (or sparkling wine)

Place the liqueur, brandy, and
strawberry in a champagne glass
and freeze. After it is frozen, top
off with the champagne.

## French Kiss

BAR NOIR AT MAISON 140,
BEVERLY HILLS, CALIFORNIA

1 ounce Courvoisier V.S.
½ ounce sweetened lemon juice
4 ounces Pommery Pop
  champagne
Lemon twist

Combine the first three ingredients in a champagne flute and garnish with the lemon twist.

## Jade

DORCHESTER HOTEL, LONDON

Dash of melon liqueur
Dash of blue curaçao
Dash of lime juice
Dash of bitters

Champagne (or sparkling wine)
Lime slice
1 green cherry

Mix the melon liqueur, curaçao, juice, and bitters in a shaker with crushed ice. Strain the mixture into a tall champagne glass and top off with the champagne. Garnish with the lime and green cherry.

## Lady Killer

PARK HOTEL VITZNAU,
VITZNAU, SWITZERLAND

2 small strawberries
Champagne
White wine

In a wineglass, place the 2 strawberries. Fill the glass half with the champagne and half with the wine. (You can adjust the amount of champagne or wine as desired.)

## Lady Macbeth

4 ounces champagne
2 ounces wood-aged ruby port
Twist of lemon

In a champagne flute, combine the champagne and ruby port. Stir gently. Squeeze the twist over the cocktail before dropping it in for garnish.

## Rose

WESTIN ST. FRANCIS, SAN FRANCISCO

¼ ounce black raspberry liqueur
Brut champagne (or sparkling wine)
Twist of lemon

Pour the liqueur into a champagne flute. Fill the remainder of the glass with the champagne. Garnish with the lemon twist.

## Strawberry Mimosa

NEW YORK HILTON, NEW YORK CITY

3½ ounces orange juice
3 to 4 large strawberries
3½ ounces brut champagne (or sparkling wine)

In a blender, mix the orange juice and strawberries with a little crushed ice. Pour the blend into a chilled wineglass. Top off with the cold champagne or sparkling wine and stir gently.

# Punches

## *Champagne Cup*

*Makes 10 servings*

3 ½ ounces brut champagne
  (or sparkling wine)
1½ ounces Grand Marnier
1½ ounces maraschino liqueur
3 ounces curaçao
6 ounces brandy
1 tablespoon confectioners' sugar
Orange slices
Pineapple slices
Cucumber peel
4 mint sprigs

Combine the first six ingredients in a large pitcher with several ice cubes. Stir well and garnish with the orange, pineapple, cucumber, and mint.

## *Roman Punch*

*Makes 30 (5-ounce) servings*

2 pounds sugar
Juice of 10 lemons
Juice of 3 oranges
10 egg whites
1 quart champagne (or sparkling wine)
1 quart golden rum
½ ounce orange bitters

In a large punch bowl, dissolve the sugar in the fruit juices. Add the rind of 1 of the oranges to the punch bowl. Separately beat the egg whites, then add them to the punch. Pour in the champagne, rum, and bitters and stir well. Keep the punch cold by surrounding the bowl with crushed ice.

# Vermouth

## *Achampanado*

3 to 4 ounces dry vermouth
½ teaspoon sugar syrup
Juice of ¼ lime
Club soda

Pour the vermouth into a chilled collins glass with ice. Add the syrup and lime juice. Stir until the syrup is dissolved. Top off with the cold club soda.

## Addington

2 ounces dry vermouth
2 ounces sweet vermouth
Club soda
Twist of orange peel

Pour the vermouths into a chilled collins glass over ice. Top off with the cold club soda and stir. Twist the orange peel over the glass and drop it in.

## Americano

⅔ ounce sweet vermouth
⅓ ounce Campari
Splash of Perrier
Orange slice
Lime slice

Pour the first three ingredients into an ice-filled cocktail glass. Stir well and garnish with the orange and lime slices.

## Chrysanthemum Cocktail

2 ounces dry vermouth
1½ ounces Benedictine
Several dashes of Pernod
Twist of orange peel

Stir the vermouth and Benedictine in a mixing glass with ice. Strain the mixture into a chilled cocktail glass. Add the Pernod and stir. Drop the orange twist into the drink.

## Duchess Cocktail

⅓ ounce dry vermouth
⅓ ounce sweet vermouth
⅓ ounce Pernod

Combine all ingredients in a shaker with crushed ice. Mix well and strain into a chilled cocktail glass.

## Harvard Wine

1 ounce dry vermouth
¾ ounce brandy
Dash of orange bitters
Club soda

In a mixing glass with ice, stir the vermouth, brandy, and bitters. Pour the mixture into a chilled cocktail glass and top off with the cold club soda.

## Hong Kong

1 ounce dry vermouth
1 ounce gin
¼ ounce lime juice
1 dash of bitters
¼ teaspoon sugar

In a shaker with crushed ice, mix all ingredients. Pour the mixture into a chilled cocktail glass.

## Lamb's Club

¾ ounce dry vermouth
¾ ounce sweet vermouth
¾ ounce gin
¼ ounce Benedictine

Stir all ingredients in a mixing glass with ice. Pour the mixture into a chilled cocktail glass.

## Lone Tree

¾ ounce dry vermouth
¾ ounce sweet vermouth
¾ ounce gin
Several dashes of orange bitters
1 scoop crushed ice
1 olive

Mix all ingredients, except the olive, in a shaker. Strain the mix-ture into a chilled cocktail glass and garnish with the olive.

## Picon

1 ounce sweet vermouth
1 ounce Amer Picon
1 scoop crushed ice

In a shaker, mix all ingredients. Pour the mixture into a chilled cocktail glass.

## San Francisco

1 ounce dry vermouth
1 ounce sweet vermouth
1 ounce sloe gin
Several dashes of bitters
Several dashes of orange bitters
1 scoop crushed ice

In a shaker, mix all ingredients. Pour the mixture into a chilled cocktail glass.

## Serpent's Tooth

1½ ounces sweet vermouth
¾ ounce Irish whiskey
½ ounce kümmel
¾ ounce lemon juice
Several dashes of bitters
1 scoop crushed ice
Lemon peel

Mix all ingredients, except the lemon peel, in a shaker. Pour the mixture into a chilled old-fashioned glass. Twist the lemon peel over the drink and drop it in.

## Third Edition

1 ounce sweet vermouth
1 ounce dry vermouth
1 ounce gin
1 teaspoon white crème de menthe
Several dashes of orange bitters

Pour all ingredients into a mixing glass with several ice cubes. Strain the mixture into a chilled cocktail glass.

## Third Rail

2 to 3 ounces dry vermouth
Several dashes of curaçao
Several dashes of peppermint schnapps
Lemon or orange peel

Stir the vermouth, curaçao, and schnapps with ice cubes in a mixing glass. Strain into a chilled cocktail glass. Twist the lemon or orange peel over the drink and drop it in.

## Vermouth Cassis

3 ounces dry vermouth
1 ounce crème de cassis
Club soda

Mix the vermouth and crème de cassis in a chilled highball glass with ice. Top off the glass with the cold club soda.

# White Wine

## Kir

5 ounces dry white wine
½ ounce crème de cassis

Chill both ingredients. Mix them in a chilled wineglass.

# White Wine •
# Signature Drinks

## *Dorchester Coupe aux Fraises*

DORCHESTER HOTEL, LONDON

3 or 4 strawberries
½ ounce brandy
½ ounce orange liqueur
2½ ounces white wine
2½ ounces sparkling wine
Mint sprig

Marinate the strawberries in the brandy and liqueur. After several hours, place the strawberries in a champagne glass and top with the wines. Garnish with the fresh mint sprig.

## *Occidental White Sangria*

OCCIDENTAL GRILL, WASHINGTON, D.C.

*Makes 4 servings*

18 ounces dry but fruity wine such as Chenin Blanc or Sauvignon Blanc
1½ ounces gin
1½ ounces brandy
¾ ounce liquid sour mix
2 ounces 7 UP
2 ounces ginger ale
½ ounce diced apple
1½ ounces diced lemon
1½ ounces diced orange

Fill a 44-ounce pitcher with ice. Add the all ingredients and stir well. You may also dice and add such summer fruits as pears, apricots, and peaches.

## *Vino Fresca*

EL DORADO CANTINA, BRENTWOOD

*Makes 4 servings*

18 ounces white wine
12 kiwis
1 cup of grapes, cut in half
½ pomegranates' worth of seeds
1 green apple
1 banana
3 blood oranges
2 ounces brandy
2 ounces freshly squeezed orange juice
2 ounces freshly squeezed lime juice
¼ cup sugar
Mint leaves

Pour white wine into a glass container (such as a sun tea jar or glass barrel). Add the fruit, brandy, juices, and sugar and let the mixture sit overnight in the refrigerator. Serve over ice in a red-wine glasses. Garnish with mint leaves.

# NONALCOHOLIC DRINKS

In direct contrast to the surge in popularity of mixed drinks and premium spirits, the last decade has also witnessed the growing popularity of nonalcoholic drinks. Teahouses and coffee bars are being joined by juice bars and smoothie outlets. You can wander into one of these brightly colored havens of health and grab a shot of wheat grass juice or place your order for a giant blended smoothie concocted from frozen fruits, yogurt, and juice, but it's just as easy to make your own at home.

Now more than ever, myriad options exist for the permanent or temporary teetotaler. Why opt for boring bottled water or dreary soft drinks when you can sip tasty concoctions made from natural tea and fresh fruits and vegetables? The same creative energy that went into many of the mixed drinks in this book have also had a role in stirring up the following intriguing combinations of nonalcoholic ingredients.

## Classics

### Almost Cape Cod

3 ounces cranberry juice
3 ounces white grape juice
Orange peel, spiraled

Pour the juices into a chilled cocktail glass over ice cubes. Twist the orange peel over the drink, then drape it over the glass.

### Black Cow

10 ounces cold root beer
1 scoop vanilla ice cream

Pour 3½ ounces of the root beer into a 14-ounce chilled tall glass. Add 2 teaspoons of the ice cream and stir. When it is creamy, add the remaining root beer and ice cream.

## Bloody Mary—Not!

*Makes 4 servings*

1 quart tomato juice
¼ cup bottled horseradish or 2
    tablespoons freshly grated
    horseradish
¼ cup chopped green bell pepper
¼ cup chopped celery
¼ cup chopped scallions
2 teaspoons hot pepper sauce, or
    to taste
4 celery ribs

In a blender, blend half the tomato juice with the horseradish, pepper, celery, and scallions. Add the hot pepper sauce to taste. Pour the blend into an ice cube tray and freeze. Place 4 wineglasses into the freezer to frost. When the cubes are frozen solid, empty them into the blender and add the rest of the tomato juice. Blend until smooth. Pour the mixture into the frosted wineglasses and garnish with the celery ribs.

## Lemonade

Juice of 1 lemon
2 tablespoons sugar
1 scoop crushed ice
6 ounces water
1 lemon peel spiral
1 lemon slice

In a shaker, mix together the lemon juice, sugar, and crushed ice. Strain the mixture into a tall, chilled collins glass. Fill the glass with the water and stir well. Garnish with the lemon peel and slice.

## Shirley Temple

1½ ounces grenadine
5 ½ ounces lemon-lime soda
4 or 5 ice cubes
1 maraschino cherry

Pour the grenadine and lemon-lime soda into a chilled cocktail glass with the ice cubes. Stir well and garnish with the cherry.

## Virgin Eggnog

10 ounces milk
1 egg
1 scoop crushed ice
1 teaspoon grated nutmeg or
    ground cinnamon

Combine the milk, egg, and crushed ice in a shaker. Shake well and strain into a tall, chilled collins glass. Sprinkle the nutmeg or cinnamon on top.

## Virgin Mary

3 ounces tomato juice or V8 juice
3 ounces clam juice
3 dashes of Tabasco
3 dashes of Worcestershire sauce
½ teaspoon lemon juice
1 scoop crushed ice
1 teaspoon finely chopped fresh
  dill

Mix all ingredients, except the dill, in a shaker. Shake well and pour into a chilled old-fashioned glass. Top off with the dill.

## Wassail

*Makes 14 (4-ounce) servings*

3 cups apple cider
1 cup unsweetened pineapple
  juice
1½ cups orange juice
½ cup grapefruit juice
½ cup lemon juice
2 cinnamon sticks
1½ teaspoons allspice
½ teaspoon ground cloves
½ cup superfine sugar, or to taste
1 orange
14 cloves

Put the cider, juices, and cinnamon sticks in a large saucepan. Tie the allspice and ground cloves in a

cheesecloth and drop it into the saucepan as well. Bring the mixture to a boil, then reduce the heat and simmer for 5 minutes. Taste the wassail and add the sugar to taste. Slice the orange into 7 cross-sectional slices. Cut each orange slice in half and pierce each half with 1 of the cloves. Pour half a cup of the hot wassail into each punch cup and garnish with the clove-studded orange section.

# Creative Concoctions

## *Big Banana*

½ ripe banana, peeled and sliced
4 ounces cold milk
1 ounce pineapple juice
1 teaspoon coconut extract
4 ounces crushed ice

Combine all ingredients in a blender and blend until smooth. Pour the mixture into a tall, chilled collins glass.

## *Corona Punch*

*Makes 46 servings*

2 quarts fresh orange juice
1 quart fresh grapefruit juice
1 quart ginger ale
1 cup fresh lime juice
1 cup orgeat or sugar syrup to taste
½ cup grenadine
1 large cake of ice

Chill the first six ingredients and pour them into a chilled punch bowl. Add the cake of ice to the bowl.

## *Ger Bowl*

ROYAL PARC EVIAN HOTEL,
EVIAN-LES-BAINS, FRANCE

2 ounces fresh pineapple, cut into pieces
2 ounces fresh raspberries
3 ½ ounces hibiscus tea
1 pink grapefruit
5 ice cubes

In an electric blender, combine the pineapple, raspberries, and tea. Squeeze the grapefruit and add 1 ¾ ounces of the juice to the blender along with the ice cubes. Blend for 30 seconds. Strain into a large glass.

## *Goddaughter*

½ cup cranberry juice
½ cup grapefruit juice
4 or 5 ice cubes

Mix the juices in a blender until foamy. Pour the mixture into a large cocktail glass with the ice cubes.

## Herbal Cooler

*Makes 4 (6-ounce) servings*

1 cup brewed peppermint tea
1 cup brewed Red Zinger tea
1 cup cranberry juice
Lemon wedge

Mix the first three ingredients together and serve over ice with the wedge of lemon.

## Long Boat

SAVOY HOTEL, LONDON

2 ounces lime juice cordial
2 ice cubes
5 ounces ginger beer or ginger ale
1 fresh mint sprig

Pour the cordial into a tall collins glass over the ice cubes. Top off with the ginger beer or ginger ale and garnish with the mint sprig.

## Ivoire

ROYAL PARC EVIAN HOTEL,
EVIAN-LES-BAINS, FRANCE

1 large pear
1 ¾ ounces soy milk
1 small piece of ginger
3 ½ ounces Evian water
5 ice cubes

Peel the pear and cut it into pieces. Put them through a juice extractor and juice until you have 1¾ ounces of juice. Pour this juice into a blender, and add the soy milk. Peel the ginger and add it to taste. (Start with just a little.) Pour in the Evian water and ice cubes and blend for 30 seconds. Strain the cocktail into a large glass.

## Mickey Mouse

5 ounces cola
4 ice cubes
1 scoop vanilla ice cream
2 tablespoons whipped cream
2 maraschino cherries

Pour the cola into a tall collins glass over the ice cubes. Add the ice cream. Top off with the whipped cream and garnish with the cherries.

## Orange Fizz

3 ounces orange juice
3 ounces ginger ale
4 ice cubes
1 orange slice
1 maraschino cherry

Put the juice, ginger ale, and ice in a large wineglass and stir gently. Garnish with the orange slice and cherry.

## Orange Glow

*Makes 6 servings*

4 cups fresh orange juice
1½ cups unsweetened pineapple juice
½ cup fresh lemon juice
2 tablespoons grenadine
24 ice cubes

In a large pitcher, combine the juices and grenadine. Stir well and pour into a chilled cocktail glass over 4 ice cubes per serving.

## Orange-Strawberry Smoothie

*Makes 4 servings*

1 quart freshly squeezed orange juice
1 cup frozen sliced strawberries

Combine the juice and strawberries in a blender and blend until smooth. Chill the mixture in the refrigerator. When it is ready, pour the blend into a chilled tall collins glass.

## Party Punch

*Makes 8 servings*

1 cup fresh orange juice
Juice of 2 lemons
2 cups cranberry juice cocktail
1 cup superfine sugar
2 cups ice cubes
1 quart club soda
1 orange slice
1 lemon slice

In a large pitcher, mix the juices and sugar. Stir well to dissolve the sugar. Add the ice and pour in the chilled club soda. Float the orange and lemon slices on top for garnish.

## Pippi Longstocking

4 ounces cold apple juice
1 teaspoon grenadine
1 teaspoon lemon juice
4 ounces ginger ale
1 apple slice

Pour the apple juice, grenadine, and lemon juice into a champagne flute and stir well. Top off the glass with the cold ginger ale and garnish with the apple slice.

## Pussy Foot

SAVOY HOTEL, LONDON

2 ounces fresh orange juice
2 ounces fresh lemon juice
2 ounces fresh lime juice
Dash of grenadine
1 egg yolk
Splash of club soda
1 maraschino cherry
1 orange slice

Combine all ingredients, except the soda, cherry, and orange, in a shaker. Shake well and strain into a chilled cocktail glass. Top off with the soda, and garnish with the cherry and orange slice.

## Santa Claus Cider

2 ounces half-and-half
1 egg
½ teaspoon superfine sugar
3 ounces crushed ice
6 ounces apple cider
Freshly grated nutmeg

Combine all ingredients, except the cider and nutmeg, in a shaker. Shake well and strain into a chilled tall collins glass. Pour the cider into the glass and top with the grated nutmeg.

## Strawberry-Banana-Pineapple Smoothie

*Makes 4 (6-ounce) servings*

1½ cups sliced strawberries, stems removed
1 ripe banana, sliced
Juice of 1 lemon
2 tablespoons sugar
1 cup pineapple juice

Blend the strawberries, banana, lemon juice, and sugar in a blender or food processor. Slowly add the pineapple juice. Mix until smooth, then pour the blend into a mixing bowl and freeze for an hour. When it is ready to serve, fold into a chilled tall collins glass.

## *Tropical Treat*

*Makes 3 servings*

1 ripe mango, pitted and sliced
1 banana
1 cup plain nonfat or low-fat
    yogurt
1 cup lowfat milk
2 ice cubes

Add all ingredients to an electric blender. Blend until thick and creamy. Pour the mixture into chilled tall collins glasses.

# Hot Drinks

## *Café au Lait*

4 ounces hot coffee
2 ounces hot milk
2 teaspoons superfine sugar, or to
    taste

Pour the coffee and milk into a coffee mug. Add the sugar to taste. Stir to dissolve the sugar.

In a mixing bowl, beat the heavy cream until it is almost stiff. Add the sugar and vanilla extract and beat until the cream holds its shape. In a separate bowl, beat the egg whites so that they are in peaks. Fold the egg whites into the whipped cream mixture. Divide the mixture into 6 warm coffee cups. Pour the coffee into the cups.

## *Café Toulouse*

*Makes 6 servings*

8 ounces heavy cream
2 tablespoons superfine sugar
1 teaspoon vanilla extract
2 egg whites
4¼ cups hot French-roast coffee

## *Mocha Coffee*

½ cup hot chocolate
½ cup hot coffee
1 tablespoon whipped cream
Dash of powdered cinnamon
Dash of grated nutmeg
Dash of grated orange peel

Pour the hot chocolate and coffee into a warm mug. Stir well. Top off the drink with the whipped cream, then sprinkle on the cinnamon, nutmeg, and orange peel.

## Orange Flame

*Makes 4 (6-ounce) servings*

18 ounces cold orange juice
⅓ cup superfine sugar
6 mint sprigs
2 ounces lemon juice
20 ice cubes
4 orange peel strips

In an enamel pan over low heat, bring 8 ounces of the orange juice, the sugar, and the mint sprigs to a boil, stirring constantly. Pour the remaining orange juice and the lemon juice into the pan. Put 5 ice cubes in each chilled highball glass and pour in the drink mixture. Light a match and twist 1 of the orange peels over each drink, next to the flame. Drop 1 peel into each glass.

## Philadelphia Winter Coat

*Makes 8 servings*

½ cup brown sugar
1 dash of nutmeg
2 quarts cider
1 teaspoon whole allspice
1 teaspoon whole cloves
8 orange slices
1 cinnamon stick

Combine the sugar, nutmeg, and cider in a pan. Tie the spices in a cheesecloth and add to the mix. Slowly bring to a boil. Cover and simmer 20 minutes. Remove the spices. Serve hot with the floating orange slices and the cinnamon stick.

# Index